Character

Other Books by Gail Sheehy

Spirit of Survival
Pathfinders
Passages: Predictable Crises of Adult Life
Hustling: Prostitution in Our Wide Open Society
Panthermania: The Clash of Black Against Black in One American City
Speed Is of the Essence
Lovesounds

Character

America's Search for Leadership

by
Gail Sheehy

WILLIAM MORROW AND COMPANY, INC.
NEW YORK

Library of Congress Cataloging-in-Publication Data

Sheehy, Gail
    Character: America's search for leadership.
    1. Presidential candidates—United States—
Psychology.   2. Political leadership—United States.
3. Presidents—United States—Election—1988.
I. Title.
E880.S54 1988   324.973′0927   88–9221
ISBN 0–688–08072–3

Printed in the United States of America

First Edition

1 2 3 4 5 6 7 8 9 10

BOOK DESIGN BY ANN GOLD

For my mentor, Clay Felker

Acknowledgments

It has been my rare good fortune to have not one but three editors in the course of this work. Tina Brown, the galvanizing spirit of *Vanity Fair,* gave me support and generous space in her magazine for the original reporting upon which this book draws. Elise O'Shaughnessy, whose refined sensibilities bridge political and literary journalism, was my constant and valued editorial companion from inception to completion of each character portrait. Alan Williams at William Morrow brought his broad historical view to bear on the shaping and extending of this material into a book.

And because my publishers, Lawrence Hughes and Howard Kaminsky, believed in submitting these character references to public debate *before* the parties nominate their presidential candidates, this book was brought into being with awesome swiftness and teamwork.

I would like also to thank Susan Carswell for her multiple skills and commitment as my assistant, Morgan Ryan and Donna Cornacchio for their help, and Ella Council for her nourishing support to us all.

My appreciation also goes to the crack editorial, research, design, and production teams at *Vanity Fair.* Finally, my thanks to Lesley Stahl for being godmother to this book.

Contents

ONE

Six Candidates in Search of Character

Sow an act, and you reap a habit. Sow a habit, and you reap a character. Sow a character, and you reap a destiny.
—CHARLES READE, 1814–1884

Character has been an important consideration in our selection of national leaders since the time of George Washington. Even our first president—by nature a retiring man—drew on the reserves of respect and trust he had stored up among the people as he campaigned in the churches of Philadelphia to sell the Constitution.

At this point in our political history, however, the concentration on character issues is unparalleled in its intensity. The reason, as I see it, is simple and stark.

By the time they become national leaders, the candidates' characters are sown. And if character is destiny, the destiny they reap will be our own.

As a journalist, I have been writing about presidential candidates since my political baptism in 1968, when I traveled with Bobby Kennedy's campaign in the last week before his tragic assassination. As an author, however, my concentration has been on character and psychological development. In 1984 these two parallel tracks in my work happily came together. *Vanity Fair* magazine asked me to find out who Gary Hart really was, and gave me a month in which to do it. I knew there were superb political analysts already dissecting the issues. And the traveling press was tracking day-to-day developments with computerized precision. Research had already shown that in presidential elections, most people were not voting on issues. They were voting on character. And character is a perceived combination of those traits—together with the values he or she represents—that set a person apart, and motivate his or her behavior. So I decided to pursue my own liveliest interest in writing about this candidate: What made Gary Hart tick?

It was a tantalizing assignment. Hart himself had been quoted as saying, "I'm an obscure man, and I intend to remain that way. I never reveal who I really am." The mystery became more intriguing as I heard the same refrain from one political associate of Hart's after another: "When you find out who Gary Hart is, let me know."

The first clue dropped on April 11, in the back of the chartered plane in which Hart had been virtually sealed since his candidacy had caught fire in New Hampshire two months earlier. His upset victory brought the full effulgence of the American media upon a man whose campaign had been ignored for a year: Gary Hart burst onto the national stage as the Gentleman Caller of American politics—the illusory romantic figure with "new ideas" who might offer escape from the decadent old ways. The glow lasted almost a month. But Hart was beginning to lose it in New York and was drowning in Pennsylvania; now his campaign capsule was headed home to Denver for a day's rest.

Both Hart and his wife were sick with honking bronchitis. The strain of the campaign showed in Lee Hart, in the grooves of fatigue around her mouth, the weedy hair. Hoarse and fidgety, she could not stop trying to please. She attempted to edge onto the armrest next to her husband. He ignored her. She struggled to lift the armrest and back her hip close to his. He was oblivious, talking issues.

Then Gary Hart came walking back to the press section, not a wrinkle in his fitted western shirt, the only sign of wear and tear in the run-down heels of his cowboy boots—a man as controlled physically as he was emotionally.

I dropped a name: Marilyn Youngbird.

"Do you know Marilyn?" Suddenly his voice was buoyant,

spontaneous. "She's been my spiritual adviser for the last few years."

My jaw dropped. Hart gushed on, in a most uncharacteristic fashion. Marilyn was a full-blooded American Indian who had introduced him to Indian religion, he said. "Marilyn's given me eagle feathers and, well"—an embarrassed smile caught up with his ebullience—"other religious artifacts."

"A prayer robe?"

"Yes, a beautiful robe."

I could scarcely believe my ears. When I first interviewed her, the mysterious Marilyn assured me that between 1978 and 1980 she was Hart's closest friend, a soul mate. They had met the day after he first entered the Senate, and she told me she had awakened in Hart a reverence for the sun, the trees, all forms of life. She also described in melodramatic detail the peak moment at an Indian ceremony that brought them close both personally and spiritually. She had invited Hart to a sunrise powwow in a Denver park with the Comanches.

"It was so romantic," she said. "They brushed the front and back of our bodies with eagle feathers. It was sensual. He would look at me, smiling from ear to ear. We didn't know whether to laugh or cry."

I had been certain these were the tales of a lonely female supporter who becomes infatuated with a handsome presidential candidate and wildly exaggerates her importance to him. Now, I wasn't sure.

"Marilyn asked me to tell you that you should take time for a spiritual-healing ceremony."

"I know." He sighed. "Marilyn's been telling me for a long time I need a spiritual purification. I'm carrying a note from her in my pocket right now."

Suddenly I remembered the message Marilyn had given me to pass on to Hart. When she'd shown me its contents, I thought I would never have the nerve to hand it to a serious man running for the most serious elective office in the land. But he was eager to read it.

> Get away from everybody. Go to nature.
> Hug a tree.

"I'm his conscience," Marilyn had assured me. What was more, her parents, both medicine people, had heard the prophecy. The Great Spirit, their god, had chosen Gary Hart to save nature from destruction. I repeated the prophecy for Hart.

"I know," he said gravely. "She keeps telling me that."

"Do you believe it?"

"Yes."

When his own words were reported in my story that July, Hart's immediate response was to say he had not read the article and did not intend to. But he was quick to charge, "It's terribly inaccurate journalism." He might well have said, "I'm a Colorado senator and American Indians are an important part of my constituency. Of course I'm interested in the environment and conservation, just as they are." Instead, he lied. It was the first evidence of what we all later learned was Hart's knee-jerk reaction to being caught at anything. Lie first, then blame others.

Once *Newsweek* and *Time* both verified the accuracy of my reporting, Walter Mondale's campaign managers began dropping references in front-page news stories to "the flake factor" that was giving them serious doubts about Gary Hart as a running mate. In fact, campaign chairman Robert Beckel later disclosed that from the moment Hart emerged as a real contender in New Hampshire, the Mondale campaign had been deluged with "scurrilous material" about the Colorado senator's escapades with various women. Beckel had decided against leaking it to reporters, fearing a backlash if the Mondale campaign was found to be the source.

The month I spent following Hart for that first story in 1984 gave me two other clues to his character. First, here was a man very much still in search of himself, and drawn to those, like Marilyn, who would support a grandiose notion of his superiority and render him morally lovable as well as unimpeachable. Then I caught a glimpse of other inner barriers when I did my first one-on-one interview. There were three seats across on the plane. I sat down next to Hart. He shrank back. His body language commanded me to move a seat away. Later, his Senate staffers mentioned that when they would be working late at night over a bill, infused with excitement and camaraderie, they would crowd around Hart at the desk. All at once he would stiffen. The molecular field would force them back. They had come too close. Gradually, I began to notice how these simple incidents had their analog in the chaos of the Hart campaign. It was an intentional chaos: The ambiguous chain of command seemed designed to keep his advisers snarled up in power struggles among themselves, and at a distance from him.

Here was a man determined to keep everyone at arm's length. What was he hiding? I had to wait until the 1988 election season for the chance to look more closely.

By that time, as the campaign approached full swing, everybody seemed to be interested in the character issue. News magazines were writing about it. Candidates began crowing about it—or, as in Hart's case, decrying the focus on character at the expense of issues. And the public was not sure what to think. Was this healthy, or just an appetite for morsels about the private lives of public people that had turned into a senseless feeding frenzy? What is character, anyway?

The root of the word "character" is the Greek word for engraving. As applied to human beings, it refers to the enduring marks left by life that set one apart as an individual. Commonly, distinctive marks of character are carved in by parental and religious imprinting, by a child's early interactions with siblings, peers at school, and authority figures. The manners of one's social class and the soil in which one grows up often remain indelible, and certain teachers and coaches or books and ideas may leave a lasting impression. Character is also marked by where a person stood at great divides in his or her nation's history. But what matters even more, particularly in a would-be leader, is how many of the passages of adult life have been met and mastered, and what he or she has done with the life accidents dealt by fate.

Inborn temperament also influences the way people turn out. Certain broad characteristics of one's temperament—the tendency to be sociable or withdrawn, optimistic or depressive, open to change and risk or given to following rules and staying within safe bounds—now appear, from studies of identical twins raised apart, to be profoundly influenced by heredity. But the individual who finds himself handicapped by a trait such as stubbornness or an aversion to risk can go a long way toward teaching himself more constructive ways to behave.

Massachusetts Governor Michael Dukakis, for example, was born stubborn. *Monos mou*—Greek for "by myself"—were the first words he learned, the governor told me. The grown Dukakis will always tend toward stubbornness. But he discovered that this inborn characteristic got in the way of the things he most wanted. So he set about trying to modify that trait and has achieved some success.

Senator Robert Dole was born with his basic mood set in the depressive rather than optimistic range, and a cruel life accident and a long, unhappy first marriage only exacerbated a tendency to brood. While basic mood is one of those personality characteristics largely influenced by heredity, the capacity for intimacy is the least influenced by genes and largely learned from the closeness or distance maintained in one's first family circle. Dole's father never hugged. "Around the Dole house," writes Bob Dole in his autobiography, "we were taught that compliments can be devalued by overuse. So if you mowed the lawn to perfection, on time and with every blade of grass in place, you treasured Dad's 'Pretty good.' " To this day, his faithful assistant of twenty-one years cannot remember hearing a word of praise from Bob Dole.

Taken together, the temperamental disposition to brooding and the learned reticence to express affection gave Bob Dole a harsh edge even before his war injuries embittered him. But that was not the end of the story. His success as a leader in that most clubby of clubs—the U.S. Senate—and his remarriage to Elizabeth Hanford, which brought a bubbly and socially secure presence into his life, have softened some of those darker shadows in his character. As a close friend says, "This is happy for Dole."

And so it is not just the hand dealt, but the way one plays it that gradually shapes character. How people engage the great psychological issues of adulthood—or deny, defy, or elude them—establishes a pattern of behavior. That pattern impresses deeply on the mind the distinguishing marks of character. And enough of those mental and moral distinguishing marks are evident by the time individuals seek or rise to high office to predict whether a leader might be weak or strong, sincere or tricky, good or bad.

For example, Lyndon Johnson's character—and in particular that aspect of his character most deeply engraved and evident as a pattern throughout his youth and adulthood—played a crucial role in the disillusionment of a political generation. But neither the press nor the public was as sophisticated twenty-five years ago as they are today, and we had to wait for the first volume of Robert Caro's definitive biography to learn that Johnson's extraordinary preoccupation with, and talent for, secrecy was an inborn aspect of his temperament. He was not just an occasional liar when growing up; indeed, in college he was known as the biggest liar on campus—"Bullshit" Johnson.

Like Gary Hart, Lyndon Johnson employed his energy and wits in a lifelong effort to hide the truth about his behavior and to reconstruct hundreds of details about his youth. This compulsion carried over, inevitably, into his public conduct. The habit of deceit translated into the fateful policy he pursued as president during the war in Vietnam. In the campaign of 1964 Johnson bombarded the public with messages of hope and promise, presenting himself as the determined seeker after peace. Immediately upon assuming the role of Commander in Chief, he began expanding America's military involvement. In this public duplicity, he employed the same striking talent for prevarication that he had displayed all through his personal life.

Had people been aware of this predisposition in his character, they might have elected him anyway, on his many other merits, but wouldn't they have received his pronouncements on the war more skeptically? Instead, his presidency not only failed and left the Democratic party bitterly divided, it left Americans with a gaping "credibility gap." And that legacy, the start of a long-term mistrust of the president that would profoundly influence the nation's history, can be laid directly at the door of one man's character.

When I was asked to cover the '88 election, my idea was to measure the leadership potential of the presidential hopefuls against their own life histories. Some have asked, how can "psychoanalyzing these candidates from afar" really answer the questions of character? To begin with, I don't pretend to be a psychoanalyst, nor do I work like one. I base my character analyses on evidence—evidence I go out and dig up.

For a psychiatrist, the whole story is filtered through the patient's eyes—my sister grabbed all the attention, my mother never really loved me, my wife is self-centered. In contrast, I build my portrait of an individual on evidence culled from interviewing thirty, forty, or fifty people who have known him at different stages of his life—a parent, an uncle, a rivalrous brother, schoolmates; I seek out the significant teacher, the high-school coach who forged him into a competitor, the first wife, and the people who've worked with him, or for him, through all his successes and setbacks. I compare my perceptions with theirs. It's like working on a psychological thriller. Strangely enough, one soon realizes that very few of these people—maybe not even the person closest to him—know the whole story of what makes the man tick.

It is then, and only then, that I test out my insights on the person whose character development I am tracing. None of these portraits is drawn "from afar." In each instance, I have been fortunate to have had at least two long interviews with the presidential candidate himself, and to have traveled with him extensively under many different conditions. His response has always been illuminating and told a good deal about how well the man knows, or wants to know, himself.

Many odd bits of behavior turn up when one researches a person's entire life history. Everybody, after all, is engaged in the act of autobiography, and the way we tell our life stories as adults reveals what we feel is important now and in the future, as well as the difficulties we have in reinterpreting our stories as we go along. Political figures in particular are at pains to edit out the rougher edges of their past life. Some of them try to "erase" marks of character that might contradict the smooth, consistent images they want to project. Any odd bit of behavior, therefore, might be a clue to a larger truth. And when enough of those bits of behavior are connected, an outline begins to take shape that suggests the *personal myth* the individual is trying to create for him- or herself.

It is inevitable, then, that the journalist will come across something that is at odds with the candidate's public autobiography. The examples are many: differences in Hart's name, age, and signature. Contradictory stories about Jesse Jackson's appearance in a bloody shirt after the assassination of Martin Luther King. The Reverend Pat Robertson's concealment of the fact that he married his wife ten weeks before their first child was born. The question to be asked about such discoveries is always the same: Are they *relevant*?

The best gauge is the candidate himself. If he seems relaxed when questioned, and gives a simple, plausible explanation for his action, it may not bear mentioning. But if he gets tongue-tied or testy, as Hart did when CBS's Lesley Stahl first questioned him about his name change, there's probably a deeper significance. With Jackson, I returned in several separate interviews to the "bloody shirt" incident, and each time he gave me an explanation that contradicted his previous one. Pat Robertson claims that his indiscretion occurred long ago, in the years when he was "involved in wine, women and song on several continents" before he was "born again," and therefore has no relevance to his presidential qualifications. That might hold water except that he has spent most of his career as a minister railing against premarital sex and now lectures all Americans about their moral behavior. The same suggestion of a split personality is evident in a more serious contradiction. Here is a man who made his living for a quarter century as a television evangelist, and who articulated the goal, in 1980, of a White House and Congress run by nothing but "Spirit-filled Christians." When he later denies that identity in favor of presenting himself as a purely secular candidate, we are doubly alerted to Robertson's efforts to revise his life story.

Interviewing people and writing about human behavior for twenty-five years, along with the study of psychology, has allowed me the opportunity to test my insights constantly against a popular audience. Gradually I have learned how to look at an individual as a collection of selves—added or altered or outgrown at different stages of life. Anthropology gave me yet another set of tools, particularly useful in examining subcultures within our American society. Each of these candidates comes from a distinct subculture, and that has left an imprint, often a definitive imprint, on his character.

Gary Hart, for instance, came out of a powerful religious subculture: the Church of the Nazarene. When I traveled to Ottawa, Kansas, to look for clues to Hart's mysterious behavior, I found that almost none of the people who had known him as a child realized that the Hartpence family's church was very different from theirs. It was only in searching out others who had left strict Fundamentalist churches in adulthood that I was able to understand the lifelong, either/or struggle that can ensue from that kind of upbringing.

Michael Dukakis, son of two immigrants, was raised in a well-established suburb among affluent Yankees and Jewish Bostonians. His father, although he had talked himself into Harvard Medical School, was never able to shed his Old World Greek accent. His mother's belatedly learned English was almost stilted in its correctness. Michael Dukakis appears to have been assigned the role of moving the family out of the immigrant subculture and into the core culture. The goal was to prove that a Greek boy could be not just as good as but smarter and better than the others.

Jesse Jackson's charisma and drive were nourished in the subculture of the segregated black South. By spending time in his hometown of Greenville, South Carolina, I discovered that Jackson was one of those children whose special qualities are recognized by the community, and who is consequently designated to be "saved." The townsfolk protected and promoted little Jesse, recognizing that he had the qualities necessary to escape the limitations of poverty and skin color.

The study of character, as I see it, involves placing the individual in his subculture, then studying his development through each stage of his life, looking for the pivotal turning points, and marking what has changed and what remains repetitive or inflexible about his responses. The object is to pull through the important threads of experience that form a *pattern of behavior.*

After thinking about it for several years, I see three key reasons why it is not only useful, but essential, that we examine the character of those who ask us to put our country in their hands. Chiefly, it is to protect ourselves from electing a person whose character flaws, once subjected to the pressures of leading a superpower through the nuclear age, can weaken or endanger the course of our future.

Second, we need the cold slap of insight to wake us up from the smoothly contrived images projected by highly paid professional media experts who market the candidates like perfumed soap.

Third, we can benefit personally as we peer into the mirror afforded by our leaders, whose aspirations are more highly motivated and magnified versions of what we all dream of doing. What these people are made to reveal about themselves can offer us tools to do a better job in developing ourselves.

Let's look first at why we must protect ourselves. We live in a global electronic marketplace where money now moves faster than the human mind, where terrorism can hold a whole nation hostage to an aggrieved group whose name we can't even pronounce, where missiles are programmed to lift off in a matter of minutes after the command is given. In a world so often electrified by the suddenness of events and the swiftness of change, a great burden is placed on our leaders. The issues are too complex and the response time too condensed for us to put our faith in a candidate's position papers. We are left to search out those we can believe in as strong and sincere, fair and compassionate: real leaders to whom we can leave the responsibility to use good judgment when crises catch us unaware. We must therefore know our would-be leaders in a deeper way than ever before.

What really drives them to run for the highest office? Is it a healthy need to prove themselves? Or a pathological compulsion? Do they live in reality or invent rationalizations? Do their inner natures impel them to take high risks? Or to retreat from confrontation? Do they lie some of the time, or all of the time? What do we really demand of them, and what can we forgive them?

We have suffered repeated disillusionments with recent presidents because we failed to enter into the compact aware of even their most obvious patterns of behavior. The current fascination with character may be an instinctual reaction from Americans who have bought one president after another for

21

neatly packaged virtues they turned out not to have. The "new" Nixon. Lyndon "the peacemaker." The competent Carter. The realistic Reagan.

There is a second, equally important reason why we are dissecting these individuals as never before. Political parties have seldom been more interchangeable. Ideological differences have become blurred. Reform has eviscerated the power of party bosses. And the issues are too complicated to submit to clever political slogans. Indeed, a content analysis of twenty nomination acceptance speeches delivered between 1928 and 1964 by candidates of both parties found a consistent change: The issues have become increasingly diffuse.

The only thing that is certain is that nothing is certain for long. So the candidates play it safe, relying on their rhetorical skills to produce the greatest number of "sound bites" that say as little as possible. The Republican National Committee chairman, Frank Fahrenkopf, Jr., encouraged his candidates not to get into any ideological debates, and they agreed. In January of 1988, Republicans couldn't be certain whether by the summer they would want to run on, or from, the economy. And Democrats, forever warning about "the chickens coming home to roost," feared they might find themselves crying wolf all the way to an economic downturn that is not expected until *after* the election.

The Republican field, furthermore, is uniformly gray-haired, white, Anglo-Saxon, Protestant, and male. The two strongest candidates as the primary season began were both fuzzy on "the vision thing," as George Bush peevishly called it.

Bush is a status-quotician, remaining safely bland on all issues. Robert Dole is a deal-maker, who started in politics with no particular intellectual or ideological foundation and became a natural student of the art of compromise. Both have been unable to show voters that they have vision, that gut feeling for how the world works, for cause and effect, formed even before reasoning begins.

Neither Dole nor Bush had really discussed personal issues with the press before I did my character portraits of them. Dole, for example, is monosyllabic—a man straight out of a Hemingway novel—and unlikely to talk to a strange writer about the most intimate and anguished part of his past. I approached him as a survivor, having just written a book on the subject, and hoped I could strike a chord of empathy that might open him up. Little by little, the story of his war injuries and his long period of dependency during the recovery came out. It told me that here was a man who had become fiercely independent, but who still did not consider himself whole.

Once the article appeared, in March of 1987, Elizabeth Dole heard from many people that it "humanized" her husband. She told him, "Bob, this is what you've got to tell the American people. This is how they will understand you and what made you strong." Bob Dole finally gave in and thereafter used his experience in overcoming adversity as a central theme in his campaign.

The vice-president, too, was skittish when I first interviewed him. "So, this is gonna be a deal on where I'm coming from, a psychiatric layout?" he asked. He told me he was terrible at telling stories about his past, and that there were some sacred family moments he could not share. So I got him talking about his war experiences and his personal relationship with Ronald Reagan. His wife, Barbara, told me the painful story of the death of their child. Again, the word came back from his chief of staff that the article had "humanized" their man. Bush was soon projecting himself through character in interview after interview—as a World War II hero and a man whose personal loss of a daughter to leukemia had made him a stronger and better person.

So it was not by accident that character came to dominate the '88 campaign. Campaign strategists elected to make the character issue central. Jack Kemp and Pete du Pont's managers, and certainly Gary Hart, may have hoped to keep the focus strictly on issues. But the major candidates' managers wanted to make personal qualities dominant. The party is an abstraction, the issues are blurred—a "Dukakis" or a "Dole" is specific.

The Democrats started the '88 election season with a younger, multiracial, multireligious field of men. Nonetheless, the "front-runner" label bounced back and forth between Jesse Jackson, an international celebrity, and Gary Hart, an international sensation. While their notoriety used up a precious commodity in very short supply—public attention—the other five candidates, all new faces on the national scene, had terrible trouble breaking out and acquiring presidential stature. They, too, began to make use of the character issue.

Michael Dukakis hardly set the skin to tingling when he talked about chasing tax cheats and proposals for solid-waste disposal. His advisers knew that character was his best issue: Talking about the solid values he learned from his immigrant parents was the way to humanize this unemotional technocrat. Paul Simon presented himself as the good uncle, always talking about "caring" and pledging to balance the budget painlessly by lowering interest rates (which is not an executive privilege). Bruce Babbitt was a Jiminy Cricket character, America's conscience, the last honest man. Richard Gephardt—despite his record as an opportunistic Washington insider who has flip-flopped on abortion, busing, and Reaganomics—obdurately packaged himself as a prairie protectionist.

And so, for all the flaunted and disparaged "power of the media," it is the candidates themselves, and their managers or wives, who have learned to use character to their own advantage. And they can use it just as easily to exploit our emotions as to enlighten our understanding of them.

Today's highly manipulative personality marketing, through paid TV commercials as well as the massaging of the press, often misleads voters as to the true character of a candidate until he or she is in office. At that point, TV can be used as a personal instrument to put a spin on the news. A president can pursue policies that may have more to do with private obsessions than the public will. Richard Nixon was always motivated to use political office to make money; this fact, along with his paranoia and a penchant for secrecy and trickiness, had all been vividly displayed by the time of his defeat by John F. Kennedy in 1960. Yet the man who would later cover up the most famous burglary ever originating in the White House was able to come back, seven years later, and persuade the press that he was a "new" Nixon.

James David Barber, the most original and prescient student of the presidency in the last decade, predicted the dangers of a Nixonian character in the White House. Although this prediction—along with others made in his *The Presidential Character*—has been borne out, Barber still despairs at the laxness of political journalists in getting out the relevant information in time. Often asked by his history students at Duke University, "Well, everything is image, isn't it?" Barber has boiled down his point of view to four words: "Is Charlton Heston Moses?"

Charlton Heston is not Moses; but the distinction between image and reality has become as blurred in the political world as it ever was in Hollywood. There is always a lot of talk by the candidates about how they stand for the "basic American values." Yet over the last twenty years or so of cultural drift, the values that Americans could count on *other* Americans to share have been dwindling, and breaking up. When the *Los Angeles Times* did a massive study of over four thousand voters in 1987, it found that Americans were divided into *nine* different value orientations. It may be that the only commonly held values remaining are entertainment values. Particularly after seven years of exposure to a professional actor in the White House, performance values have taken hold across the board. And so, as fickle as directors at a casting session, we watch the candidates turn handsprings to get our attention as we click the channels. If it's not a good act, he's not going to get a callback.

Al Gore, for example, like several of his rivals, just wasn't flashy enough to attract many major magazine or TV profiles.

"You're too boring, Al," a *60 Minutes* producer told him. "Dole has The Arm, Jesse says, 'I'm a bastard,' even Dukakis had a failure. Nothing really interesting has happened to you."

"I went to Vietnam," Gore said.

"Yeah, but you were a *journalist*."

In fact, what I discovered from interviewing Al Gore's parents, army buddies, wife, and ex-girlfriend, and the candidate himself, is that his six months in Vietnam as a U.S. Army combat journalist had a profound effect on him. Both personally and politically. But the simple fact of Gore having been to Vietnam does not, in itself, tell us much at all about the man.

Similarly, the simple fact of Jesse Jackson having been born illegitimate does not begin to explain his unquenchable yearning for legitimacy.

What one has to search out is the individual *context*.

Certainly, to be an "outside child" in a black family in the Deep South was nothing unusual. The other children didn't start taunting him until Jesse was five. By then he lived with his mother and stepfather in an intact, two-income family, and in a neat wood-frame house. But when I went to Greenville, I found there was another house, in a neighborhood where the more favored black residents lived, a house so grand folks would stand and stare. This was the palace of Jesse's blood father— and the garden in which Jesse had spotted his half brother, playing like a prince.

Once Jesse had seen how his *own* other half lived, his was not a fine childhood at all. The sting was in the difference between the status of his half brother—a lighter-skinned, expensively dressed, private-school kid who could move back and forth between black and white worlds at a time when the color barrier was monolithic—and the stepson of a postal worker.

Just as we need to find the context to understand Jesse Jackson's hunger for legitimacy, we need to look beyond the preppy jokes to find the context for George Bush's passivity.

Bush's father was a towering man with a basso-profundo voice who brandished a belt to punish his children. The vice-president confirmed it for me: "Dad was really scary." Children of authoritarian fathers find different ways to adapt—even in the same family. One son may also become authoritarian. Another son might fight back or break off with his father. A third son may submit, appease, learn to please.

George Bush was the son who submitted. His older brother, Pressy, *did* argue with their father, but George, according to his younger brother, Jonathan—never. We can see the same pattern all through Bush's public life. It seems that George Bush has never met a president to whom he couldn't show unquestioning loyalty. When Republicans' infatuation with Barry Goldwater seemed to assure the Arizonan's presidential nomination, Bush declared himself a "Goldwater Republican." When Democrats were agonizing over Lyndon Johnson's Vietnam War policy,

Bush, then a first-term congressman, waved the flag for him: "I will back the President no matter what weapons we use in Southeast Asia." And during the Watergate scandal, when Bush was G.O.P. chairman, even his mother tried to persuade him that "tricky Dick" was lying. But Bush was the last man in the party to believe ill of Richard Nixon.

In judging character, one can never be sure the judgment is 100 percent accurate. Naturally, similar family circumstances will have very different effects on different people. My work is to collect not just single incidents but "characteristics," meaning stable, internal factors, and to figure out how they have been woven together over the years to form that pattern of behavior.

Some readers will make their own connections between the many details offered in these portraits, and come out with a very different assessment of a candidate's character. I have written portraits I considered, on balance, negative; but readers will write in saying, "Now I'm convinced, he'd make a great president."

Finally, examining how character is formed in our national leaders is an effective way to learn about ourselves. On the premise that character reaps destiny, we can see that destiny played out most vividly in the life histories of the men and women in whom millions invest their trust and their dreams. The stories of our leaders' lives—like movies—offer a common point of reference, since we all know something about them.

Part of the fascination lies in comparing ourselves with these larger-than-life figures:

What do they have that you and I don't?

What is different—bold, cunning, courageous, even bizarre or pathological—about the way these people take on the great psychological issues of adulthood and battle their way to positions of power and respect? Or, when luck or chance thrusts power into their laps, why are they ready and able to seize the moment? We can learn from these case histories what is demanded, what works, and what is the price for avoiding or denying confrontation with life's major passages. Far from being cowed, felled, or fatally scarred by a major psychological crisis, most of the leaders I have studied *confronted* a personal crisis and were powerfully galvanized by it.

We often assume that those who rise to great prominence have had a head start in their family background, or at least no obstacles to slow them down. But consider the father of Mike Dukakis, who came to America at fifteen and used to run every day from the restaurant where he worked to English classes at the Y.M.C.A. Or Albert Gore, Sr., whose educational horizons were reduced by the Depression; he drove fifty miles a night to the Y.M.C.A. to study law. Hart's parents didn't finish high school. Gephardt's father worked as a milkman. Jackson's great-grandmother was a slave.

Furthermore, many of the candidates have overlooked or overcome physical limitations, which speaks volumes for the triumph of intention over circumstance. Dukakis had himself programmed to reach a height of five feet eleven, but slowed down in junior high when he hit five feet seven. Notwithstanding, when the gym teacher ordered the tall kids to line up for basketball, Dukakis unashamedly joined them. To compensate for his height, he would go out in the snow, in gloves, and shoot baskets off his garage. Jesse Jackson had to overcome a stutter. Dole survived when doctors had all but left him to die.

So the prominent politician is not necessarily a product of privilege, and often has had fewer advantages than many Americans. Indeed, at least three of the candidates examined here are driven by the need to overcome a negative identity from their past. Hart, Jackson, and Dole all knew shame before they were able to do much about it. And for those who have experienced it, shame comes to drive many other emotions.

A ferocious competitive spirit, however, is one thing they all have in common. George Bush was practically born with a bat in one hand and a tennis/squash/Ping-Pong racket in the other; whatever the competition, he loves to win. Bob Dole as a boy pumped iron with cement blocks and lead pipe in his basement. Al Gore competed with his best friend in doing contortions on water skis; he never gave in, simply carried over a loss in one contest to the next playing field. Jesse Jackson still has to win when he shoots basketballs at home with his own kids; more than once, his wife has had to call an ambulance when he has thrown his back out.

Sports metaphors figure prominently in the way each of these men tells his story. Jack Kemp can hardly make a point without referring to football. The male public relates to athletic prowess far more readily than to intellectual brilliance. Probably the main qualification Bill Bradley has in the minds of American men who were hoping he would enter the '88 race as a dark horse is his performance in the 1969 Knicks season.

Certainly the tedious, exhausting, and often demeaning process of campaigning demands a stamina and discipline equal to those of most professional athletes. No off-season for the would-be president. The six or eight months of building name recognition now runs straight into six months of primaries, then into the conventions, then on to the national campaign—during which even the losers are expected to work hard. Presidential candidates stick their hands over the flame, get burned, stick out their hands again, and keep them there for a year, two years. This is how they are different from you and me.

And what makes them just the same as you and me?

Most of these would-be leaders think of themselves as having godlike attributes. But they face the same tasks of development and must find ways to deal with the same predictable crises of adult life—leaving home, establishing an identity distinct from their parents, developing the capacity for intimacy, finding the proper course in life, making commitments, then rebounding from failures, surviving successes, and facing the resurgence of adolescent discontents in midlife under the shadow of their increasingly real mortality. That is what makes these portraits relevant even after the nominations and the general election: They are case histories that instruct us in how, and how not, to conduct ourselves to win at life. We can use these characters as mirrors of our own character— reflecting both our flaws and our strengths. Seeing how their various attempts to change and adapt have played out from earliest childhood through public life can be a catalyst for taking steps to change ourselves.

Each of us has a characteristic manner in which we attack the tasks of development and react to our own efforts. Some of us take a series of cautious, planful steps forward, then one or two back, always minimizing risk. Others thrive on setting up sink-or-swim situations: Watch me, I can do it! We all know people who seem to live by accident, waiting for life to happen to them and reacting only when they absolutely must. Still others appear to be changing dramatically, but it's all an act, a series of one-night stands, perhaps before enthusiastic audiences, but serving only to mask the essential fear of confronting the real "me" of childhood frustrations.

I have called this characteristic mode of reacting to "the changes and chances of this mortal life" a person's *step-style.* The six candidates in search of character together with the sitting president, whose portraits make up this book, are arranged according to step-styles. This schema should enable the reader to focus on what he or she can learn *from* them as well as about them.

FALSE CHANGE

Grandiose characters often appear, as they wish to, larger than life. In their public behavior, they seem high-spirited and extroverted, wholly confident of their cleverness, attractiveness, and ability to excel in whatever they attempt. But in private, the morning after, the sense of futility and emptiness can return and throw them into depression and introversion. Feelings of shame or anger carried along since childhood flood into the void all over again. This is because, despite his boldness in taking many risky steps in his outer behavior, the grandiose character may never have changed much inside. His self-presentation is of a "false self."

Alice Miller, a Swiss psychoanalyst, describes the deeper dilemma of the grandiose personality in her *Prisoners of Childhood*. "If his success the previous night only serves as the denial of childhood frustrations, then, like every substitute, it can only bring momentary satiation. True satiation is no longer possible, since the right time for that now lies irrevocably in the past. The former child no longer exists, nor do the former parents."

The grandiose person's sexual partners must be many, because he is constantly occupied with gaining admiration. Casanova depicted both the bravura antics and the sudden collapses of self-esteem common to this step-style. But whatever the wound of childhood that drives him, the grandiose character cannot heal it with outer success or sexual admiration. The enemy is within, where the true self has remained unconscious, and therefore undeveloped. A new basis for self-respect must be built on truth.

Gary Hart and Jesse Jackson both illustrate a tendency toward and facility for false change. Both have invented and repeatedly reinvented themselves, both routinely falsify their pasts, and both use the political process as therapy for the private demons they cannot lay to rest.

Gary Hart is a double man. All his life he has lived a lie. Severely restricted by his upbringing from experimenting in any of the ways normal for a bright, imaginative boy, Hart broke out at twenty-four, and seems to be stuck in a perpetual adolescence. He tried to narrow his problem to one "damn fool" escapade and the admission he had committed adultery. But the real issue is character: a pattern of recklessness and high-risk behavior that causes him to self-destruct just when what he supposedly wants is within his grasp. His compulsion is rooted not in seeking illicit sex, but in proving he is so superior, so utterly worthy, that he can break all the rules of personal and political conduct and still satisfy that inner censor who keeps him a prisoner of his childhood.

Similarly, Jesse Jackson must continually demonstrate, first to the father who rejected him, and then to the world at large, that he is worthy to be seated at the banquet table of ultimate power. To do so, he crashes the game at higher and higher levels. He has largely succeeded already—whatever the outcome of the elections, he will be at the table when the Democratic power brokers sit down before and after their convention. But Jackson's quest is insatiable. He cannot rest until he proves that he is *somebody* so singular, none of the usual "white man's" rules apply to him.

FORCED CHANGE

Forced change is often the result of a serious life accident. Bob Dole grew up believing he was a great athlete and putting little effort into his mediocre grades. Then he went away to war, where his gift was shattered.

"You change the way you measure everything," as Dole described the turning point to me. "Life becomes about learning how to use what you have left."

A survivor of forced change develops the strength and self-directedness necessary to fix his sights and chart a course without depending on outside forces—indeed, often in spite of them. He may go so far as to reject all but his own inner judgments.

PASSIVE CHANGE

The passive changer makes himself over into whatever the dominant power figure wants him to be, even at the expense of developing any strongly defended beliefs or standards of his own. He may attempt one grand step—jumping out of the parental mold and into a very different kind of work or life-style for a while—but the task of separating oneself from the inner censors of childhood cannot be completed with one step. Indeed, developmental gains won in one stage of life can later be lost—and are not always rewon.

George Bush is the quintessential compliant changer. Although he made several early attempts to establish his own identity, it was so much easier for him to defer to those in power—to be a lifelong teacher's pet. Bush's refusal to confront the central psychological crisis of his life, however, has a price. The deeper marks of individuality can be gradually erased and the strength of character weakened.

ACCELERATED CHANGE

A circumstance sometimes dictates that a person develop more quickly than is demanded by the average life course. Abandonment by a parent, whether by divorce or untimely death, may dictate that a child assume an adult role prematurely. Or a famous or powerful parent may leave such giant footsteps to be filled that the child is driven to work twice as hard and fast to prove his own self-worth. Alternatively, or sometimes even simultaneously, the drive may be to make up for the parent's failure.

This step-style usually produces accelerated growth, but that growth is uneven. If intense effort is focused on intellectual development, for example, the building of strong friendships may of necessity be neglected, and the individual left without adequate support during a life crisis. Nevertheless, people who truly excel at what they do usually have an accelerated learning curve.

Albert Gore, Jr., son of an awesomely self-assured senator, has been at pains all his life to do twice as well as expected, so as to prove he is not coasting on his father's coattails. His intellectual and political growth has always proceeded at double time. In this campaign, he believes, he is developing faster than ever. But he is not well liked by his colleagues on Capitol Hill, some of whom are jealous and resentful of his premature national recognition. Any highly successful young challenger has to be prepared to face equal parts admiration and jealousy. If the latter is not disarmed, it can become a deadly weapon against him.

CHANGE AFTER FAILURE

What happens when a wunderkind, who has always been good at everything he did and achieved his goals ahead of schedule, slams into a stunning defeat? He can fall apart, look for scapegoats, turn bitter and vindictive, seek frantic escapes from the truth, or give up and join the walking dead. Or, he can take time out to get to know himself, and work on the characteristics that led to his failure.

The making over of Michael Dukakis is almost a clinical case history of a man who, having hit failure when he lost reelection as governor of Massachusetts in 1977, stopped, picked himself up, and took the blame. After months of numbness he began painstakingly, cognitively, to take apart those aspects of his character about which so many had complained for so long, and to put the pieces back together differently. His story shows what kind of adaptation is possible, even of inborn traits.

REFUSAL TO CHANGE

The mind is formed to an astonishing degree by the act of inventing oneself. In telling and retelling our stories, we create our own plot line, and that plot line lays down a track within which our *intentions* shape our perceptions. From the time we learn to speak, we begin working at getting our narrative straight: that is, trying to fit together what we *do* with what we *think* about what we do. (Am I the hero, the villain, the victim, or just the bystander of my story?) As we move along in life, the highest act of memory is to sort out from the grab bag of our experiences those events and people *we* determine are of significance, and to assign meanings to them.

An eminent psychologist who has been studying the way people tell their life stories, Dr. Jerome Bruner of New York University, finds that our self-reports soon turn into self-fulfilling prophecies. The ways people tell their stories "become so habitual that they finally become recipes for structuring experience itself, for laying down routes into memory," and finally, for guiding their lives.

Performers and deniers are uniquely defended against having to change their actual behavior, because they are so clever at reinterpreting their plot lines and rewriting their memories. To change what we really think about what we do requires daring. Simply to change how we package and present what we do requires only imagination and the endless ability to rationalize. The model of this step-style is Ronald Reagan.

Reagan appears never to have changed at any deep level. He has simply reinvented himself, constantly improving on the plot line and script of his long, highly successful performance. He is by nature a dreamer, by training a performer. These two central aspects of his character are evident in everything he has done, from early childhood onward. First his mother, then his community, and finally the world rewarded Ronald Reagan for denying unpleasant realities and creating pleasing illusions.

The yearnings of Americans to compensate for the failings of their current president, by electing his antithesis, provided the climate in which Ronald Reagan's personality showed to best advantage. Most Americans voted *against* Jimmy Carter. In a country depressed and withdrawn, after a period of disgrace spanning the withdrawal from Vietnam and the humiliation by hostage-takers in Iran, candidate Reagan struck just the right chord of unapologetic patriotism and old-time religion.

But even the candidate himself warned us in 1980: "What makes you think that whatever image is presented is the true image? . . . Don't become the sucker generation." We didn't listen. Once more, we looked to one man to make everything right. We believed the image he projected had a foundation. It did not. Ronald Reagan has always stayed on the surface of events, absorbed facts selectively, and denied the dark side of life. Denial of unpleasant realities long ago became his characteristic problem-solving style. He is a man greatly gifted in making others believe the illusions in which *he* needs to believe. Americans, too, wanted so badly to believe, we let him convince us of propositions that were patently absurd.

Once people began to catch on, many simply lowered their expectations. Reagan was so charming, so superficially genial; if he managed to remember what country he was talking about, stayed awake, and stuck to the script, that made his meetings a success. After all, didn't every foreign leader seem to want to have his picture taken with this symbolically strong superpower leader? Reagan was always judged on form, not substance.

Finally, however, in his last term, even his own illusions began to unravel. Americans faced the now ritual disenchantment with yet another president who wouldn't play it straight.

There exists between each of us and our leaders a powerful *personal* connection. Given the hair-trigger global village that we now all inhabit, it is crucial that each of us be able to discern and weigh the innermost natures of our would-be leaders *before* they dominate our television screens and take control of our fates.

But character is more than just a factor in our evaluation of how we are going to vote. It affects us all as an essential ingredient in how we work, play, and deal with other people. Reading about how seven characters have learned and changed may suggest a new perspective from which to judge our associates as well as ourselves, a context within which to clarify our own values, and a more informed basis on which to decide how we want our country to change. It is in that spirit that I present my work.

TWO

Gary Hart:
The Road to Bimini

Six weeks before Gary Hart killed off his presidential candidacy, in May 1987, I had a story in the works describing the war that raged within this double man. It was a war to the death. After studying Hart on and off for three years, I had become convinced that this time around it was not a question of *if* Gary Hart would destroy himself but a question of when.

He accomplished the stunning feat of political self-destruction in only twenty-six days. Why would any man in his right mind defy a *New York Times* reporter who asked about his alleged womanizing to "put a tail on me," then cancel his weekend campaign appearances and arrange a tryst at his Washington town house with a Miami party girl? What demon was loose in the fifty-year-old front-runner of the Democratic party, who lurched across the chartered yacht *Monkey Business,* drink in hand, and boasted to a model friend of Donna Rice's that this was her big chance to sleep with the next president of the United States?

When he was caught and cut and ran, I thought that put an end to my story. Then debate broke out. Adamant that he had in no way transgressed, Hart lashed out last May at the wrongheadedness and prurience of the press and stalked off the public stage in anger and defiance. Hart's own divided mind found its analog in his defenders who still believe a Chinese wall can exist between public and private selves. Husbands and wives bickered over what adultery has to do with whether or not a person would make a good president.

Almost immediately, Hart himself began to doubt the necessity for halting his campaign. He spent the first weekend at
home with his wife and children, behind drawn curtains in their
cabin in Troublesome Gulch. It was the longest time they had
all been together in years. Hart was surprised to discover his
kids—Andrea, twenty-three, who was in and out of the University of Colorado, and John, twenty-one, who was doing poorly
at the University of Massachusetts—were furious with their
father for quitting. Warren Beatty, Hart's closest adviser, told
him he was crazy not to get back in.

And so, two days after his formal withdrawal, the isolated
Coloradan began talking about a very different path to the White
House. He would mount a "light infantry campaign," according
to a former campaign worker who sat in on a strategy meeting
at Hart's home: no manager, no media adviser, no lieutenants
at all, just Gary making speeches. "He had it all figured out,"
recalled the aide. ". . . I thought he might mean 1992 or '96."
But Hart, who had received condolences from Richard Nixon,
was not planning to lie low as long as the disgraced Watergate
president had. Nixon stayed out of sight for three years. Hart
would be even shrewder: He would use the press to attack the
press. The harsher the media attacks on Hart, the better they
would play into his strategy, according to John Emerson, a
leftover from the '84 campaign who talked with the candidate
after the May disaster. "Gary hoped he would get into a situation where everybody was against him but the people."

After months of playing peek-a-boo, Hart charged into the
middle of the pre-primary playing field just before Christmas,
taking aim against anyone who dared raise matters of personal
character, temperament, and patterns of behavior, and insisting
they were irrelevant to the presidency. Brandishing his own
ninety-four-page campaign Bible, he claimed he had "done my
penance on television," by admitting he was an adulterer in an
interview with Ted Koppel. He pronounced himself "forgiven
by God." And as a result of his self-made destruction and
telegenic resurrection, he wanted the voters to believe he was
now *more* qualified to be their leader.

Hart's public psychodrama remains an object of intense

curiosity because the central question is so disturbing: How could a man so dangerously flawed, and so insistent upon his private right to to lie, cheat, and walk away from one commitment after another, come so close to persuading the people that he was fit to lead a superpower through the perils of the nuclear age? The key to the downfall of Gary Hart is not adultery. It is character. And that is an issue that does not go away.

A pathological deficit in Hart's character riddled the public man as thoroughly as it ruled the private one. Through both his races for the presidency, to appease the inner dictator of his sore guilty soul, Hart sought out pretty spiritual playmates like Marilyn Youngbird, the Native American divorcée, who would worship his driven-to-do-good side and play back the message that he was worthy, even exalted, in his quest for power. Such worshipers were not, finally, a fair match against wilder demons that drew him to the satyrs, procurers, hustlers, and bimbos always first to spot a weakness in a powerful man and eager to exploit it.

The people close to Hart knew of his bizarre behavior patterns. Almost every one of the key players from his 1984 campaign had turned his back on Hart and walked away in puzzlement or silent disgust. The new players in his 1988 campaign rationalized to themselves and lied to us. His wife, Lee, a woman with a twenty-eight-year investment to protect, continued to be his accomplice in the sham that here was a healthy, happy man with a rehabilitated marriage who was our next great hope for leader of the free world.

Clues to Hart's fatal character flaw were strewn all across his public life. If one missed the signs there, he had been flaunting the same weakness in his private escapades for at least fifteen years. Yet millions of Americans, manipulated by highly paid media advisers and Hart's millionaire movie and video producer friends, did miss the clues. And when he reentered the race in December, the sheer force of celebrity catapulted him virtually overnight past the six winter soldiers in his party to a smug first-place position in national polls. That is why it is a serious exercise to try to solve the psychological mystery of this double man. At a deeper level, the revelations raise the question of how much we really know about the character of any of the candidates running for presidential office. How hard are we willing to work to save ourselves from waking up, once more, with the terrible aftertaste of a night on the town with yet another un-revealed and perfidious president?

Retracing his steps, I traveled through the various worlds of Gary Hart. The population of each world was alien to and unaware of the others. With the help of his sister, aunts, uncles, and cousins, his pastor and old Sunday-school chums from the Church of the Nazarene, and his closest classmates in Ottawa, Kansas, I reexamined the mental and moral distinguishing marks left on his character by an upbringing far from normal. Then I went on to the disciples who had believed in his worthy side as he cut a bold and even sacrificial swath across American politics. Feeling betrayed, most wanted to share what had always puzzled them about Hart.

To both of these groups the world of Donna Rice was about as familiar as a black hole. It is a demimonde that thrives on the illusion that beautiful young women and drugs are effort-lessly available, as party favors. Since Donna was determined to come out of the scandal squeaky clean, a celebrity who is "buddy-buddy" with Barbara Walters, she and the agent she hired as a "crisis manager" were not forthcoming, and clearly had a manufactured story to tell. So I sought out her father, who admitted his own doubts about his daughter's life-style. And, with the help of Miami and Fort Lauderdale prosecutors and drug-enforcement agents, I explored Donna's live-in love affair with a big-time cocaine dealer, who is currently serving ten years in a federal penitentiary. Five of Donna's friends illuminated the rest of the smoke and mirrors in this high-rolling nether-world. It might be seen as the forbidden picture show to which Hart's hidden, sybaritic side had always longed for admission. Indeed, it might be one in a dizzying series of mirrors on which, according to a senior political consultant who has known and watched him for over a decade, "Gary Hart has been writing in lipstick for years, 'Stop me before I fuck again.' "

Out of the lull of a thousand miles of plains the visitor is jolted into Ottawa, Kansas, by bumping over a railroad crossing. They crisscross the town, these old tracks that hum with the importance of faraway places—Chicago, St. Louis, New York, even California—but the trains do not stop here. Ottawa is one of those respectable blurs glimpsed by people who pass through; no hope of greatness in it. The tracks serve only to fence in this flat farm town, as if to keep it safe from worldly contamination, safe even from the future.

Scarcely a thing has changed in Ottawa in the twenty-five years since Gary Hart broke out. The houses are still bungalow-like clapboard boxes with gliders on their sagging porches, proud, tired, and perpetually in need of a fresh coat of paint. Apart from a few tire swings and mechanical rotating daisies, precious little is squandered on pleasure here. People still eat the same syrup-soaked foods and drive '47 Chevys (now rebuilt) and set fans on their floors against the creep of heat. The girls still have doughy legs and the boys Fuller brush cuts, and the fifty-year-old men who were boys with Gary Hartpence get to-gether down at the Main Street bakery every morning and have the same conversation they've been having for the past quarter of a century. The fourth of May was different. The guys were all waiting on Walt Dengel with a wallbanger of news.

"I see your buddy Gary did it to himself," one taunted.

"You've got to be kidding me," said the respected town mortician. Dengel, who has known Gary since fourth grade, had been about to open a local Hart headquarters.

"No, man, he got caught with his pants down."

"Dumb," Dengel muttered.

"Midlife crisis, I bet" was Walt Dengel's theory by the time we met. "But if it'd been me, I'd a come out swinging." Suddenly he banged on the counter. "It just ticks me off, how he did it. Did he want to get caught? Get it over with? Is that it?"

Two weeks after the scandal broke, these men who are contemporaries of Hart's, stumped by his mystifying behavior, were scouring their memories all over again to offer me clues. The first words that came to mind when his schoolmates described Gary Hartpence were invariably "always neat and clean." Skinny and fine-boned, the boy always wore a long-sleeved dress shirt and perfectly pressed slacks, with his hair cropped short above jug ears—a creature resembling in no way the rangy, cowboy-booted desperado of later years.

41

They discovered that not one of them had been close to him. Not one had gone home with him. The more Gary's schoolmates scratched their heads, the more they questioned if the boy they thought they had known, the boy they had given back to the press in tidy anecdotes, ever really existed.

His athletic record, for instance, is pure fiction. Hartpence played a fair game of touch football in eighth grade, but didn't even come out in the ninth. The only league in which he played basketball was the church league, which admitted boys for superlative attendance at Sunday school. No, his schoolmates corrected the record, Gary wasn't good enough to make any varsity team except tennis, which was a sport for leftovers. Classmate Kent Granger reminisced over their last tennis game, in which he beat Hartpence 6–0. Granger remembers because he had already contracted the polio virus at the time.

Granger believes he knew Gary as well as any of his classmates did. But they weren't in the same "carload," and the social-classification system in Ottawa came down to who was in which car draggin' Main Street. Granger belonged to the jock crowd. "We smoked and had successful relationships with ladies." Being that Ottawa had no bars, there were only a few outlets for boys to show their virility. One was to let a little air out of the car tires and hump them over the railroad tracks next to Skunk Run, then gun it eight miles to the next town, hoping a train didn't catch you first. In a recent autobiographical sketch, Hart passed himself off as a participant in this daredevil pursuit. "Not Gary," swears Walt Dengel. "He wasn't nocturnal then." He chuckles. "Not like he is now. He didn't drag Main Street, either. He'd only come out for special occasions."

The Youth Center was the social cornice of Ottawa, equivalent to the dance assembly, the country club, meeting under the clock at the Biltmore, the essence of being "in." Elbowed back by the tracks of the Santa Fe line, the Youth Center still functions today, with Ping-Pong tables and a record player and chaperons. When Gary's classmates gathered there, everybody danced. Everybody? I ask.

"Maybe Gary didn't," amends Dengel. Gary and his sister, Nancy Lee, were never welcomed by the clique at the Youth

Center. "They thought they were fancier people," Nancy Lee recalls with a wilted bitterness.

Gary never talked about his feelings. Nice kid, but he never gave much. Granger pegs him as the slowest in maturing of anyone in their class, in every respect except intellectually. One thing they all agree upon for certain: The "mischievous" boy Hart tried to manufacture for the press at his staged homecoming in the spring of 1987 was an outright lie.

"When the mischief started," recalls Kent Granger, "Gary always faded away."

Granted, he belonged to the strictest church in town, but the whole town was conservative, a dry town in a dry state, with standardized Christian manners that equated dullness with godliness. The other kids assumed Gary Hartpence's church was pretty much like theirs, the First United Methodist or the First Baptist. But by their very stature and social prestige, the two redoubtable spinster churches, which still dominate the town, bear no resemblance to the grocery-box plainness of the Church of the Nazarene.

In fact, the Nazarene church at that time in Ottawa had no more than fifty members. Of the four young people who belonged, two were Gary and his sister. The entire sect had a national membership of around 233,000. Its rules of Christian conduct, meant to protect initiates from going to hell, forbade dancing, listening to the radio, seeing movies—one never knew when something satanic might come on—and, of course, drinking. Some of the Nazarenes in Ottawa today told me they had never seen a picture show. Well, maybe one Roy Rogers movie, but only because the children insisted on seeing Trigger. Nobody could remember Gary so much as taking a beer all during high school. He implored select schoolmates to give him blow-by-blow descriptions of the movies they saw. He never told anyone why. He made up excuses. Even then, he lived a lie.

I called on a spry lady who at one point lived two doors down from the Hartpences and had been close to Gary's mother. Using the terminology of their church, I asked if she thought Gary had backslid seriously.

"Honey, well, yes, I do. Gary was a good boy. I hope there's some good in him left. As long as he was a Christian, we'd have known he wouldn't do this. But as you get into these worldly jobs, you backslide. Power gets to a man." Her lips pinched tight. "I could just pull his ears."

I had asked Hart in an interview in 1984 about his own boyhood conception of God.

"Was He punitive?"

"Yeah, if you did bad." He laughed. "He was a God of mercy, but of wrath as well."

Born with an introverted temperament, his early upbringing reinforced his cool, distant nature.

"Was your mother demonstrative?" I asked Hart in one of our 1984 interviews.

"Not really."

I had been warned repeatedly not to ask the next question: "Did she hug you?"

Warily, "Did she what? Oh, yeah. But not demonstrative in a loud way."

I asked about his first memory of Ottawa, Kansas.

"Very cold," he blurted. "I remember one cold winter day— Dad wasn't there. I came downstairs. I was about five. I put on an old coat sweater hanging from a hook and a mouse ran out of the sleeve. My mother screamed. I remember that vividly."

His mother had drilled into the young Gary her own dark evangelical beliefs: that man is born with a sinful nature, that natural functions and appetites must "continue to be controlled" by "putting to death the deeds of the body." The only refuge the boy found from the cold, from the frozen dogma of a bleak church, from the instability of frequent moving and the constant state of alert created by his ailing mother, was in books.

"I read all of Zane Grey, then I got off on science fiction," he told me. "I loved to go up to Kansas City 'visiting.' All I'd do is sit and read the magazines. My family was too poor to afford magazines."

Friends could not remember a girl ever making a play for the straitlaced Gary. "Lots of laughs but not a looker" was how the kinder kids described the girl he dated his senior year, Kay Shaughnessy. Kay became a career navy officer and never did marry.

The name of Ann Warren was mentioned. She spent time

around Hart when he came back to Ottawa for his class reunion in 1984, and noticed that he didn't say much, just sat back, detached and looking uncomfortable, as he always had been.

"I did date Gary in high school," she acknowledged. "But he wasn't romantic, no, definitely he wasn't." Still, when the extroverted Ann went on to date another boy, Hart had a fit.

"I wonder about all these affairs, if he really enjoyed them," mused the widow Warren. "Maybe it was just revenge for all the things he never had. I think he's still thumbing his nose at the world."

Nina (pronounced Nye-nah) Pritchard Hartpence, Gary's mother, was someone Walt Dengel knew rather well. She made frequent use of the ambulance owned by his father's funeral home. "It was more of a delivery-service type thing," Dengel said, by way of explaining Nina Hartpence's frequent calls demanding to be taken into Kansas City to the hospital. "She was frail, kinda chronic. I couldn't even tell you what we took her to the hospital for." This was not surprising, since Mrs. Hartpence, who had always complained of vague ailments, kept her family on call for such trips throughout the last fifteen years of her life.

The local newspaper found out the famous politician's mother had moved the family at least sixteen times before Gary got out of high school. Nina Hartpence would take a place, clean it up, then move—once in the course of a single day—and start cleaning again. Nina had an extraordinary hold over her family. When she wasn't turning the whole household upside down to meet her standards of perfection, she would take to her bed and control everyone around her by complaints of headaches, or asthma, or heart palpitations, and, ultimately, thyroid problems. Relatives still talk about how Carl Hartpence, Gary's father, waited on her hand and foot. He couldn't even get out of the house to go fishing for fear of leaving her alone.

"She was strictly religious," her brother-in-law, Ralph Hartpence, told me. "She'd always quote out of the Bible. She'd hold services in the church and get Gary to preach with her."

Did other members of the family think Nina's strictness strange? I asked Uncle Ralph, who comes from the more passive father's side of the family.

"It sure showed on Gary," said his uncle. "He stayed with us at our trailer house in Colorado in '48, when he was ten or 'leven. Never saw such a well-behaved boy in my life." Gary dared not take more than one toy out of the box at a time.

"Why don't you take the whole box outdoors?" his uncle Ralph kept coaxing. "Take out all the toys, like my kids do, and have a ball."

"I'm afraid of getting dirty," he remembers Gary saying.

"That boy needed to be turned loose."

Not according to Aunt Erma Louise, who of all the relatives remains closest in spirit to Nina Pritchard Hartpence. "Gary's mother was compulsively clean," she said approvingly, and Gary was always a good boy, she emphasized. I asked what she thought of his recent behavior.

"Somebody set him up." (This was not a phrase that came naturally from a lady with hair the yellowed white of never-used linen.) "I'll never see and never believe, just like Nina wouldn't have believed it." Her demeanor perfectly expressed the contentment of the walking dead, a condition distinct from that of her sister-in-law, Gary's deceased mother, only by the outstanding balance to be settled on her account with her Maker.

Outside the gaunt parsonage that was once a home of the Hartpences, I met the current pastor. Gary Hartpence is a dead soul as far as the Church of the Nazarene is concerned. He died the day—the Reverend Earl Copsey remembers the date exactly, September 20, 1968—"he left the church to go back out to the world of sin."

The truly singular feature of the Nazarene sect is that its members believe one can, and should, achieve perfection in this life. No wonder Hart admitted to me in 1984, "The one Protestant quality I suppose I've got my share of is guilt."

People raised in such strict Fundamentalist families never experience the turbulence common to normal adolescence. And since the stage of rebellion and identity formation is not allowed, adult breakaways like Hart often behave for years like teenagers. Rebellious, angry, and irresponsible as grownups, they commonly harbor an extreme fear of commitment, and buck any sort of structure. Yet, even as they are compelled to break rules and backslide toward Satan, the voice of a wrathful God is almost impossible to silence. The hold that this kind of authoritarian upbringing has on a person can last thirty or forty years after the formal church tie has been severed.

Charleen Peterson Roberts, a teenager a little older than Gary at the time, left the Nazarene church even before he did. But the church never really leaves a person. The world is black and white, and there are only two ways to go. Charleen's voice lowered superciliously. "Gary's going to hell, that's all, it's pretty plain. If he doesn't get right with God."

Donna Rice, or "the woman in question," as Hart dehumanized her in his public references, was cast as the villain of the piece. "Irate" is how Gary's sister described herself when I phoned the day the infamous picture appeared in *The National Enquirer.* "Girls like her are a dime a dozen. I can tell you, when Gary and I sat and talked on April 12, he said what an asset Lee was."

Then why, I asked, would Hart have taken such a cruel and reckless chance? Nancy Lee said she meant to ask him. A week later she was calm and implacable.

"Are you reading that crap in the newspapers?" Hart had demanded of her. "Well, don't, just don't," he directed. He and Lee had gotten on the phone and given her the family line: Their marriage is stronger than ever; the real truth will eventually come out; the "setup" was planned by Hart's enemies even before he announced.

"Why would Gary give up something like Lee for that lowlife," Nancy Lee asked rhetorically, "a twenty-nine-year-old tramp?"

But the evidence is that when Gary Hart did break out into the worldly world, he gravitated toward its farthest extreme, using hedonists and fixers to find him girls. They led him into the kind of suspect scenes where party drugs were ubiquitous. With a lust for danger, he plunged finally into the world of Donna Rice, a world even her father feared to look at too closely.

Spindle-legged and buck-toothed as a young girl in Irmo, South Carolina, Donna Rice made mostly A's and did missionary work for the Southern Baptists one summer. She blossomed by the age of twenty-one into a willowy if flat-chested blonde, not beautiful but pretty, not unintelligent but undirected. Of what use was a Phi Beta Kappa key (offered to about 140 students—or 6 percent of her senior class) if it couldn't buy her fame? She figured the easiest way to come by celebrity, according to her friends, was to use her looks to make the right connections to meet "people of significance."

In a lengthy interview with her father, Bill Rice, a highway engineer for the federal government in South Carolina, the nebulous outlines of her reported life-style began to take on definition. "She won that beauty contest and they put her up in New York and that's when her life started to change."

A New York businessman, according to one newspaper report, met Donna at a party and took pity on the struggling newcomer. He invited her to stay at his East Side apartment for a few days. She moved in and stayed for two years. The anonymous businessman described Donna as "always up." She would go to discos all night, sleep late, and use his telephone constantly. Her room was always a mess, and although she turned up at "go-sees," he said she didn't need to take more than one modeling job every three months.

"I've been a little disturbed by her life-style," her father admitted. In June 1981, Donna called him from New York and warbled, "Guess who I went out with last night? Prince Albert."

"Who in hell is Prince Albert?" her father drawled. But that was typical of the calls Donna made to her friends and family, itemizing each "date" with a famous person: the prince of Monaco, Tony Curtis, rock musician Don Henley. "She was always out having a good time," her father recalled. "Driven to dating celebrities," said the businessman. "They went from club to club every night," remembered Shirley Semones, mother of Donna's friend Julie.

"She drifted into acting because it's what everybody else was doing," added Julie Semones. "She hasn't really been serious about it." Donna didn't trouble to take classes or do plays, but she was nothing if not persistent about using people to get to the right parties, Julie recalled. "She'd meet people through me and she'd say, 'Why don't you stay in touch with these people? They're good connections.'"

Finally, through some Arab connections, Julie introduced

Donna to Nabila Khashoggi, daughter of one of the richest men in the world. Bang. Donna was invited to Adnan Khashoggi's forty-sixth birthday party, aboard his opulent new yacht, the *Nabila,* her ticket and expenses to Cannes paid for.

"Her trips to Europe and Vegas were at the request of Khashoggi's daughter," Donna's father confirmed, "and Donna's part of it was paid."

I asked Mr. Rice if Donna had a trust fund.

"What's that?" her father asked. "You were under the mistaken impression we were rich?"

How, then, did Donna support herself for two years in Manhattan? I inquired.

"I don't want to get into that," he said.

Had he talked to his daughter about it?

"I didn't ask her those questions. It was never discussed." All at once, Donna's father revealed his own worst fears. "What *was* she doing in New York to make a living? Have you got some information indicating she was a hooker?"

I said I didn't know.

"She just doesn't think!" her father exploded in frustration. "Her mother and I tell her about appearances, but she's so naïve it makes you want to throw up." His voice went limp with resignation. "Looking back, of course, I can see where I went wrong. I could have advised her. But, hell, she's twenty-nine years old."

Subsequently, I received a call from a woman on the West Coast who claimed to know Donna and the crowd she was seen with from time to time. "None of us were models or actresses, we were looking for a score. Donna made many trips with Khashoggi. I was there a lot too, and Julie Semones, who recruited a lot of girls. Nobody was ever invited to Khashoggi's boat unless they were sexually available."

My West Coast informant had been young and in New York at the same time as Donna, and described how girls in their crowd teamed up. "One of us would meet a guy and try to get him to take care of us, while we hit on the next one. Some would get pretty angry after the fact—being trapped by this seemingly innocent girl—when we'd move out because they'd run out of money."

Khashoggi's frequent dinner parties were high points. Twenty girls would be assembled, usually by one or two men who passed themselves off as theatrical agents, but who used girls to induce potentates like Khashoggi to finance their movie or record deals. Model Christina Cox, who knew Donna in those days, said of one such man, John LaRocca, "I wouldn't never sign with him, the guy's like a pimp."

When dinner was over, Khashoggi would point at the chosen girls around the table: "This one, this one, and that one." He would have them chauffeured to his home or hotel room, and after a rather strenuous night of mixed sex, he would reward them with $1,000 to $5,000, depending upon his whim. The rejects were given $200 "cab fare" for their trouble.

"Just to have dinner for two hundred dollars was real nice, and in a real nice restaurant," said the West Coast woman, with a pathetic pride. She was making between $200,000 and $300,000 in cold cash in those days. "I blew it all—clothes, travel, parties." Married now, she says she found it a "very lonely and desperate life-style, always looking."

What was that life-style? I asked pointedly.

"Mmmm, I'm trying to circumvent the words 'high-priced call girl.' "

My West Coast informant called me twice, and the names and telephone numbers she offered to back up her story checked out. Why, I asked, had she gone to such trouble?

"I used to be part of that crowd, and I can't stand seeing Donna cashing in on a situation like that." This, too, rang true. Those in the free-lance party-girl business are as competitive as they are jealous, or as my informant put it, "The guys all wanted your body and the girls are all backstabbers."

Donna, she said, was going for bigger and bigger scores. "She always got herself attached to married men. They were the best because you could blackmail them afterwards." She couldn't stifle a giggle. "Some would get pretty angry, being trapped by this seemingly innocent young girl."

Fine-boned, well-spoken, and fair, Donna was quite good at passing herself off as a southern belle. Michael Griffith, an attorney who met Miss Rice at a Bridgehampton party in 1980, told a New York newspaper that he believed she came from a wealthy South Carolina family and therefore didn't have to work while she waited for her break.

In 1983 Donna moved to Plantation, Florida, outside Fort Lauderdale, and stayed briefly with a friend, Debi Dalton. Debi introduced her to a handsome, laid-back neighbor, James Bradley Parks. He had a two-bedroom condo on University Drive and a big, flashy motorcycle. Donna moved right in. For the two years she lived with Parks, neither of them had any legitimate source of steady income. She had supposedly gone to Florida in hopes of getting a Screen Actors Guild card. But her modeling work was "real sporadic," according to Debi. She got Brad a chance to make a beer commercial, begged him to go, but Brad preferred other, more adventurous and lucrative activities.

Caught red-handed in 1979 picking up a thousand-pound load of marijuana smuggled in on a low-flying plane from Colombia, Parks impressed authorities as "a real cocky guy."

When I reached Parks's attorney, Bruce Wagner, he was baffled at first about why I'd be calling him for a story on Gary Hart. Then a whistle came through the phone. "Oh, *that* Donna. I know she went out with Brad all during the time his appeal was being prepared. Sure, she was at the sentencing."

The sentencing hearing, on March 30, 1984, did not go well for Brad and Donna. Brad protested he was a scapegoat and said he'd straightened out and was getting modeling jobs. But all the evidence from government witnesses suggested that Brad's drug-dealing activities had only increased since his 1979 arrest. Judge José Gonzalez, Jr., gave James Bradley Parks ten years in Eglin Federal Prison.

"Brad Parks was what we in the Drug Enforcement Administration consider a significant drug trafficker," says Special Agent Billy Yout. "Which means, in Florida"—he is careful to qualify—"hundreds of kilos of coke a year and millions of dollars."

After Brad, times were tough for Donna. She had to get her own digs for the first time. And, according to her talent agent, Peggi McKinley, "her career was pretty much flat. It didn't develop." She was still sent on casting calls to try for parts as the all-American girl or a young mom, but she was number fifteen on McKinley's list. A serious professional model in Miami can make over $100,000 a year. In 1986 Donna Rice earned no more than a few thousand dollars with McKinley. During the first five months of 1987, she brought in only $800, says the agent. And in the commercials business, as on the party-girl scene, a girl over twenty-five is no longer young.

So, Donna had to take her first steady job, as a sales rep for Wyeth Laboratories. Boring, but it gave her rent money and a company car, and she could work on her own schedule. "She was always flying off somewhere," the maintenance man at her unprepossessing apartment in North Miami told a reporter. There was no man in her life after Brad. "She didn't like to have relationships with men," offers Debi Dalton.

At her twenty-ninth birthday party, Donna was without a date. The Miami man she spent more time with than any other, Steve Klengson, did show up. He was a self-described naïve country boy with whom she'd had a platonic friendship since their South Carolina days. At that point in her life, Klengson said, Donna was focused not on finding a relationship, but on advancing her career. She told him she'd had news that Brad might get out of prison by next fall.

Klengson was the easygoing, movie-date pal Donna had leaned on, the year before, when she decided to have breast implants. "She was self-conscious about it," he said, "but she thought a smaller-chested woman just didn't make it." When he married one of Donna's casual acquaintances, two weeks after the party, "that put a strain on our friendship," Klengson acknowledged. He felt partially to blame for not warning Donna off the path to Gary Hart.

Over Super Bowl weekend in January, Donna and her model friends Dana Weems and Lynn Armandt had flown out to Los Angeles looking for action. Julie Semones took them to the private club Helena's, where Donna met a Hollywood screenwriter, Eric Hughes. "She is sweet, but vacant," he observed. Donna told him it was time for her to move to L.A., to really get her career off the pad. "She's probably still too naïve to understand she should be desperate," the Hollywood veteran told me. The four women ended up watching the Super Bowl on TV.

In Miami Donna hung out at the Turnberry Isle resort complex, a world of make-believe concocted on 234 acres of landfill on the Intracoastal Waterway beside Miami Beach, where rich men migrate for winter weekends. From the four gigantic condo towers rising out of the flatness to the celebrities' lounge, with its promise of "animated conversation" with guests like tennis star Vitas Gerulaitis or actor James Caan or dethroned Miss America Vanessa Williams, to the spa, billed as "one of the most lavish dens of self-indulgence in the world," to the ocean club, where, the brochure promises (in not very ambiguous phrases), one can "create, with the help of our staff, a very private affair," to the highly publicized "model nights," when pretty girls drift out of the disco to the boats, their backs soft as butter, the whole concept is to induce the most expensive fantasies, fulfill them, and then collect. Mitchell Kaplan, owner of Books & Books in Coral Gables, told me, "To people who know Miami, the fact that Hart was hanging out at a sleazy place like Turnberry said more about his character than Donna Rice."

Turnberry Isle's guest list is not limited to shady celebrities and models, according to D.E.A. Special Agent Billy Yout. "A lot of drug traffickers frequent and stay at Turnberry, and with dealers come drugs. The atmosphere caters to their fast-lane life. These are people who can buy virtually anything, including the companionship of supposedly legitimate women."

For certain pretty Miami girls, the $100,000 membership fee is waived. "Donnie's girls," recruited by Turnberry developer Donald Soffer, play an important role in creating the glitzy atmosphere. Their function is to help the wealthy swingers who come for winter vacations to "relax." Donna Rice was one of these decorative fixtures.

To save them the time and anxiety of "dating," busy men can charter an entire party along with the yacht *Monkey Business,* which is owned by Soffer. The models who hang out at the Turnberry show up, and the party begins. Lynn Armandt, whom the press has described as a model, was the party-girl connection. No stranger to the world of drug-trafficking, Lynn had been married to a Chilean drug dealer who disappeared in 1982. "Dead?" I asked her. "Well," she drawled, "I *assume.*" Armandt's Too Hot Bikini Shop was nothing more than a tent with a few racks of bikinis on which she paid Soffer a nominal commission, while he provided her with a base on some of the most expensive square footage in Florida.

The fateful night in March when Donna went aboard the *Monkey Business,* she didn't even know who had chartered it. Another model friend, the woman who later tipped off Tom Fiedler of the Miami *Herald,* was aghast that Gary Hart could be at a party like that. "They weren't the kind of people you'd think a presidential candidate would want to be around." Many onboard were drunk or using drugs, according to Fiedler's source. She drew back in disgust at the arrogance of Hart's come-on. But Donna, upon hearing his boast about being a presidential candidate, made a beeline for him.

"Hi, we met in Aspen," she said for openers. The rest is history.

Donna told anyone who would listen of her great coup. Now she had really hit it lucky. She even called her father when she got back from Bimini. "Guess who I had a date with?" Upon hearing, Mr. Rice said, "Donna, you look out for those damned politicians. I'd better look up this boy's history." She told Debi Dalton that one of her friends was so excited she said, "Just think, Donna, you could be First Lady." Debi dumped on Donna's naïveté. "You won't ever be anything but a sidekick."

But let us not forget that the man who chartered the party boat for Hart was William Broadhurst, a friend and political intimate. Billed as "Mr. Fix It" for Edwin Edwards, the notorious Louisiana governor who beat a corruption charge, Broadhurst specialized in getting close to politicians who were out of control. "Billy B." arranged planes for the governor's gambling trips and enjoyed his jokes about Edwards's well-publicized womanizing. In the midst of the Hart–*Monkey Business* flap, a state senator asked the governor what he thought of his boy, Broadhurst. A vintage Edwards comment came back: "Oh, Billy B., he was more careful when he was pimping for me."

Broadhurst had picked Gary Hart as his favorite for the White House. The lawyer had been throwing around a lot of money on Hart. One frequent visitor to Governor Edwards's mansion who was close to "Billy B." informed *The Washington Monthly* that Broadhurst "told me that I should support Hart because [Broadhurst] was going to be one of three people I would have to go through to see the president." Broadhurst's law firm subsequently challenged his use of its money for such political entertainment, and after the scandal, the partners reorganized and dropped him from the partnership.

Given the company Gary Hart had chosen, he was heading for a crash. "The woman in question" does not even qualify as a villain, since she is a character with no center, an "action girl," just drifting from party to party in a perpetual state of expectation that the next introduction will lead to the next connection, which will land her in the lap of the next great score. On that game board, Donna started out at the top with royalty, followed by one of the richest men in the world; it was downhill from there. Nearly six years after her debut aboard the *Nabila,* she was a woman still waiting to hit a lucky streak. The *Monkey Business,* a mere $2,000-a-day charter, was a dinghy compared with Khashoggi's $70 million yacht.

Donna Rice did not know how to protect herself, and, worse, she had nothing to protect. She collided with the world of a man who had everything to lose, and was ready to lose it.

The tempting, tortured journey by which Gary Hartpence crossed the tracks of Ottawa to the world of Donna Rice took him twenty-five years. He began on August 9, 1961, with an appearance at the courthouse in Ottawa to petition for a change of his name. Nina Hartpence, it was so noted, had an illness and was not present.

Years later, when the press discovered the name change, Hart was still covering up his very first act of independence, dared finally at the age of twenty-four.

His first attempt to leave had taken him to Yale Divinity School, but he went with the blessing of his mother by promising to live out her dream for him to be a preacher. It was a common path for young men like Hart who wished to go beyond the mind-set of their upbringing, but were terrified to make a complete break. At Bethany Nazarene College, he had met Oletha (Lee) Ludwig. Lee came from a classy Kansas City family, and her father was general secretary of the Nazarene sect nation-wide. She wouldn't give that "hick" the time of day.

What Gary had not shared with his mother were the Dosto-evskian visions already planted in his head by one J. Prescott Johnson, the philosophy professor who claims he "broke him" back at Bethany. The college was a bulwark of religious recti-tude intended to protect its flock from the wickedness of univer-sities; the dress code forbade girls to wear sleeveless blouses or blue jeans. Not only did Johnson introduce Hart to the seductive existentialists, he left the boy alone for the first time with a woman, Lee.

"Gary saw Lee as a challenge," says Nancy Lee, his sister. He took up that challenge, and they were married two months after their college graduation.

Gary and Lee packed up and drove their jalopy to New Haven, where Lee began a six-year stint of supporting them both while Gary attended two graduate schools. Almost immedi-ately Hart expressed frustration at being tied down. He told a friend, Tom Boyd, "You do everything right, you go with a girl, you get married. Then, six months later, you wake up in the middle of the night and ask yourself, 'My God, what have I done?' "

And so when Gary headed back east to attend Yale Law School in 1961, it was "with the idea of starting a new life," says Nancy Lee. Hart's overwhelming need at that stage was to find an identity to replace his necrotic Nazarene past. As a volunteer in John Kennedy's 1960 campaign, he had found his first model. With the utter surrender of a sword-swallower at the circus, Hart internalized J.F.K.'s values and attitudes, then tried to conjure up the same charisma by copying his gestures and even the Bostonian twang.

"We used to drive up and down Main Street and Gary would imitate President Kennedy's voice, saying 'Cuber,' 'Africer,' and 'South Americer,' " Duane Hoobing, an old Ottawa ac-quaintance, recalls of Hart's visits home.

Marking well that here was a presidential candidate who could play around with impunity, Hart also took Jack and Jackie's marriage as a model.

Following his graduation in 1964, and after two years in

Washington at the Justice Department, Hart struck out for Colorado. It was 1967. Colorado in the swinging sixties was the frontier for a covey of young, idealistic lawyers looking for a place to resettle, do good, and "be free." Patricia Schroeder, now a congresswoman, and Richard Lamm, later governor, were a part of that movement. But, for all the group's nonconformist élan, its members saw Gary Hart as the biggest risk-taker.

No sooner had Hart served a year within the confines of a traditional law firm than he walked away, moving into a basement to start his own practice. Hart himself told me that was the greatest turning point in his life. He was thirty-one, and the father of two. But that bold move was only the beginning of an accelerated flight from his past. In the same year, 1968, he formally left the Nazarene church.

His mother, already disappointed at his straying into the secular woods, set a cold sentence upon him. She told Aunt Erma Louise, "He's changed." From Nina, that was a condemnation.

In 1970, abandoning his new practice, he left his wife and family and moved out on the trail to work for an apparently hopeless cause called the McGovern campaign. "We thought he was nuts," says Pat Schroeder. Not remotely interested in ideas in those days, Hart prided himself on being a cool technocrat. The intoxication of disencumbering himself of all obligations— human, financial, and spiritual—swept Hart into that high, sweet air the Scriptures call "lighter than vanity." And in this weightless state, he met his mirror image.

Warren Beatty, star and sybarite, was a daredevil from Hollywood taking a year out of his life to work for George McGovern and indulge his earliest childhood wish: to be president. He could introduce Hart to the glamour of Hollywood, and Hart could offer him political credibility—a magnificent symbiosis. It was the beginning of a long association. In age and temperament, Beatty and Hart were a perfect match; Beatty, too, had always made use of secrecy in his life, and when criticized for being inhuman he once remarked, "But I have no need to seem more human." Gary copied Warren's seductive body language and eventually metamorphosed into the kind of character

Beatty played in *Shampoo:* a philanderer hiding from his own promiscuity.

"Hart had a real Don Juan complex," observes Amanda Smith, now a feminist lecturer and the wife of political scientist James David Barber, but back in 1971 the women's-issues person in McGovern's Washington headquarters. "It's something he couldn't stop, but the women weren't people to him at all." Hart would speak for McGovern at a college political-science club, then spend the weekend with the club president. Monday morning, time and again, these breathless, brainy little buds would turn up in Washington to commit their lives to working for Gary Hart. Time and again, they would find themselves stuffing envelopes and weeping as they watched Gary pass their desk—without so much as a hello.

"Over and over the women who stayed with the campaign found themselves consoling the women who had been bewitched by Gary," said Smith. "Some were local campaign workers, some married, some pretty fancy. They were anybody."

The ugly duckling, Gary Hartpence, had developed, as if overnight, into a dazzlingly handsome young man whose picture appeared even in *Playboy*. Gary had been a sensitive and intelligent boy; his need to break out was inevitable, yet he could not use the new freedom to experience sex and pleasure within the context of a full human relationship.

It was sudden and inexplicable, the way Nina Hartpence withdrew from her mortal coil. On the eve of the '72 primaries, just as Gary was moving into high gear, he had to slam into reverse and rush home to Ottawa, toward a reckoning that never took place. Dashing up the steps of the local hospital, he was met by his mother's nurse's aide. Nina had already expired.

Gary hurried away without giving a eulogy at her funeral (although he later did so at his father's). But his father seemed to make an effortless transformation. Carl went fishing, he went dancing, he romanced the nurse's aide, and she made him laugh again. With his wife in the ground only six months, he and Faye Brown, the aide, aged seventy-two, had themselves a church wedding. Nancy Lee thought the ceremony "extravagant," but Gary gave his unqualified approval. "She was pretty, fun-loving," sniffs Aunt Erma Louise, "nothing like Nina." The newly-wed couple enjoyed exactly one day of bliss before the hitherto perfectly healthy Carl Hartpence suffered a heart attack. Five days later he was dead.

Clearly there would be no simple escape from the awesome power Nina Hartpence wielded over her son and husband. Both men had to go to dangerous extremes to free themselves. Indeed, Carl Hartpence may have died from the attempt. And if Gary had hoped that his mother's death would release him at last from the cold steel band of guilt around his heart, the fate of his father must have been a dark omen.

A strict Fundamentalist is taught that any window left open in one's own faith can let in the evil that strikes down loved ones. Years after a person "comes out" from a Fundamentalist background, a traumatic event or even a familiar verse from the Bible or evangelical exhortations can trigger a panic over the remembered feeling of suffocation. Such a panic may have been what brought Gary back to Lee and the children after his parents' unexpected deaths. But it didn't keep him from letting his aides sweat out the danger when Gary was traveling for McGovern without his wife, and Lee would suddenly turn up in the lobby of his hotel. One top McGovern aide remembers the panic of knowing Hart was upstairs in his room with a famous film star. Nor did it stop Hart from showing up with a stewardess at a serious staff dinner after the '72 Democratic convention. At least one close colleague remembers being stunned to learn that Hart was married. From then on, without regard to the status of his marriage, there were always other women.

Even before their separations, when Hart would return to the marital home, he would keep up his escapades with a parade of women. A longtime neighbor, Evelyn Essig, from the Park Hill section of Denver where the Harts lived between 1967 and '77, describes a commonplace, if tawdry, scene. Gary would be home minding Andrea and John, then only toddlers, while Lee went back to Kansas to visit her family. "No sooner did Lee walk out the door than young women would start tramping in, one at a time," said Essig. "Fifteen minutes before Lee was due home, the last lady would be out the door."

Another pattern began to emerge, as fascinating as it would

ultimately be fatal. Hard as he tried to experiment more successfully with the world of free relationships, Hart never seemed to
shake the tail from his own past, the constant reminder that he
was a sinner. His efforts to break from that past became more
desperate, more self-destructive. One fleeting resolution of such
an inner contradiction is to live dangerously, always on the edge
of exposure.

"Just as challenge and insecurity frighten most people, security and safety frighten me," he told a *Washington Post* reporter
in 1972.

Over and over again he took daring chances, then tore up
everything he had built and walked away from it. What he was
walking away from, hoping each time to give the slip, was his
still-unresolved self.

When the McGovern campaign crashed, Hart handled the
failure in a memorable way. "Everything was over for him,"
recalls Harold Himmelman, a Washington lawyer. "Gary had
nothing—no career, no money, no future. He was then the
architect of the world's worst political campaign." Yet Hart
seemed, somehow, stronger, lighter, even happier—like a man
broken loose from all rules and obligations, and free to reinvent
himself. Even then, Hart was dropping tantalizing clues to his
danger-seeking side.

During the cathartic period of winding down that followed
the campaign, Hart called a law-school classmate, Oliver
"Pudge" Henkel, and his wife, Sally, to invite them to join the
Harts on vacation in Jamaica. The Henkels were surprised; they
hadn't seen the Harts since Yale and didn't consider them good
friends, but they accepted. During the trip, Hart withdrew from
the group, spent time alone, silently pondering his future, and
came back to announce that he was thinking of a political career
for himself. To the amazement of those around him, with a
negative net worth and no political base, Hart set out to capture
a seat in the U.S. Senate. When he was elected in 1974, Hart's
worthy side cast his victory as a purification: "Receiving the
oath of office was, for me, the secular equivalent of acceptance
into church membership."

The purifying effects of election to what Hart considered the most select club in America did not inhibit the new senator's adventures. In the Senate dining room, he always ate alone. At night in the cafeteria, he would sit with Senator William Cohen and plot novels, far removed from the tedium of waiting for a floor vote. In public life, he made no friends, formed no coalitions, and left no lasting legislative record. But in private, he began to roam farther afield, exploring American Indian religion and putting himself into the hands of a glossy Englishwoman, Diana Phipps, who would introduce him to European society.

Yet on the subject of guilt, "Gary seemed so young and immature," says an old friend and former staff member. At one point, when he had been separated from Lee for six months, he closed the door of his Senate office and told this good soldier, "You've heard Lee and I are separating. You'll no doubt want to make other arrangements." The Fundamentalist buried within him must have assumed the staffer would want to move away from such a sinful person. Simultaneously, he was asking his secretary to find him excuses to fly to L.A. for weekends. From 1981 on, Warren Beatty gave him free run of his Beverly Hills house. Sitting by the pool, which was often populated with topless starlets, Hart and Beatty were overheard discussing other men's scores, with Hart admiringly reporting on another senator who would go to New York, line up five or six girls, "and just have himself a weekend."

The more broadly Hart roamed, the more exaggerated was his denial that he had any problem. When he decided to gird up for the first presidential run, his friend Mike Medavoy, executive vice-president of Orion Pictures, warned him to keep some distance from Beatty because of the actor's atrocious reputation. Hart took offense, as he always did, and said, "I don't have to worry about appearances if I'm not doing anything wrong."

His real-life struggle was mirrored in his two novels, one in collaboration with Senator Cohen (even titled *The Double Man*). The plots would always involve his hero in spying, manipulation, and dangerous intimacies with females on the other side. Hart and his heroes had a compulsion rooted not in seeking illicit sex but in proving they were so utterly worthy that they could break all the rules. For all Hart's superficial arrogance, however, the evidence suggests that he could never believe he was worthy enough.

By the time Gary first decided to run for president, Lee had made a significant, twenty-four-year investment in his future. She had quit teaching in 1964 to have her first child and had not gone back to work until 1979, when she and her husband separated officially.

They had reconciled in time for her to campaign for Hart's reelection to the Senate. Less than a year later, Lee was shuffled off once more; Hart's office announced they were divorcing. She turned to real estate. But life as a hardworking career woman held no appeal for her.

"If there is anything tougher than campaigning ten hours a day," Lee Hart told me in an interview in 1984, "it's competing eighteen hours a day, seven days a week, with those real-estate sharks along the Potomac." The Harts patched it up again shortly before Gary began his first presidential campaign.

Hart had always proudly worn the label of poorest member of the Senate. My question to Lee Hart in 1984 about her husband's much-vaunted indifference to material things struck a raw nerve.

"Sure, I'd like to have the freedom that money can bring," she said, her voice a scornful singsong. "I can't go to Colo*rado* and *ski* like I'd like to, because I can't *afford* to. I can't go to New *York* and take in a *play,* as I would love to, because I can't *afford* to."

Lee seemed clearly to want the White House as much as Gary did. That would explain why she was willing to be humiliated in private and ignored in public. During joint campaign appearances, Lee would come forward, on cue, and be acknowledged by Gary only as "already deserving the job of First Lady" for her hard work. She would hold up her hands like the trapeze lady from the Flying Wallenda family, then drop back into the shadows. Not infrequently, her husband would forget to introduce her altogether.

"Lee Hart was always able to separate what she felt for Gary as a husband and what she felt for him as a politician," according to Raymond Strother, a friend and campaign consultant. Lee and Gary's relationship seemed to have become mutually exploitive. Since neither one expected honesty or intimacy from the other, Lee Hart never saw herself as a victim. She had tried independence and found it a tough row to hoe. It would be easier to achieve her own ends by advancing her husband.

But his hidden side was never far out of her mind. When Gary told her of his decision in '82 to run for president, Lee warned him, according to friends, "Your downfall will be sex."

Almost two decades after Gary Hart severed formal ties with his Fundamentalist church, he was still ambivalent about worldly success. The part of him that could not believe he deserved to be successful, because he was a sinner and a backslider, would now begin to sabotage his grander political ambitions. Even during the fastest-rising arc of his career—those few magical weeks in 1984 after his upset victory in the New Hampshire primary—while he was the nation's hottest political star with a full-strength media spotlight upon him, he was compelled to flout the rules of normal public behavior.

A Washington woman he'd been seeing since 1982 was startled to have him turn up on her Washington doorstep at such a vulnerable moment. She could see the Secret Service van parked right down the street from her stately Georgetown town house. Hart stayed the night and blithely walked out her front door the next morning.

The same woman later spilled her hurt to one of Hart's former advisers. She described her association with Hart as "sporadically affectionate." This meant that when Hart was separated from Lee, he told the other woman he was planning a divorce and that she was the only woman in his life. When he went back to his wife, he never told her. When he came back to the mistress, he never told his wife. The more intimate their occasions together, the more brutally he would withdraw. As they parted he would say, "Call me and we'll get together very soon." She would demur, saying she knew how busy he was. No, he'd insist, just call and he'd find a way they could be together. So she would call. And then he'd duck her.

A political friend of Hart's for the last ten years says, "Gary was compulsive about seeking out women, sometimes for a sexual relationship, sometimes not. It was a compulsion, but it was not about sex, even if the relationship was sexual. The compulsion was to defy the rules and still have it all, on his terms." The pattern was always the same: the indiscriminate hunt, the rush to intimacy, the forced reassurances, then a sudden withdrawal, denial, and rapid retreat.

The capriciousness of it was what stung Hart's women, many of them smart, substantial people. When his Washington mistress heard about Hart spending the weekend, not at her town house but at his, and with a "Miami model," she was reportedly devastated. With the model of a mother as continuously demanding as she was undemonstrative, Hart could not be expected to have any notion of what a warm, close, friendly relationship with a woman was. Sex and power could be sought only outside such a relationship. Under the sway of his sensual passion, and when conquest and possession was the issue, he could be very intense, according to several of his partners' confidantes. But once the passion was consumed, the fantasy fulfilled, and the specter of the start of a relationship reared its head, Hart would shrink back and, clang! that inner steel door between his two selves would slam shut.

As Hart pursued national office, he naturally faced increasing constraints and the microscopic press scrutiny that goes with the territory. Alarm bells must have gone off. The constraints were not unlike the suffocating restrictiveness of his upbringing; the scrutiny must have been perceived as the very "prying" he'd been hiding from all his life. He grew sick of feeling guilty. His denials grew more extreme. Hart's pathology was much like that of an alcoholic who, after his seventh drink, insists with thickened tongue, "Whaddya mean I can't drive, shhur I can!"

In 1980 he told Hal Haddon, a longtime friend from Colorado, that he had stopped womanizing. Convinced that the only way Hart could become president was to clean up his act, Haddon suspended disbelief. But by 1982 Haddon, like Hart's brain truster Larry Smith, had lost faith and walked away. Hart's campaign became a vacuum, and into it were sucked *naïfs* like Pudge Henkel—who signed on as campaign director when Hart told him, "I have nothing to hide"—and an assortment of what Smith saw as "scumbags, jackals, and freebooters." Henkel himself was amazed when Hart asked him to manage the campaign. He saw later that Gary had chosen him because he already knew his personality: "He wanted someone who was not going to ask him to tailor his personal life to what a political consultant would want."

Patrick Caddell was brought on in desperation in January 1984. The veteran pollster told me that he'd gradually recognized what Hart really wanted: "maximum chaos." A campaign always takes on the character of a candidate; and in this case the campaign was designed to keep Hart free of structure, to ensure that his advisers were kept off-balance by bickering, and to guarantee that no one got close enough to see the demons Hart was hiding. The pattern was frightening in a campaign; in a presidency, such chaos could be catastrophic.

Having looked closely at his life history, we can now propose some possible explanations for Hart's behavior. Here is a man who grew up in a severely restricted manner, by virtue of his religion, his social milieu, and a mother whose treatment of her son was tantamount to child abuse. Emotionally deformed by his long boyhood, simply not equipped with any understanding of, or feeling for, the value built into human relationships, he was never able to learn in adult life how to connect with others. He can connect only with abstract ideas.

The Gary Hart who emerged from this tortured journey is a divided man. It was buried in his earliest consciousness that one was either worthy or sinful. One could not be both. Because he had to believe he was worthy of asking to be made president, he was compelled to separate the part of himself that he considered sinful from the part that was worthy.

One side of Hart, the rigid and controlling spirit of his Fundamentalist past, seeks perfection and inflicts harsh self-punishment for any natural pleasure. This is the boy who could not be coaxed to take more than one toy at a time out of the box, the boy who was always outside the picture show peering in. The other side of him, the passionate and profane side, never saw the light of day when he was an adolescent—indeed, was imprisoned for his first twenty-five years. That delinquent side began beating on the cell floor and going over the wall as far back as

1972, during the McGovern campaign. Finally, it went haywire.

The compartmentalization of Hart's private life was echoed in his public life. He could stand on a Colorado mountaintop and, in a ringing incantation, call for a "higher standard of public ethics." Then turn around and declare, when caught, that "public interest ends where a person's personal life and private life does [*sic*] not affect his or her performance in office." He scorned all along the *symbolic* nature of the presidency. The American president is also the embodiment of the nation's ideals and aspirations. As such, he becomes cloaked in the power that will allow him to persuade the people of a vision of what is good for the country.

Hart's concept of politics was unable to connect the emotional or moral expectations of those around him with the right instruments, i.e., how things should work. He contended vehemently that one was not properly connected to the other. He balked at having to phone potential supporters, and rarely thanked people who had given up months or years of their own careers to work for him.

"I was given some political talents," he had told me in '84. "I'm not always comfortable using them. I wasn't given the personality to go with them." When he gave speeches, it often seemed there was a circuit breaker inside him that shorted out the electricity audiences had built up in anticipation of his appearance. That Hart sorely lacked the easy warmth and congeniality a politician needs to win loyal supporters, and to work within the club atmosphere of Congress, made his intellectual appeal all the more impressive.

It played particularly well with members of that cool, technocratic, narcissistic stratum within the Baby Boom who came of political age in the late seventies. They saw reflected in Hart their own resistance to firm commitments, their own floating values. Like Hart, many were laser-locked onto their own success path, but insistent that their "personal development" be obedient to no laws or rules beyond their own. Gary Hart made these new aspirations and ideals respectable.

And one part of him seemed deeply to believe that he would make a magnificent leader. He worked hard at attracting experts to design sophisticated ideational grids. Above all, he subscribed to the Gatsby theory of self-reinvention. Whenever the bonds and obligations of any new relationship with the world pulled too tight, and he felt again chased and cornered, he'd be off to a new place, seeking a new adventure, and putting on a different face for the world.

Tom Fiedler, a Miami *Herald* reporter who had covered the candidate for two years, at first didn't recognize Hart when they came face-to-face on that fateful night in May outside his town house. Hart was disheveled. When confronted, he clutched himself with both arms, and his speech was halting and disjointed.

But by the time he phoned his wife that Saturday night he was able to tell her, coolly, to ignore the imminent scandal. This moment cannot have come as any great shock to Lee Hart.

Another call Hart made that night was to his campaign director, Bill Dixon, assuring him there was nothing to the story. Dixon prepared the counterattack on the press, then resigned two days later. According to a former top aide, "We never really considered telling the whole truth."

When Hart appeared before sixteen hundred publishers at the Waldorf-Astoria two days later, he made a slashing attack on what he called "a misleading and false story that hurt my family and other innocent people, and reflected badly on my character. . . . It is clearly one of the reasons many talented people in this nation opt out of public service."

At a formal fund-raising dinner the very same night, Hart seemed unusually relaxed, even buoyant. Making a dashing getaway, Hart then turned to the man at the wheel, a high-powered news executive. They were planning a trip through Europe together that summer.

"Where are we going to find girls?" were the first words out of Hart's mouth.

Half-choking, half-chuckling, the news executive quipped, "You know, Hart, I'd like you to have two operations. The second one would be to have your tongue cut out."

Hart smirked. "If I had a choice, I'd take the second one."

"Hi, babe" was the breezy greeting he gave his wife when she emerged from three days of seclusion to join him in New

Hampshire the following day. Lee's face, set like aspic, looked as if its last buoyancy was about to collapse.

Hart then faced reporters, who asked the candidate if he had ever committed adultery. He refused to answer. At dinner that night on the Vermont border, he was full of brittle laughter and joked about his imbroglio with Donna Rice. In his utter disgrace, he was oddly devil-may-care. Then Lee told him, according to a participant, that his children were devastated. Hart was startled. It was the first indication he was registering even faintly the human impact of his actions.

Shortly after eleven that night, Hart's press secretary went to him in his motel and laid out a new set of facts. Photographs of him entering and leaving the house of a Washington woman were now in the possession of *The Washington Post*.

"This thing is never going to end, is it?" Hart said to his press secretary. Then, with a remark so stunningly cavalier one can almost hear him thumbing his nose, Gary Hart said, "Look, let's just go home."

Faced with a crisis of his own making, Hart simply walked away from those hundreds who had used up the credit on their charge cards to stake him to the caprice of a presidential campaign, dismissed a million-and-a-half-dollar campaign debt, and slammed the door on thousands of volunteers who had squandered on him the idealism of their twenties.

Holed up in the Rockies for the next month, Hart established a one-way communication with the world: He took a secret telephone number, turned away requests for interviews, phoned out to dozens of his financial contributors, and sent several thousand supporters a letter of apology as impersonal as a "Dear Occupant" mailing, and signed off by quoting the Scriptures. Beatty loaned his buddy $265,000 to buy a buffer of land around his cabin in Troublesome Gulch to secure privacy from the media.

When the first visual evidence of his romantic relationship with Rice appeared in *The National Enquirer*, Gary Hart simply withdrew into his ever smaller, isolated world and, miraculously, according to friends, managed to insulate his family from exposure to the pictures. Lee Hart was very angry, but her anger was externalized, according to a former Senate staffer who stayed with Hart until the bitter end. Lee was convinced that the debacle was all the fault of the press and of Washington. She insisted he sell the tainted town house; she never wanted to see Washington again.

Andrea Hart, when asked later if she was disappointed in her father's behavior, replied, "It's none of my business. He said" —she stopped, then went on—"I listened to whatever he said."

Had Hart gotten away with his ludicrous explanation (he and Donna slept on separate boats; it was a completely innocent "mistake" of appearances), poor Donna Rice would have lost the chance for which she had worked ten years. For a woman and her friends who have made their living by "scoring" off men they have compromised, this was the moment to go for "googol." Nineteen eighty-seven was a very good year for the bimbo business.

Donna's later protestations that her privacy had been "beaten down by the press" rang rather hollow. It was Donna, not the press or her pals, who dropped the bombshell about her weekend cruise with Hart on the *Monkey Business.* That assured her of the national celebrity she had so long but lucklessly chased. Her distress was not over the publicity, but over the fact that, to her continuing astonishment, it was negative.

Sending up a trial balloon to test his reentry potential in early fall, Hart agreed to a one-hour appearance on ABC News's *Nightline*—under his conditions. Just he and Ted Koppel, *mano a mano,* but with Koppel agreeing not to "debate" Hart. After giving a prepared diplomatic statement, Hart couldn't help lashing out at the press, while insisting that he had never tried to shift the blame away from himself. Koppel refreshed his memory about having blamed the media for his downfall. Well, said Hart, that was because he had been "angry" and "mixed up" about being "hunted."

More revealing was how heavily laden with religious references his language was. "We've been talking about sin here this evening, I guess it's what it gets down to—not crime, but sin—"

"And bad judgment," Koppel reminded him.

Hart rambled on, as if debating himself. "But the Bible that says that being unfaithful is a sin also says we're all sinners

. . . it says further that one of the greatest sins is to waste God-given talent."

If his transgressions could be discounted as "commonplace sins," and his political talents endorsed as so singular that the nation would recognize God's larger purpose working through him, then at last Gary Hart might be pronounced morally adequate. He tried to set things right that night by casting himself in a light even nobler than that of the nation's leader. "I've got to figure out a way to contribute. I think there's one higher office than president, and I would call that patriot, and that's all I ever want said about me."

And once again, he lied.

Koppel asked why a presidential candidate with any sense of balance would go to a club in Miami well known for traffic in drugs and as a place where wealthy businessmen go to meet young women.

"All I can tell you, Mr. Koppel, is that . . . I'd never even heard of the place."

The next night, invited onto the same show, I had the opportunity to point out that Hart's picture hangs on the wall in the office of the manager of that Miami resort. According to the Miami *Herald,* the staff boasts about the fact that he was there with Warren Beatty during the '84 campaign.

The political pros were as astonished as the public when Gary Hart jumped back into the presidential contest seven months after he'd abandoned it. Speculation was rife: His publishing contract had been canceled, his book outline had been rejected; his lecture audiences were shrinking—all true. His status at his Denver law firm, where managing partner Donald O'Connor said Hart has brought in some oil business since the scandal, was uncertain. Hart needed a job. He wanted to qualify for matching campaign funds. According to his friends, he realized that the only way to reinject himself into the political spotlight was to revive his presidential campaign. But more than anything, Hart seemed compelled to return from limbo and make one more round through the circles of hell to play out his own inner drama.

With his few disciples claiming that his reemergence showed great courage, Hart walked the main streets of New Hampshire,

his wife clamped to his side, his shield against the most embarrassing of questions. He soared to front-runner status in a matter
of days. The most common explanations were name recognition—and Hart's entertainment value. But a fair number of
party activists were prepared to believe Hart was their Moses,
come down from the mountain after all, with a tweedy new
wardrobe and his ninety-four-page tablet of "new ideas," to
deliver them from terminal dullness.

Described by political pundits when he reentered as the
"five-hundred-pound gorilla" that the other Democrats would
have to beat, Hart was treated to several weeks of one-on-one
network television interviews, in which images told the public
he was the biggest man in the Democratic contest: The proof was
right on their screens.

On several TV call-in shows, people pressed journalists to
ask Hart the very question a Republican retiree had wanted to
pose at a high-school gathering in Portsmouth, New Hampshire:
"Why won't you people in the press ask him if he couldn't be
compromised or blackmailed as president by that Florida gal or
one of his other women?" Even Hart, attempting to defend
himself, raised the same specter: "If anyone has something in
their background they could be blackmailed about, they
shouldn't be president."

But the one question no one dared ask was, how could Hart
be trusted when he continually walked away from his human
commitments? The surrogate question became "How can we
trust a man who walks away from his creditors?"

By the time Hart joined the ring with his six Democratic
rivals for the first time, at the Des Moines *Register* debate in
mid-January, a funny thing had happened on the way to the
circus: All six former "dwarfs" had gained in stature. And Hart
shrank before their very eyes. Instead of a five-hundred-pound
gorilla, he looked more like the sad clown. Glassy-eyed, slightly
disheveled, not a spark of warmth or humor in his long dis-
courses on ideas that now sounded as rusty as he did, Hart was
also ignored by his opponents. The very first question of the
debate undercut him—he was asked about his statement that he
would "not be the first adulterer in the White House." His
hollow answer didn't matter much; what registered was that

GAIL SHEEHY

Donna Rice would always be with him, her half-image blinking on his forehead like a neon nightclub sign.

Hart had tried, at first, to freeze the character issue. Failing that, he attempted to turn it to his own advantage. "I don't know any major leader who hasn't had a setback, some major adversity," he said. "It either weakens or strengthens you. A test of character is not whether you make a mistake. Of course we make mistakes. I'm a human being. Don't expect me to be flawless. It's how you deal with adversity."

He classified himself with Winston Churchill, Abraham Lincoln, and Charles de Gaulle in the certainty he had gained from his adversity. Churchill spent ten years being shunned by his party until he was called to leadership during World War II. De Gaulle withdrew into a brooding retirement for ten years before he was called upon, during the revolt in Algeria, to save France. And Lincoln, a manic-depressive, faced the tortuous decision of civil war or secession, knowing that either path might rend the nation asunder for good. Hart was asking people to accept as equivalent to those epic tests the seven months he spent after "the business last May" being deprived of the national spotlight, losing his book contract, watching his lecture audiences dwindle away, and having to face the anger of his children for letting them down.

The final irony was that the man who had tried for so many years to duck the character question ended up building his own TV commercial around it. The cheaply produced spot that was airing before the Iowa caucuses focused tightly on the candidate's face as he adjured the American people, "Character is the test."

His other constant message had been that he was taking his case straight to the voters—"Let the American people decide." They did. In a mere five weeks, Hart's support had dropped by more than half from the soaring 34 percent of Democrats who'd expressed belief in his candidacy around the first of January. In the Iowa caucuses, he took less than 1 percent of the vote. And in New Hampshire, a miserable 4 percent.

To reporters who followed his campaign in those final weeks, the double nature of the man showed through the "all-

72

but-hooted-at days," as Paul Hendrickson put it in *The Washington Post*. Whether it was stopping to play pool, or to shoot a few baskets in an Irish bar, the rigid, perfection-seeking side of Hart would make a mission out of trying, failing, trying again, and again, as if sinking a basketball were a metaphor for the existential effort to *make* the American political system work for him as therapy. On the other hand, there was something much looser, more relaxed, even more likable about Hart that several journalists picked up. "What would explain this?" mused Hendrickson rhetorically. The end was near. Hart had walked his cruel mile, dragging the cross of his wife all the way. He had taken the lashings of the crowd, forsaken by his party. And now, his purification nearly over, escape within sight, he could look forward to the incredible lightness of being, once more—a free spirit!

Hart has always been at his most attractive just before he's doomed. It was right in character.

On March 11, 1988, stepping up in a Denver restaurant to make his second, snappish withdrawal speech in one year, Hart took as his motto the downwardly mobile, mopily adolescent lyric made popular by Janis Joplin:

> Freedom's just another word for
> nothin' left to lose.

It is hard not to feel some compassion for a man so alienated from his past he has nowhere to go. If Gary were still a member of the Nazarene church in Ottawa, the Reverend Mr. Copsey would personally confront him. "I would ask, 'Are you guilty of goin' to bed with this woman? Havin' these affairs?' I would read Scripture to him and ask him to ask the Lord's forgiveness."

Just suppose for the sake of argument, I proposed to Hart's aunt Erma Louise, that all these things about Gary are true. What would he have to do to redeem himself? Aunt Erma Louise, in whom negation has been canonized as the one positive virtue, pronounced the judgment that Hart must be fleeing to this day.

"He'd have to go back to the way he lived before. When he was a boy."

It would seem unthinkable for a man of Hart's hard-won independence to go home again, to "put to death the deeds of the body." Born a sensitive boy with a bright inquiring mind and a healthy appetite for adventure, he was crippled a long time before the Donna Rice escapade. But the presidency is not the place to work out one's personal pathology, as Richard Nixon demonstrated so well. Rather than insist that he be elevated to a plane above ordinary mortals, Hart needs to find a way to feel his common humanity, and to search out a middle path between Nazarene perfection and Beatty-esque amorality. That journey requires humility.

Only time will tell, and only one person will know in the end, if Gary Hart can beat the Devil in Gary Hartpence.

FALSE CHANGE

Both Gary Hart and Jesse Jackson are driven by the need to overcome the negative identity of their pasts. Their arrogant exteriors mask inner fears that they are not worthy—and that if they let anyone close to them, they might be found out.

Both are wizards of deception and masters of self-invention and reinvention.

Both are very smart and have shown superior instincts for playing the game of contemporary politics.

Both are loners, cannot bear to share power or control.

Both make it up as they go along, kick over every convention, and protest loudly that they, alone, can break all the rules.

And as prisoners of the Oval Office, not only would they have to submit to rules and constant scrutiny of their behavior, past and present, but they would be charged with upholding the rules and laws of the land.

Why, then, did they alternate as the Democratic front-runners for the first nine months of the '88 campaign? Jesse Jackson, for most blacks—and a growing number of whites—personifies the underdog; he is their way of sending a message that the system stinks and that they feel left out. Hart tapped into the most cherished romance in the Great American Narrative: the lone individual against the Establishment. Both men were living out those fantasies the American public loves most of all.

Both have covered up the shame they suffered as children with a façade of false superiority. The sense of shame drives some people to build an inflated self-image through the pursuit of fame or money or sexual admiration, hoping to convince themselves of their lovability. The emotion, ignored by psychology until very recently, is now seen as a "master emotion." If shame is carved in early, it is father to all the other emotions. For Jesse Jackson, its child was envy.

Jackson has lived all his life as an outsider, yearning to be accepted. No one ever gave him respect he didn't demand. By now, his achievements *force* acceptance. At the halfway point in the primary races, Jackson had proved himself the largest popular vote getter among his Democratic rivals. His phenomenal success on Super Tuesday compelled political professionals to take him seriously as a presidential contender. As his message became more mainstream liberal, balancing soak-the-rich populism with a crusading anti-drug, anti-instant gratification personal conservatism, he continued to broaden his appeal among young, educated, and liberal whites, although 29 percent of Democrats were adamant they would never vote for Jackson. But Jackson's journey has the potential of transcending far more than practical politics. It may be symbiotic with a revival of the civil rights spirit of the sixties.

More than anything he says, Jesse *himself* is the message—he is his own medium—and arguably the most inspiring political speaker on the national stage today. The fact that he has climbed so far, with none of the footholds available to a conventional white politician, has opened a window in our national consciousness. A younger black generation can see that their efforts to rise to success and acceptance can be worth it, while their elders can lift up children to see him, the way they were once lifted to see Jackie Robinson, and say, "See, he's a black man, and he's done it."

Jackson is both handicapped and protected by his color. Being black, he is still not believed by party insiders to have any chance of being the Democratic nominee. But were he white, the fast and loose way Jackson originally parlayed himself into national prominence would have eliminated him from the race. Jackson's closest parallel in a white politician is George Wallace; yet the media has not been as harsh with Jackson as they were with Wallace, for fear of appearing racist.

I approached Jackson through long interviews with the people who have been closest to him throughout his life—his mother, his blood father, his half-brother, his coach, and so on right up through his wife and present campaign manager. My portrait of him shows many shadings of his character, the baggage he carries as well as the genius of personality he has honed. It has no secret racist agenda, nor does it back off and treat him like an exception. I think that's ultimately the way most black Americans want to be treated, as truly being *in* the game and subject to the same rules, not just as a sideshow.

Many Americans of all colors are eager to see his personal saga as evidence that Jackson has been transformed from a self-promoting hustler to a national pathleader with true moral authority. The fact remains that Jackson has never stopped long enough to institutionalize his charisma, build a movement, or set up a grass-roots organization to carry through on his message. Jackson craves adulation as insatiably as any rock star. And in the past, like a rock star, he has not shown any interest in sticking around town after his "gig" is over. That inattention to the greater good in favor of pursuing personal glory reflects a character weakness that has nothing to do with color.

It remains to be seen whether this is a weakness that he can overcome. Has Jackson changed only his act? Or might the slow earthquake of change set in motion by his historic candidacy truly reshape the character of the man?

THREE

Jesse Jackson: The Power or the Glory?

Davenport, Iowa, is the kind of town where adults at the dinner table will say, with a straight face, "I never saw one until I was eight or nine. And then I jumped for fright." They are speaking of black people. The Jefferson Elementary School sits in a depressed pocket of Davenport, so about half of its student body is now black or Hispanic or Asian. One day in the fall of 1987, the Reverend Jesse Jackson came to visit. The teachers had the children all lined up. Each one held out a drawing festooned with crepe paper, saying, "I'm proud of you, Jesse Jackson," or "You're nice, Jesse Jackson," or "Welcome to Jefferson School, Jesse Jackson."

Their faces were a mural of smiles. But talking to them individually, one soon found that while some kids saw Jackson as a hero, others didn't want to discuss him at all. I sat in the auditorium next to a freckle-faced redheaded boy, just a squirt, eight years old. In front of us were two black girls. As a local white pastor preceded Jackson down the aisle, one of the girls turned to ask, "Is that him?"

"No, he's black," I said.

Her mouth fell open and her fingers hooked over her lower teeth. Heaven had opened up. To the group around me, I addressed the question "Do you think that Reverend Jackson could be president?"

"Yeah! Yeah! We think so," everyone squealed. "Why not? That'd be cool. He could be."

"No way."

Startled, I turned to see that the hard words had come from the freckle-faced boy. "What makes you so sure?"

"If a black man gets to be president, white folks would be slaves," he announced.

"Where did you hear that, sweetheart? At home?"

He said, "That's right." Then his mouth clamped shut above his hard little set-back chin.

Down front, Jesse Jackson connected immediately with the kids. He put out amusing parables from his own boyhood and then bore down with his motivational pitch. "Running the race of life is never like a hundred-yard dash—who can get there the fastest. Because there are traps, and there are tricks, and there are land mines. If you are trying to get to graduation and you stop off for liquor, you really can't get there. If you're trying to get there and you stop off for drugs, you really can't get there. If you're trying to get there and you stop off and choose to practice basketball three and four hours a day, and don't spend any time on reading, and writing, and counting, you really can't get there. So you must make the decisions this day."

This is the kernel of a psychodrama Jackson has been performing in schools several times a week for the last fifteen years, the basic tool of his PUSH-Excel program for motivating minority youth. The 1988 version hits hard on drugs.

"How many of you, in this room, know someone who is in jail because of drugs? Stand." As usual, several students stand. "If you know someone who is dead because of drugs, stand." Again, a handful of students stand. When he asks the last question, "If you tried drugs, be fair unto yourself and stand," it starts with ten, then grows to twenty. Finally, he makes what is known in the church as an altar call. "If you have the will to say no to dope, if you have the will to change your disposition, I wish you'd come forward. Talk to me, don't hide, come forward."

In a high school of five hundred students, he can bring a hundred kids out in front of their peers, shuffling and sobbing. Teachers watch, flabbergasted. All look up to this man, this mysterious dark angel who can do what none of the parents or teachers or town police can do, as he directs the kids to join hands in prayer and commit themselves to stop drugs and start learning.

"Tell me you're going to make your school the only drug-free school of academic A students," he exhorts the Jefferson Elementary School kids. "Say 'I am.' "

Kids: I am.

Jesse: Oh, you're just a little too quiet for me. Say "I am."

Kids: I *am*!

Jesse: Some*body*.

Kids: Some*body*!

Jesse: My mind.

Kids: My *mind*!

Jesse: Is a pearl.

Kids: Is a *pearl*!

Jesse: I can learn anything.

Kids: *I can learn anything!*

Jesse: In the world.

Kids: In the *world*!

He has every child in the hall standing tall, chanting at the top of his lungs, flushed with self-importance, completely transported—the freckle-faced boy among them.

In closing, Jackson comes back to the phrase he has shouted so often one wonders if it isn't a poultice for some long-ago, private wound of pride: "I am."

Kids: I *am*!

Jesse: Some*body*.

Kids: Some*body*!

Jesse: God bless America.

Kids: *God bless America.*

Over the din of applause, I inquire of the freckle-faced boy, "Did you like him a little better than you thought you would?"

"He's O.K." The kids are still howling.

"Would you like to meet him in person?"

"Yeah!" His eyes light up.

And so, as Jackson is coming down the aisle, I signal to him. "Reverend, would you say hello to this young man? He's heard that if a black person becomes president, white people become slaves."

Instantly, Jackson bends over and clasps the boy's arm and

croons, "Oh, that's not true. I love you very much, buddy. O.K.? All right?"

Tears gush out, and the boy buries his face, his whole world of thought-stultifying prejudice suddenly in collapse. "Feel better," soothes Jackson. "God bless you, Brother. I love you, buddy, O.K.?"

There isn't a dry eye all around us.

Jesse Jackson has always had a feel for the hurting ones. Some call it empathy; others believe there is divinity in the man. He also has one eye out at all times for the limelight. Within an hour of this moving encounter, Jesse Jackson, then Democratic front-runner in the presidential race, was bragging to reporters about how beautifully he handled it.

Jesse Jackson may be the hungriest man in the world. He is as hungry for the crowds as they are for him. The distortions of segregation in the South in the forties left their mark, to be sure, but behind his tropism for the limelight, underneath all the braggadocio that is mistaken for arrogance, lies Jesse Louis Jackson's greatest longing in life—the lust for legitimacy.

His personal psychological need happens to coincide with the experience of blacks in America, a tremendous yearning to be affirmed as full-fledged members of the national constituency. All these years Jackson has been tunneling up, and in the long climb he has clung tenaciously to everything he could use, stepped over warm bodies, greedily dipped his fingers in the blood of his hallowed predecessor, Martin Luther King, Jr., shaken down businessmen, black and white, absorbed some of the tactics of Chicago's Boss Daley, and brought with him baggage that is decidedly distasteful. He has never held a conventional job or stood for elective office. The organizations he has created and spearheaded—PUSH and the Rainbow Coalition— have functioned above all as personality cults for Jesse Jackson. Yet, with his superhuman drive and charisma, and the verbal pyrotechnics that allow him to move from lofty oration to tub-thumping money-raising, he has carved out a unique position for himself in American political life and earned the attention of the whole world.

Now, finally, he has surfaced under the banquet table of the

Democratic party and demanded a seat. The party claims to be looking around for an extra chair, and Jesse Jackson is being terribly polite. He has made adjustments: cuffs on his pants and clodhopper shoes, plus a conscious effort to slow down his speech to a safe white drone. Image, Noah, proper image, he keeps telling his half brother.

"Polite" is the word Jesse Jackson equates with being a politician. He admits now, at least in private meetings with members of the Congressional Black Caucus, that he didn't do enough courting in 1984. The big ego, the loose cannon, seeking after the limelight at the expense of substance—"I know those are some things I might be accused of," he candidly acknowledges in meetings with his campaign advisers. But he is not completely willing to give those things up. And so he is in transition. Indeed, he seems to be in the middle of at least three passages at once: personal, political, and historical.

He has lived all his life as an outsider and learned to capitalize on it. Now he is within reach of what he has always wanted, to be accepted.

He is also in transition from preacher to politician. After being the song-and-dance man who livened up a dull act in the '84 debates, he was determined in the '88 election to be taken as a deadly serious candidate who brings a message. Working it out as he went along, he hammered at populist themes of putting people to work and curbing the flow of jobs to foreign countries, adding them to his antidrug crusade. He campaigned in the early-primary states like any other candidate, concentrating on the white middle class. For Jackson, that was known as "working the margin."

There may be a historic shift in the making as well. The retreat from equality that began under the Reagan administration was dangerously polarizing the nation by 1984. While everyone was arguing about racial or sexual rejection, Jackson pulled out of his hat something called the "Rainbow Coalition." Though only token whites and Hispanics and the rare Asian or Native American appeared onstage among his backdrop of black faces, Jackson did plant a seed.

And the seed flowered. Among eighteen- to twenty-five-year-old black males, the voter turnout in 1984 was 25 percent; turnout among white male voters of the same age was only 22 percent. Jackson's unforgettable political baptisms helped to foment in the South a new coalition of activated blacks and scared white officeholders. Together, they helped give the Democrats control of the Senate in '86, and led the larger coalition responsible for the resounding rejection of Supreme Court nominee Robert Bork. By spinning out an illusion of American prosperity while hunger, disease, homelessness, and greed all flourish, Ronald Reagan set the stage for a messiah. Enter the Reverend Jesse Jackson.

"The world around us has changed," Jackson observed in late 1987. "Who would have thought, this time twenty years ago—try four years ago—that I would be leading in the polls? That Bill Gray would be chairman of the House Budget Committee? Or that Bill Cosby would be the number one entertainer?"

Still, there is the asterisk problem. Front-runner status—if you happen to be black—comes with an invisible asterisk next to your name that means "not seriously expected to win." "Jesse wants the media to pronounce that he's legitimate, bona fide, that he *can* win," I'd been told by one of his intimates. "He wants to be known as one who can fly, leap tall buildings—he wants to be seen as Superman."

So let's take his campaign at face value. Would a color-blind America elect Jesse Jackson?

"**H**ello, Miss Gail." He took my hand and, from a distance, kissed it. Courtly. Southern. A subtle put-on. Charming but aloof.

"So, we finally meet," he said.

I had been trying to catch up with him for two and a half weeks. Until Jesse gave the word you were O.K., a journalist who called his headquarters for his schedule would have done better to check the newspaper. In the fall of '87, he had staffers, but they functioned as factotums. Nothing happened unless the Reverend said so. Following his campaign was like broken-field running in a football game. It began to make sense only when you started to think the same way Jackson does, like a quarterback. He agreed with my assessment: "One side is cheering, the other side is jeering, everything's in motion, and all eyes are on the one who's got the ball." But no sooner did you think you knew the play than Jesse would call an audible at the line of scrimmage—huh, what's happening, why is that man running the other way?—and there he'd go, having changed the play at the last second within earshot of only a handful of teammates. For all the frustrations, following the Jackson campaign was never dull.

"Can I explain to you what kind of story I want to do?" I asked him.

He nodded.

I told him that my focus is finding the people and events that have made a lasting impression on character and shaped an individual's uniqueness. I handed him a list of names that would grow, ultimately, into over fifty interviews. He looked startled, then added a few. When I asked for help in contacting his half brother, Noah Robinson, Jr., he backed off, vaguely suggesting that Noah had moved out of Chicago to New Mexico. (In fact, Robinson still runs his multimillion-dollar business operations out of Chicago, and at the time he was involved in a black gangland murder investigation.)

And so we were off on a six-week jet stream. The chaotic, high-risk Jackson campaign was at the other extreme from the movable country club on George Bush's Air Force Two, with one's name card over the seat and a minute-by-minute break-down of the day on a computerized dance card—ho hum, another filet mignon luncheon, starting at precisely 1:02.

Jesse Jackson is a walking affront waiting to happen. He has come so far, yet he looks out and sees a world that has so far to go. He travels to South Africa and recasts the story of his childhood as living under apartheid. He meets with Palestinians and identifies with people denied a homeland and beaten when they demonstrate for equality, just as blacks were in the South. He forces us to think, nettles us to change. One senses the slow seething just below his surface. Publicly the extroverted boaster, privately he is an introverted brooder. Quick to cry but slow to love, he is a snappish, sleepless, noctambulant, driven man.

For millions he is the only flame of hope. For others he is an extremely threatening figure. Among the black professionals and politicos he has worked with, some are suspicious of his personal motives. The doubt that has dogged Jesse Jackson all along remains today: What is it all for—Jesse or the movement? Jesse or the party? Jesse or the American people?

As we settled that first day into his chartered plane, he began spinning out his philosophy of survival. His large, meaty hands moved like a quarterback's. Never a smile. Eyes straight ahead. Cold. Calculating. Looking for the edge.

He couldn't help reading over my shoulder as I studied an old review of Barbara Reynolds's 1975 biography of Jackson. A former *Chicago Tribune* reporter, Reynolds had idolized Jackson. After five years of following him—finding that the man did not live up to the myth—she became his most severe critic. When *Jesse Jackson: America's David* was published, a campaign of censorship began: first threatening phone calls to her publisher, then the cancellation of her book party. After hitting number four on the local best-seller lists, the book suddenly disappeared from Chicago bookstores. Reynolds has confirmed that then, as now, Jackson expected black journalists to be black first, journalists second.

"How old is that?!" Jackson demanded. The clip was from 1975. He began speaking in sesquipedalian words, and wound up with a little lecture on Shakespeare's *Tempest:* "Now, *there* was a writer. It isn't enough to have skills." Both his meaning and manipulation were clear when he added, "To be a great writer, you have to have a great subject."

Greenville, South Carolina, is a dozy town tucked along the foothills of the Blue Ridge Mountains between the more dynamic cities of Charlotte and Atlanta. By the mid-thirties it had peaked as the textile capital of the world. The 15 percent of the population then called "Negro," though poor by white standards, lived mostly in one-family frame houses, "kept their place," and pulled together in a tightly knit social fabric centered on their churches. Into this narrow social wedge was born a boy, child of a passionate but misbegotten moment.

Helen Jackson was a beauty. "Tall, long-haired, and stacked," recalls Clenty Fair, who went to the same hairdressing school. She was aggressive for her day. And her voice was such a gift that five music colleges had offered her scholarships. Helen's illiterate mother, who worked as a maid for an affluent white family, poured all her hopes into her single angel of a daughter. Truth told, Helen was one of the "outside children," born without a father, who are not in the least uncommon in the South.

The day the sixteen-year-old Helen announced she was pregnant brought her mother's hopes down in a rage. Their churches expelled both the girl and the baby's father, a married man almost twenty years her senior, who lived—oh, the iniquity of it!—right next door, with his wife and three stepchildren. He was a boxer of some repute, a tall, handsome, golden-skinned man. The two lovebirds ran off to Chicago.

They soon returned. Helen confessed, "I've sinned against the church," and was restored. But her mother's rage was not dissolved; is not to this day. The cycle of shame had repeated itself. "It's your responsibility," she said of the baby to come. And washed her hands of it.

"I gladly accepted," Helen Jackson told me during a long interview at her lovely suburban home in Greenville. "I said, O.K., that singing career is over. I was committed to being a real mother."

The boy born to Helen on October 8, 1941, had a face as broad as the moon and a twirl of black hair at the back of his neck. Alma Smiley, one of Helen's pals, watched the baby from her house across the street. "He was a charmer from the start. Always casing everything. He'd give you a little old sexy smile. I couldn't stand it. I'd run up those steps and bite him."

Jesse's first memory of Charles Jackson was from a picture his mother showed him at about the age of three. "Your father's coming home soon," she said. He stared at the soldier in uniform and was proud. It was when he was five, near as Jackson himself can remember, that the taunts began.

"Children oftentimes are cruel," he says now. "But it always comes down to their parents." *Your dad-dy ain't none of your dad-dy. You ain't nothing but a no-body, nothing but a no-body.* That taunt came from the boys playing in Happy Hearts Park.

"We finally told him," says his mother. Helen had married Charles Henry Jackson on October 2, 1943, when Jesse was almost two years old. From then on, Jesse called the man in his house "Charlie Henry."

By the age of five, Jesse—nicknamed "Bo-Diddley" for the guitarist—was a mischievous child, always impatient and quick to lose his temper, but never, ever, a bully. How did he fight back? I asked his mother. "He cried a lot. He would try to be very brave. He never came home and repeated the things they said. You had to read the expression on his face."

The most favored black residents lived in another section of Greenville. One house in particular, on the generous corner lot at Gower and Douthit streets, attracted sightseers from all over town. A fieldstone suburban home with a brick wall running all around it, and pillars, and a basketball court in the backyard, and a brook running under a big oak, it took black folks' breath away. On the chimney was a wrought-iron R for Robinson. Here was the palace of Jesse's blood father, Noah Robinson.

One day when Noah Robinson, Jr., was seven years old, and Jesse was eight, he was playing at the far end of his yard and something happened after which nothing would ever be the same. "I saw this kid come up from the playground, came to look at me from across the street," Noah told me. "I waved at him first. I took the initiative. He waved, and then he ran away."

At the dinner table that night, Noah junior spoke up. "Today I saw a little guy across the street, looked just like me." The slurp of soup stopped. His mother choked. His father spat out the word, "Shit."

Mrs. Robinson went into the hospital that night to deliver another child. Noah Robinson, Sr., sat down with his namesake and told him the whole story. "You have a brother," he said, and he broke into tears.

Today, Noah Robinson, Sr., is seventy-nine and comfortably retired after forty years as a cotton grader. He gave me his own version of the affair. "I didn't have any children by my own wife. Helen, she was pretty, she was a baby—we just got to liking each other, and it all started. Then Helen said to me, 'I'll have a child for you.' I said, 'Hell, you know I'm married. I can't do that kind of thing.' Well, it happened. Everybody in town knew. That kept me kind of shameful. But not shamed enough to ever deny. Before he was born, I owned up to it."

His voice went to a hush. Tension still hovered in the house, with his wife sitting in the next room. "I told my wife, 'I'm not going to deny Jesse, because he's my very own. First, I'm going to ask your forgiveness.' " When she said she could accept the situation, he told her, "I'm going to try and see him, and give him everything he asks for." Robinson senior lifted his spectacles and brushed away the tears.

No one in town commanded the respect from both the black and white communities that Jesse's blood father did. Noah is a mulatto, his grandmother a slave of part Cherokee blood, and his grandfather an Irish sheriff. He enjoyed a "passport" from his employer, John J. Ryan, that was tantamount to an individual manumission. Moreover, according to Noah junior, "Few whites got funny with Daddy. He'd punch them out."

Robinson Sr. would slip around to peek at Jesse in the schoolyard. "I'd want to be with him so bad," he sighed. But there were always arguments with his wife over the money he tried to slip to Jesse. ("Little nickels," Jesse called the handouts.) At Thanksgiving and Easter, a basket would arrive at the Jacksons' with no card. Mrs. Robinson forbade the half brothers to play together, and Noah junior was sent off to an expensive Catholic school.

The *Crescent* was the finest of trains. No Negroes allowed. But Mr. Ryan gave Noah Robinson, Sr., tickets for his whole family to ride in a double bedroom on the Pullman car. "He's a colored boy, but he's got principles just like a white man," Mr. Ryan told the shocked ticket agent. There were stories in the papers about the first Negro family to ride the *Crescent*. Every summer thereafter, Noah senior and Noah junior and the other sons would pass right onto the grandest train in the South and ride in high style all the way to Philadelphia. Bo-Diddley was left behind to cry.

For Jesse, once he'd seen how his own other half lived, his was not a fine childhood at all. His nose pressed to the glass, he watched Noah junior's privileged existence. In truth, Jesse had a wonderful mother and a more-than-serviceable stepfather. The rent collector who chased others on the street never stopped at 20 Haynie Street, where the Jacksons' immaculate, four-room frame house perched on a hill. The sting was in the difference between the status of the half brother—a prince who could move back and forth between black and white worlds at a time when the color barrier was monolithic—and the stepson of a postal worker.

"You sense these distinctions," Jackson acknowledged to me. "You long for the privileges other people have."

Coach J. D. Mathis was as close to the young Jesse as anyone. Being an "outside child" himself, he identified. "It was shocking to realize that this man [Robinson] cared nothing more than as if Jesse was one of his barn horses. 'That's one of mine,' he'd say—such arrogance. There was plenty and affluence over his fence. If your father says my blood is your blood, but really you're denied, it has to affect you on the inside. If you've got a lot of pride, and Jesse has that, this can get painful. I think that was the driving force behind whatever he's done."

And so young Jesse began to boast. He boasted about his clothes, strutting to school in suits and ties, and showing up at church weddings in a tuxedo jacket and spotless white pants. He bragged on about the jobs he had, the "little jewelry" he would buy his mother. As early as the age of five, he made a stunning boast to his blood father, according to Robinson Sr. " 'Didi,' he said—he never would say Daddy—'one of these days I'm going to preach.' I said, 'You talking about preaching, you don't even know your ABC's.' But he said it again. 'My granddaddy Jesse's a preacher, ain't he?' "

Many times thereafter, defiantly, Jesse would tell his blood father, "Just you watch, I'm going to be more than you think I can be." By the second year of high school, he talked about a dream. He was leading his people across the river. "I'm a born leader," the adolescent boy announced.

When I asked Jackson about his childhood, he was at first defensive. "I never was motherless or fatherless, or hungry. I was never orphaned. I was [legally] adopted when I was a teenager."

But did he feel, as a boy, that he deserved to be born with a father he could call his own?

A shudder went through him. "Our genes cry out. For confirmation." He was glad of Noah Robinson, Sr., and the antecedents Noah could hold up to his son—five preachers in the previous generation—but as far as love and affirmation from his blood father, those were beyond reach and would remain so for as long as it mattered.

The press of segregation only added fuel to Jesse's already overheated engine. "I went to catch a bus with my mother and the sign above the bus driver's head said, COLORED SEAT FROM THE REAR. My mother had to pull me to the back. I said I wanted to sit up front. She said, 'Let's go.' She pinched me. She was conditioning me to reduced options."

He admits that he had a lot of negative motivation. "You had to figure out how to get out of this situation."

I tried out on Jackson an anthropological observation that had come to me from comparing the subculture of the segregated black South with the core culture. A child who is gifted and receptive, who picks up on everything that you give him, is singled out by the community to be "saved" for better things. Everyone—the neighbors on the street, who will give him a licking for misbehavior in place of his mother, the pastor, the coach, the teachers, even the older kids—they all look out for him so that he doesn't get into any trouble. No one wants this child harmed, in body or reputation. Helen and Charles Jackson, for instance, often went out to fight Jesse's battles for him, while the boy stayed home and cried. And adults reinforced the child's sense of specialness by holding him to a higher standard. They boosted the boy onto their shoulders, and Bo-Diddley just kept tunneling up. His grandmother cajoled the boy, "For God's sake, Jesse, promise me you'll be some*body*." Soon everyone knew Jesse was designated to be saved.

"I think that's true," Jackson said. "We use a different kind of language biblically. We say someone's been blessed, set aside, touched."

He was a big, clumsy boy, pigeon-toed, and he stuttered. (When he overcame the speech defect, he gave the credit to God.) On Noah junior had settled the lighter skin, pencil-line lips, and delicately bridged nose of his father, while Jesse's nose was soft as gingerbread, his eyes bulgy, his head big, and too much of his lower lip turned over to hope he'd ever be taken for a black aristocrat. Noah, however, couldn't run the length of a football field without wheezing. Jesse was powerfully built.

"He stood head and shoulders above everybody at the age of six, and he could talk," says Coach Mathis, smiling. "I told him he was going to be the heir apparent to great things." Together, coach and starter hammered Jesse's physical advantage into the competitor's iron will. Jackson became a superior baseball player and the school's star quarterback. Mathis also taught the boy about "putting the bend into the truth."

It was hard to miss young Jesse's talents. Consider a child so verbal, often dealing with adults unable to read or write, who, when the first TVs arrived in the neighborhood, offered to read the news off the screen for the adults. "You want to know? Give me a dime." But it was his willfulness that would have caught people's attention, because everybody knew that only the strivers could overcome segregation and racism.

The two healthiest ways to overcome shame are through humor and a sense of purpose. A schoolmate, Horace Nash, never forgot how Jesse made up jokes about whites. About "how foolish and stupid they were. He used to turn things around. He actually looked down on white people, and in those days that was unusual." And Jesse believed he was set aside by God for a purpose—one of the hallmarks of the victorious personality.

Talking publicly today about his own rejection, Jackson can become intensely personal. "When I was in my mother's belly, I had no father to give me a name," he says. "People called me a bastard and rejected me."

What is that thing inside that keeps you going? I asked Jackson after our first long interview.

His answer was vague.

Do you think your ambition started with just trying to get out, to make yourself worthy, and then began to feed on itself?

"At one level it starts as survival." He began stuttering uncomfortably. "In my instance, it started from personal denial. Then group denial." He sounded like a man thirsting, his pitcher needing to be constantly refilled, but the pitcher bottomless. "I've always been loved," he affirmed. "But there's always been an air of expectation, a higher demand of me than from other people."

Long after Jesse Louis Jackson had convinced others of his worth, he would, and always will, face that most disparaging of taunters—himself—demanding new and more dazzling forms of proof.

As the time approached for him to make his getaway from Greenville, Jesse's hunger for legitimacy hardened into his vaunted ambition. However desirable the prizes people held out to him, he always had a bigger, bolder leap in mind. No one in Greenville could figure out why he would spurn a $6,000 contract to play professional baseball, for instance. Six thousand dollars was twice what his daddy made in a year. And, oh, what excitement when the major-league scouts came to town in 1959 and Jesse was invited to the tryouts. It was the first time a black player had had the chance to be matched against a white on the segregated ball field. Jackson's version of the story has become a part of his personal mythology:

The scout tells Jesse to pitch to Dickie Dietz. This guy is reputed to be a great hitter. Jesse steps up on the mound and blazes the ball past him. Dietz can't even tip the ball. Jesse strikes him out three times. Whereupon Dietz is offered $95,000 to join an A team and Jesse is offered $6,000 to go to a B team. All the kids are cheering, "Yea, Jesse!"

Jesse says, "I don't want this."

Dietz has disputed Jackson's story. "Jesse striking me out three times? No way," he told *The Washington Post*'s David Maraniss. And Jackson, when asked about Dietz's version, did not contradict him. But underneath Jackson's fable lies a fundamental truth: Jackson knew that a professional baseball career would keep him behind the race barrier. It would not take him as far as he wanted to go.

Just you watch, I'm going to be more than you think I can be.

"Six thousand seems big, but it can go fast," as he has described his strategy. "I knew a college education would be less risk and greater returns." So he held out for a football scholarship to a Big Ten school. And got it.

What he was not prepared for, when he entered the University of Illinois that fall, was the rejection. In the dormitory, the classroom, and on the football team, where Negroes were allowed only to be linebackers, he was humiliated. "It was traumatic for me," he admits, "black players being reduced to entertainers." And so he turned his back on the fine white northern school and entered North Carolina A & T, then a mediocre black land-grant college.

There he met Jacqueline Lavinia Davis, an outspoken leftist who exuded the rock-solid confidence he wanted. The daughter of Florida migrant workers, Jackie had been smothered with protection by her mother. Thrilled to be on her own for the first time, at seventeen, she became a very active student. "I was pompous and vain. Anyone who sat with me was just very fortunate. Big lips, nappy hair, the whole bit, yet I thought I was the loveliest, most exciting person in the whole world—and still do to a certain extent."

I asked Jackie if that is what Jesse coveted in her, the air of superiority. She nodded. Why, then, did she leave college instead of becoming Angela Davis? Was it because she got pregnant?

"Yes," she said. "My husband did that to me. It was not intentionally done on my part. I think he did it to catch me. I really do. Because he kept asking me, 'How are you doing?' and I would say 'I felt a little sick this morning,' but I would always think that was the strangest question." Jackson had been her first boyfriend. "I had never seen a baby. I hadn't thought about a baby. Is that the way you get babies?

"You should ask him about it," Jackie suggested. Jesse Jackson said it was too personal a subject to discuss, but he did characterize it as a victory: "We got married. Established family security. We broke the cycle."

After college, in 1964, Jackson got into the Chicago Theological Seminary through the preachers' network. He never graduated, and Professor Victor Obenhaus, Jackson's first adviser at the seminary, told David Maraniss that he considered his pupil "a tremendous con artist." Jackson insisted on "speaking" his exams, and has boasted that he failed Preaching because he did not believe in writing out sermons. But other professors, even those who found him brilliant, remember that he avoided written work in their classes as well. One of Jackson's favorite teachers, Professor Howard Schomer, pointed out that "with his ready tongue and vivid language," Jackson could "carry a thought beyond what closer scrutiny would justify."

It is a criticism that has continued to be leveled at Jackson the candidate. One major network correspondent, after a forty-five-minute interview, concluded that "his personality projection overwhelms, outweighs, what he says, and when he talks in slogans it avoids his having to get to the specifics and show how extreme he is."

His half brother could not figure out why Jesse would want to attend a seminary to begin with. All Noah junior could imagine was Daddy Grace, the notoriously flamboyant preacher who used to ride around town in a white suit on a flatbed truck, collecting money in washtubs while women wept and clutched at his long, flowing hair. "You gettin' ready to run a hustle like Daddy Grace?" he chuckled. Noah junior claims that Jackson was "absolutely, positively not religious." Jackson's response: "He didn't know me."

A Johnny-come-lately to the civil-rights movement, Jackson caught up with Martin Luther King, Jr., by jumping the line as a mere volunteer on the Selma march in 1965. He demanded the movement people find a role for him.

Dr. King was looking at Chicago as a possible beachhead in the North. Jackson became a student in nonviolent-protest workshops run by the Reverend James Bevel, who recommended the articulate apprentice to Dr. King for a major job. King began complaining to Bevel that the young seminarian was too ambitious. Bevel argued it was only immaturity, but King saw another, more alarming dimension to Jesse: "the ability to prostitute a race for one's own self-aggrandizement," as Bevel described it to me, "to build an empire at the expense of your people."

Another civil-rights leader who hired Jackson to help organize in Chicago found him exceptionally smart and hardworking, but contentious and manipulative. "The joke was you could probably lead Jesse off any bridge in town by just pointing an empty TV camera at him and saying 'Back up.' " He also found one couldn't trust an agreement made with Jackson behind closed doors. It was when Jackson stepped out into the shower of klieg lights, and only then, that one knew what he was going to say.

Of these and other charges of self-glorification, the "bloody shirt" incident raises the most serious questions about Jackson's character.

The disciples of Dr. King were always jockeying for position. Dr. Ralph Abernathy had been designated by King as his successor, and Andrew Young was Abernathy's understudy. All the others, at least in the presence of Dr. King, contained their aspirations.

Jesse Jackson came in and broke for the top.

He seized his chance, in 1968, on the evening King was assassinated. A week before, Dr. King had held a staff meeting to talk through his ideas for the Poor People's Campaign. None of the staff were really enthusiastic about the campaign, but they were "amening Doc." Jackson, who saw Dr. King not as a mentor but as a competitor, openly challenged him. According to David Garrow's biography of King, *Bearing the Cross,* the civil-rights leader became emotional and stalked out of the meeting to go see his girlfriend at their hideaway apartment. Jackson began to follow, but King turned on him: "If you are so interested in doing your own thing that you can't do what the organization is structured to do, go ahead. If you want to carve out your own niche in society, go ahead, but for God's sake don't bother me!"

On April 4 the staff was gathered at a Memphis motel, waiting for King to come downstairs to go to a big rally. Bevel was horsing around with the Reverend James Orange and Andy Young in the courtyard under King's balcony, according to Orange. Jackson stood nearby.

At 5:59 P.M., King came out and called down to Jackson in the yard, "I want you to come to dinner with me." All those present remember marking the personal invitation as King's way of making up with Jesse. Jackson called up to introduce a Chicago saxophonist, Ben Branch. King leaned over: "I want you to play my song tonight, play 'Precious Lord.' Play it real pretty."

At 6:01 a noise split the night. All at once King's feet were dangling over the balcony. "Oh my God, Martin's been shot," howled Ralph Abernathy from inside room 306. Jackson, along with the others in the courtyard, hit the ground. "Dr. Abernathy was already down over King when Andy got upstairs," recalls

Orange. A Justice Department observer, James Laue, placed a towel over the wound in King's jaw. Abernathy cradled the dying leader in his lap.

In the courtyard below, Bevel was crouched six feet from Jackson when Dr. Abernathy called down to ask him to go over to the Masonic temple where King had spoken, and calm the people. "I asked Jesse to go with me," Bevel says, because the others were lifting King onto a stretcher to go to the hospital. Jesse told Bevel, "Man, I am sick. I got to go to Chicago and check into the hospital. This has really shot my nerves."

Bevel dismissed his young staffer. But at 6:25, when camera crews from the three networks began to arrive, Jackson was still there and called out to the others, "Don't talk to them." Hosea Williams was shocked to hear Jesse then tell the TV people, "Yes, I was the last man in the world King spoke to."

That night, while all the other disciples wept and discussed funeral arrangements, Jackson was missing. The next morning, as they prepared to pick up King's body, Jesse was making news on the *Today* show in Chicago with a story the others found preposterous.

That day, and for years after, the press reported that Jackson had been on the balcony when King was shot, and that he had cradled the dying man in his arms. But it was what Jesse said later the same morning before the Chicago City Council that embittered King's other followers. Still wearing the tan turtleneck he claimed was smeared with the blood of King, he excoriated Mayor Daley and his machine, crying, "This blood is on the chest and hands of those who would not have welcomed him here yesterday."

Jackson tells different stories, even to the same journalist. He told me that blood was splattering everywhere and that's how it got on his shirt. Other participants flatly reject that description. "There was one pool of blood," says Bevel. Ben Branch, the saxophonist, told Barbara Reynolds, "My guess is Jesse smeared the blood on his shirt after getting it off the balcony. All I can say is that Jesse didn't touch him." And Laue told Michael Kramer of *U.S. News* that "I was away from the scene for maybe twenty seconds—to get that towel—and I never saw Jesse near Dr. King."

Jackson's explanation for why he left that night is also lame. "A number of the staff members went back to Atlanta that night because that was where they lived. I went to Chicago because that's where my family and my organization were." In fact, everyone else remained overnight in Memphis.

Don Rose, a Chicago political consultant who met with Jackson the day after King's assassination, recalls, "There was a deliberate decision to launch an image-making process."

"That to me is the most gruesome crime a man can commit," says Bevel today. "To lie about the crucifixion of a prophet within a race." Another prominent Chicago leader says Jackson used "the moment of the death of the leader as a vehicle to anoint himself. People were bitter about that." On the cynical level, the political leader admits, "There's no question it worked for him."

The healthy drive of Greenville's pushy little Jesse had been transmuted into a blind, almost involuntary desire for advancement. Jackson must still wrestle with himself over his decisions in the wake of King's death. But he is loath to look back. He is reminiscent of Jacob, the son of Isaac, who obtained his father's blessing by fraud, and who wrestled with God until daybreak and then bragged, "I have seen God face to face and have survived."

Few of the slain leader's other disciples today like to come right out and call Jesse a liar, mainly because the lie is by now in Jackson's head and helps him to believe in the divinity of his own destiny. More and more, he seeks out biblical analogies and snaps them down like safety catches over the loose ends of his earlier life. In the early seventies, he was introduced as the "Black Messiah" at functions in Chicago. He often tells students, "Great things happen in small places. Jesus was born in Bethlehem. Jesse Jackson was born in Greenville."

Jackson is often compared disparagingly with Martin Luther King, Jr. But King had the opportunity to develop in ways that few southern blacks ever did. His natural intellectual ability was nurtured in an upper-middle-class Atlanta aristocracy, and he went to college at fifteen. "He saw all the ambiguities," recalls Eleanor Holmes Norton, first woman director of the Equal Employment Opportunity Commission, "and that's why he was tormented and sometimes indecisive. That's the difference between him and somebody like Jackson, who is a deprived son of a teenage mother. These are just two different fish."

More important, the civil-rights agenda Dr. King activated had been waiting for a hundred years. Jackson was not so favored by history. When he emerged in the seventies, a brash young talent burning with ambition, there was no fresh movement waiting for a leader. Older disciples in King's crusade perceived a basic spiritual distinction between the two men.

"Jesse, you have no love," Dr. King himself used to tell the young spitfire. But Jackson has his own kind of brilliance. It is immediately absorptive of new and even esoteric material, and makes wildly creative connections among these seedling ideas, which then sprout forth in charming bouquets of language. So, in the absence of passion or cause, Jackson made up his own movements. Breadbasket Commercial Association focused on black capitalism. When Jimmy Carter became president, prominent blacks were suddenly getting jobs in the administration, but the Atlanta crowd controlled that patronage and they locked Jesse out. So he came up with the idea of motivating black youth: PUSH-Excel. And later, when he needed it, he *named* a movement—the Rainbow Coalition. He made it stand for everything from futuristic foreign-policy views to issues of the most interior concern to black Americans.

Coming out of the Baptist-preacher mold made it much easier to improvise. The Baptists have no hierarchy and no educational requirements for the pulpit. Anyone with good lungs and a protest to faith can become a preacher. "Black ministers are notorious chauvinists," says Julian Bond. "This guy is God's representative to you. So when the Reverend says, 'I want to talk to you in my study, Sister,' what can she do?" Bond and Young, and other new-generation southern black activists who were choosing the electoral route, were suspicious of power wielded over the masses simply because of the title "Reverend." "We felt you had to prove leadership," says Bond.

Is Jackson, then, a great leader? Or a genius hustler? He has never held a full-time pastorate and often describes what he does as a "mission." In the private and the religious spheres, as well as in the political arena, Jackson has been making up the rules as he goes along.

Eleanor Holmes Norton believes "you've got to line him up along with the remarkable American political figures who manage to capture the public imagination—all the way from F.D.R. to Huey Long. These men are vastly different. But people were fascinated with their public personalities as they are fascinated with Jackson's, because it's one of a kind." She affirms that his need for public recognition equates with his yearning for personal legitimacy. "And it's insatiable. He'll never have it. That's why he has to keep about this pursuit. It's almost existential."

St. Alban's, an elite private boys' school in Washington, D.C., is playing a public school in suburban Virginia. It is a fresh, clear September night in 1987. Jackson's third son, Yusef DuBois, already a powerfully built 220 pounds, scores a touchdown for St. Alban's minutes before his mother arrives from Chicago to join his father on the field.

"Here comes my baby," Jackson hums as his wife, Jacqueline, appears.

A five-foot-one, lusty, busty, fiery woman swaggers closer. He gives her a quick hug. She has dimples, full cheeks, flawless skin, and—incongruously—braces. Jackie Jackson is opulently dressed for a football game, diamonds blazing on both hands, chandelier earrings, and black high heels under her trousers. Jesse Jackson goes back to pacing the field, hands plunged into his jeans pockets, shouting, "Go Yusef." When Jackie shouts in her husky voice, even louder than he, he roars with delight.

Jackie makes it clear she is her husband's chief bodyguard against the character cops. She starts right in with the several women journalists present, warning them that if the subject of her husband's private behavior is raised, she will go on the warpath in her own speeches, "and I will win." She says, "You've been around the circuit, you know what goes on during these campaigns—it's life. But nobody comes into my house or my bedroom."

The Jackson home, in a posh integrated section off South Shore Drive in Chicago, has two faces. Official visitors pass under its chocolate-trimmed Tudor peaks and stained-glass windows to enter through the front door into a formal parlor. Initiates come through the back door into a dining room of funky dishabille, where golf clubs and silver tea trays teeter against Jackie's ubiquitous hatboxes and half-refinished antiques. Flunkies bide their time reading tabloids around the long, lace-covered table. Jackson rarely tires, but when he does, his mild sickle-cell-anemia trait keeps him to his bed. There he holds court. The phone is his most constant companion. At two or three or five in the morning, he'll have a brainstorm and start dialing. His nocturnal calls used to drive the deliberate Walter Mondale crazy. His own wife simply refuses to answer the phone after midnight anymore.

Jackie talks teasingly and lovingly about Jesse, and refers to him possessively as "my husband." The early years of their marriage were stormy: Jesse was rarely there. Bogged down with five children, Jackie fought being the wife of this prominent man. In recent years, she has decided she likes it. "I took a degree in Jesse Jackson," she tells me. "A Phi Beta Kappa," Jackson corrects.

That weekend, the impressively bright, polite Jackson children were flying in from private schools all over the country for a trio of birthday celebrations in Washington. They don't gather as a family often. The oldest daughter, Santita, aged twenty-four, and an English major at Howard University, arrived just as the game ended. There was tension; she was obviously there under pressure. But after a perfunctory squeeze, her father laid his head on her shoulder in a gesture of affectionate, put-on penitence. She, of course, melted.

Jesse junior, recently graduated from his father's alma mater, had committed himself to a year of helping the campaign. He was handling with grace and humility the role of trainee under his father, who believes in administering verbal lashings to him in front of the campaign staff. His father calls the twenty-three-year-old "Little Jesse." The son refers to his father with awed respect as "the Reverend."

When I arrived for a lengthy interview with Jackie Jackson, on a Sunday afternoon after a family birthday gala at the Washington Hilton, she was sleepily rubbing cream into her face. She had been up until four. "I have to stay around to hear what beefs people have, because my husband leaves early."

Three plastic containers of birthday cake sat on the table, unopened. Jackie sat hugging a pillow, tinted glasses pushed up over her full tousled head of hair, and chain-smoked. She started out waxing philosophical. "If I got pregnant, it was the right time to be pregnant. I don't understand people who plan things. Life is not about how far you fall, but how long it takes you to bounce back." She went off on a long tangent about children and how things are falling apart these days. "How did I get on this?

"It's difficult to understand my relationship with my husband, because most women do not see themselves as partners," she continued. "They see some romantic notion they bought on the television."

Asked about jealousy, she has said, "My portion of him is mine. I can't spend too much time worrying about other women if I am to develop myself; then I would be chasing all around this country." Alternatively, she has visited Lebanon and Nicaragua and more than thirty other nations and has spoken out loudly against American intervention in some Third World countries. Often carrying back-channel messages from her husband, she travels without press, meets with dissenters, and seeks out prominent women. "In every culture, women reflect the level of suffering, so you can get a feeling of what is happening."

As Jackie was talking to me in a Washington hotel room, Jesse was about to go into a demanding military-policy debate in Iowa. The phone rang. "Excuse me, that's *my husband*."

Her voice prodded with gentle maternalism. "Have you done what you were going to do? Mmmm, well, just say a little prayer, because you need it. I love you much. O.K., O.K. What did you want to do with your clothes?"

Friends circulated in and out, helping her children to pack. Jackie called out, "What time is it? What's the date today?" Life happens around her. This poetic, free-spirited, often profound woman differs dramatically in her relationship with her husband from Coretta King. Mrs. King "saw for herself a public role as a substantive figure that Dr. King didn't accept or agree with at all," according to one intimate. "Coretta was most certainly a widow long before Dr. King died."

Rumors that Jesse Jackson has had affairs have dogged him all of his married life, linking him to such famous singers as Nancy Wilson, Roberta Flack, and Aretha Franklin. In the last four years, as reported in the *Atlanta Constitution,* he has been tied to two prominent women in Washington-based black organizations, as well as a woman now involved in his campaign (no bimbos).

A close family friend says the black community knows all about Jackson as a womanizer, but he has cleaned up his act considerably in the last four or five years. He is discreet enough so that campaign followers don't buzz about any noticeable promiscuity, the way they did with Hart. "Almost every woman he's met has thrown herself at him," says the friend. "How strongly he resists is problematical."

The most persistent rumors surround his close relationship with Roberta Flack. The singer recorded a torrid love song in 1973 entitled "Jesse." In 1974 Jackson told a reporter, "Until such time as I'm ready to concede some formal relationship, I refuse to deny the rumor, or to be intimidated by it." In August of '87, Flack sang at a Jackson benefit, and that September the *Chicago Tribune* listed her as one of his leading fund-raisers.

King's well-publicized affairs with other women did not undercut his moral authority. My guess is the issue won't hurt Jackson with his natural constituency either, especially if they get the impression the white press is picking on him. In '84, for instance, just around the time that his links with Black Muslim leader Louis Farrakhan raised a storm of criticism, Jackson's black support began to build.

The hidden impulse behind many of Jackson's moves throughout his years in Chicago, 1970 to 1982, was the rivalry between himself and his half brother, Noah. Money is Noah's god. He was a business whiz with a degree from the Wharton School of Business, and had $326 in his pocket when Jesse wooed him to Chicago. To Noah, at that time, Jesse Jackson was a big shot he saw on TV and the cover of *Time.* Anointed by the media as heir to King's movement, Jesse was then running the Southern Christian Leadership Conference's Operation Breadbasket in Chicago. He dazzled Noah by taking him to dinner with Diana Ross.

"I wanted to help him," Jackson admitted to me, "and please my father as well." Now it was Jesse who had the power and who was in the position to dispense largess. *I'm going to be more than you think I can be.* Finally, Jesse persuaded his brother to join him in running the commercial arm of Operation Breadbasket. Noah, who doesn't hesitate to describe himself as a hustler, tried to entice Jesse into exploiting the movement to make money. "I told Jesse, 'If you just do the talking for us—and I handle the financial operations—we can rival the Rockefellers in riches.' "

Breadbasket Commercial Association was set up to offer marketing and management services to minority-owned businesses. Underwritten by some of the nation's leading black entrepreneurs, the B.C.A. also sought funds from small-business people, white and black. Jackson hadn't studied his nemesis, the mayor of Chicago, for nothing. Where Boss Daley extracted political patronage, the nascent boss of black Chicago began to demand economic patronage. With Jesse doing the talking, and Noah wheeling and dealing, B.C.A. obtained over $16 million in contracts for member businesses in the first six months of 1970. It was the heady pulse of success that stirred bad blood. The two boastful half brothers clashed and split. Noah's motivation from then until now, Noah told me, has been revenge. Noah and Jesse became Chicago's Cain and Abel.

The currents of love and rivalry boiled under everything Noah said about Jesse during our interview. I asked how often they see each other today. "We run into each other in airports," said Robinson.

A slight, slip-through-the-door sort of man, with a narrow moustache and a goatee, Noah Robinson, Jr., usually has a toothpick dangling jauntily from his lips. Close your eyes and listen to the familiar singsong rhyming cadence, and you would swear it was Jesse talking. Both men have a penchant for self-dramatization, are easily insulted and vindictive, and seem absent the gene for humility. "We are both able and energetic," says Jackson enigmatically.

Noah told the story of their business association to me and Linda duBuclet, my research assistant, "Jesse brought me into the movement through the back door. His staff resented me for my success. I overran them all."

Calvin Morris, Jackson's Number Two at Operation Bread-basket until 1971, recalls, "We were told to try to contain Noah or he'd run off with the church." When Noah heard this, he was stunned. "That was Jesse's management style, to pit the opposing forces in the organization against each other. I went to Jesse and pulled back the curtain: 'Is it you?' First he denied it, then he confirmed it. 'Noah,' he said, 'you're the first person I've ever had to share the stage with.' 'Me! I'm backstage clapping. That's crazy.' "

When Noah and Jesse got together in Chicago in 1970—at ages twenty-eight and twenty-nine, respectively—it was the first time that they had compared their childhoods. "I didn't know about the other Jesse Jackson, the fearful one," recounts Noah. "I just remembered this guy from high school, then I saw him grow into this star on TV. He seemed so confident. But the inner Jesse has an insecurity, an overwhelming need to reaffirm he is good, better, best. It's a *fear,* in here"—he points to his heart—"that fuels his drive." The chant "I am somebody," says Noah, is the closest thing to a confession you'll get from Jesse.

During the year the brothers worked together, Jackson had failed to consult with the S.C.L.C. board about B.C.A. or Robinson. Finally, he was called on the carpet and dethroned by Ralph Abernathy. He left the conference to form his own, rival organization, PUSH, stripping B.C.A. of its economic base of ministers-cum-businessmen. But not before trying to get the board to fire Noah.

Noah had his bags packed, ready to be run out of town. "I was too ashamed to tell Dad that Jesse fired me—it would open up old wounds." So he vowed to stay in Chicago and fight his brother for turf.

"We didn't speak to each other for five years," says Noah. "Most traumatic experience of my whole life. His people would picket one of my sites, then my people would counterpicket." Fat was thrown in the fire when the S.C.L.C. rehired Robinson to fill his brother's shoes at Operation Breadbasket. Jackson had the preachers on his side. In exchange for the ministers' supplying troops to stage boycotts, the businessmen would give the churches money. But then, as now, PUSH staggered from payroll to payroll. Noah, meanwhile, had discovered a milk cow in the movement. He began by taking advantage of minority set-asides from the Nixon administration. He crows unashamedly, "As a minority subcontractor, I made more money than most of the prime contractors, because I kept getting ten percent of this, twenty percent of that." The ugliest part of Noah's success was the shunting of taxpayers' money, intended for the development of minority businesses, to white contractors. The whites made profits faster, and cut him and his relatives in, earning Noah the reputation of a successful "movement pimp."

"I've had thirty different operations," Robinson brags. "Whenever I saw an opportunity, I grabbed it." When the *Chicago Tribune* went after him, stirring up the first of many federal, state, and local investigations into his activities, Noah thumbed his nose. "That was my first public notoriety." He preens before me. "I wasn't ashamed of making millions. And I don't intend to change my ways."

It was in 1975, five years after their split, that Jesse called Noah junior out of the blue. Noah hadn't heard his voice since 1971 except on radio and TV. He was stunned. When the brothers came face-to-face, each wearing a vest and medallions and bell-bottoms, the mirror image unnerved them both. Noah kept reassuring himself, "I'm worth three or four million, he's probably worth thirty cents."

"I'm preaching brotherhood, but I'm not practicing it," Jackson began. His voice trembled. He told Noah he wanted to make peace with his God. He said he didn't know if he could ever really forgive Noah, but he could no longer live in hypocrisy.

Behind that noble motive Jesse was also considering his image. He was planning a trade fair, with a family-day theme, for Black Expo. Calvin Morris believes the reconciliation was also in anticipation of an eventual run for the presidency. Jesse would need Noah junior and his biological father to provide a picture of family unity. Always, with Jesse, it's the picture that counts.

After their rapprochement in 1975, Jesse once more introduced Noah around as the good brother, and announced that Robinson would be his business manager. The two appeared at a luncheon together, where Robinson announced that he and a syndicate of black businessmen had acquired a large milk company, and Jackson named twenty companies, selected as new targets for PUSH.

What of the brothers Jackson/Robinson today? Both are still hyperstrivers, though the principles that guide them are very different. Jesse craves legitimacy; Noah's goal is to enter the 1990s as the hundred-million-dollar man, and to lord it over his brother. Eerily, their associations have run parallel for many years. Jesse runs a boycott of Coca-Cola and pushes the company to sign a "moral covenant"; Noah comes along behind and locks up the first black distributorship with Coca-Cola. Jesse challenges fast-food chains into signing covenants with PUSH to hire and distribute proportionally to their black customers; Noah turns up with a chain of Wendy's, Bojangle's, and Church's Fried Chicken in both Chicago and New York. Jesse makes diplomatic missions to Arab countries; Noah's name comes up in an investigation of Chicago gang members, on trial for taking a contract from Libya to commit terrorist attacks in the United States.

Most recently, Noah's name surfaced in the middle of a federal murder investigation. Robinson had employed members of the notorious El Rukn Chicago street gang over the past three years, as well as violent drug dealers (including the convicted kingpin of a heroin ring operating in four states). As reported by the *Chicago Tribune,* the murder victim, Leroy "Hambone" Barber, a childhood friend from the days in Happy Hearts Park, was first hired by Robinson in 1977 after being paroled following the shooting of two Greenville policemen. Robinson knew of his reputation as a drug dealer, and allegedly used him to beat up debtors. In 1981 Barber landed back in prison—for the attempted robbery of one Noah Robinson, Jr. After Barber was sprung in 1984, Robinson hired him back, but claims that he fired him in November 1985, and that the "attempted murderer" followed him to Greenville. They came to blows in a pool hall in a shopping plaza owned by Robinson. Less than two weeks later, Barber was called to a pay phone in a dimly lit area of the plaza and shot in the head.

Investigators suspect Robinson wanted the rubout. A top-ranking El Rukn member, now a federal informer, told authorities that El Rukn leader Jeff Fort ordered gang members to kill Barber because he was "bothering" Robinson.

Fort—who once worked for Jackson at PUSH—had become a sort of American Qaddafi in Chicago. He held court from a Muslim temple near Jackson's headquarters, his throne surrounded by larger-than-life-sized posters of himself and the Libyan leader. Louis Farrakhan, the Nation of Islam leader whose skinheads provided Jackson with physical protection during his '84 campaign, hailed Fort's El Rukn as his "divine warriors." Last November, Fort and four members of his gang were convicted of a conspiracy to commit terrorist acts against Americans under personal contract to Qaddafi.

Noah Robinson, who continued to be referred to in the national press as simply "a successful Chicago businessman," was also being investigated last winter by a Chicago grand jury on matters related to his frequent appearances in bankruptcy court. The same white businesses he cut in on federal grants were now suing him for fraud.

The U.S. attorney in Chicago, Anton Valukas, told me straight out: "Whatever we have under inquiry has nothing to do with Jesse Jackson." Jackson was categorical in his own defense. "All the businesses I created—franchises, distributorships—I don't have a stake in any of them. I could have." Whatever Noah gets, he insisted, whether or not he uses Jackson's name to get it, is Noah's affair. "I am not in business with him, never have been. We relate warmly and respectfully, which is really all I can say."

But when Jackson wants to stage a fund-raiser in Chicago, to gather the same businessmen the two have cultivated or intimidated over the years, he still gives Noah a call. Blood is thicker than water, to be sure. But if a blood relation is mixed up with drug dealers, murderers, and terrorists, why doesn't a man in Jackson's position put an unequivocal distance between them? It may be that Noah knows too much about Jesse's weaknesses, and holds that telltale power over his brother.

Noah is the chink in the façade, and they both know it.

Jackson has had his own problems with money and organization. Between 1978 and 1982, after Hubert Humphrey urged government support for PUSH, it received $5 million in grants and loans from at least three federal agencies. But an April 1980 government report found that the Reverend Jesse Jackson had failed to convert his inspirational message into a workable public-school program. A PUSH chapter would open in a new town with considerable fanfare, and with Jackson onstage, but there would be no follow-up. "PUSH didn't push, except Jesse," claims the formerly idealistic director of a Harlem youth center, who repeatedly asked for program guidelines after meeting Jackson in 1972, but never got a response. Jackson has been most effective in challenging corporations to open up white-only distributorships and franchises to blacks. An experienced former assistant secretary of labor, Ernest Green, has been helping him in that effort. But many of the able people Jackson has hired for PUSH find his authoritarian management style impossible, and leave.

When Jackson refused to let federal officials audit the PUSH books, funds were cut off. Eventually he agreed to an audit. But by then investigators could find no records. Jackson maintains he never signed any PUSH checks. According to a Department of Education spokesman, "Our problem is that the man keeping the records died, and the records don't seem to exist. The case is now in commercial litigation with the Justice Department." The Justice Department emphasizes that there is no question of a criminal investigation, and that such referrals from other agencies are not unusual.

Jackson's response to the investigations, however, "puts a bend into the truth." He denounced the Reagan administration for trying to "discredit and destroy PUSH"—never mind that the Carter administration had prepared the critical report. "I never sought the government grant," he now says scornfully. "I did not want to get bogged down in the politics of government bureaucracy. The government wanted to identify with a success story. I anticipated what was going to happen." Since government spigots to PUSH have been shut off, Syria has funneled at least two legal $100,000 donations into PUSH-Excel.

In late '83, according to Noah, Jesse said, "Noah, I got an idea. You oughta get a piece of this. I think I'm going to run for president of the United States."

Noah said, "Well, we agree you're more qualified than the present occupant. But what's your political base?"

Jesse told Noah that he had helped every black elected official in the country, paving the way for dozens of black politicians to become mayors and congressmen. Noah shot holes in his rationale: "Like John the Baptist, you made these guys Jesus. Now you're going to go back and say you want the throne. They'll resent that. They won't abdicate."

The only members of the black political establishment who did not oppose Jackson in '84 were Mayor Richard Hatcher of Gary, Indiana, Mayor Marion Barry of Washington, D.C., and a lukewarm Kenneth Gibson in Newark, New Jersey. The rest supported Mondale.

Because of his style, the prayer meetings and little ditties of poetry, pundits predicted he would run a campaign of surface issues. Then Jackson had a brainstorm. Learning that the administration was doing nothing to free a black pilot downed in Syrian-held territory, Jackson sent a cable to President Hafez al-Assad. Next thing, he was stepping out of an official U.S. government plane to pull off a sweet victory by sheer personal diplomacy.

The party's response to Jackson became even cooler. Walter Mondale never quite grasped the "Jackson phenomenon," but he knew he didn't like it, and he cut off the voter-registration funds. These were new Democrats the Mondale forces didn't necessarily want.

The deal Mondale's forces had extracted from union leaders fell apart at the rank-and-file level. Jackson won over 90 percent of black union members' votes. Tensions increased. The Mondale camp refused to accommodate Jackson on changing the rules by which delegates are committed. But being the instant innovator he is, Jackson determined to capture the masses at the convention with his words.

Robert Beckel, Mondale's campaign manager, went into intense negotiations with him over platform and publicity. "It was a frustrating forty-eight hours," says Beckel. On one particularly rushed visit to Jackson's hotel suite, Beckel brought his mother. He intended to make the deal and, at the end, to say, "Incidentally, will you say hello to my mother?"

"You left your mother sitting outside!" Jackson yelled when he heard. He chastised Beckel up one side and down the other. While Beckel fidgeted for the next forty-five minutes, leaving Mondale, the leader of the Democratic party, to cool his heels, Jackson sat and jawed with Beckel's mother about everything under the sun.

Making 'em wait.

It became clear to the Mondale forces that they weren't going to get a deal on the platform unless they offered Jesse prime time for his TV appearance at the convention. They relented and gave him the eight P.M. slot.

The night before Mondale's nomination, Beckel walked out onto the balcony of San Francisco's Fairmont Hotel with Jackson. It was a loaded moment. "You know, Reverend, this speech you're going to give . . ."

"I knew they were braced for something negative," as Jackson tells it today. "They had stolen half my delegates and said they had rammed the platform down our throats."

"Well, I'll tell you this, Beckel," he drawled that night. "You're either going to be a chimp, a chump, or a champ."

Making 'em sweat.

Jackson's speech turned out to be a stem-winder; the public went wild. Afterward, he collected. He went to the Mondale people and said, "I'll go seven days a week, twenty-two hours a day, for you-all." He started to total up what it would cost to move him and three or four people around the country. Beckel began to sweat.

"We ended up agreeing to give him roughly half a million. It was more than anybody else cost us for a surrogate," Beckel told me.

Black volunteers who had devoted themselves to Mondale's effort to capture the nomination were unceremoniously shut out. The paid staff jobs many believed they deserved were thrown to Jackson's followers, and so began the building of his national power base.

In the summer of 1987, the Democratic National Committee held a big gala and invited every past and potential presidential candidate to an intimate dinner—except Jesse Jackson. He was truly hurt. Ann Lewis, former political director of the D.N.C., told him, "They are not the party, we are. The reason there's a Democratic Senate is not six guys in a room in Washington in bow ties. If you give them the power to shut you out, you're giving them a power they don't have."

Before he announced, Jackson asked at least a dozen people to be his campaign coordinator—Ron Brown, Bob Beckel, Carl Wagner, Paul Tully, and Basil Paterson among them—super-professionals, white and black. They all turned him down. None of them believed a campaign manager could control a man as willful as Jackson, or be allowed to do more than take orders. The Jackson campaign was all in Jesse's head.

In the fall of 1987, few of his high-powered supporters had even wanted to be identified as having a role in his campaign. Jackson had told me his finance chairman was Percy Sutton, a former Manhattan borough president. Sutton said not. Jackson also told me Basil Paterson, a sharp politico now in private law practice, was heading up his New York campaign. Paterson said not.

Paterson, who had staged fund-raisers for Jackson, found him "an absolutely exasperating person, one of the most undisciplined people I've ever seen in public life. Yet there's nobody on the public scene right now who comes up with ideas any better. He is a brilliant man."

By November 1987, however, it seemed that the Jackson campaign was finally going to be whipped into shape. Jackson announced that Willie Brown, speaker of the California Assembly, would be his campaign chairman. Brown, who is highly regarded politically, had agreed to serve in a nominal capacity, but only if Jackson brought in a professional campaign manager—something the candidate had always refused to do. That resulted in the hiring of Jerry Austin, who is white. Austin made organizational and staff changes that gave Jackson's candidacy a more professional edge, though the chief spokesman is still Frank Watkins, a white minister who has been with Jackson for twenty years and is referred to as his "Linus blanket."

The only time Jackson has ever shared power was with Noah junior in Chicago. That lasted for about a year. Is there ever going to be anyone around Jesse Jackson who can tell him when the emperor has no clothes?

"I tell him," insisted Jackie Jackson. "We all tell him things. He's slow to act on them. He has to be stubborn."

Jackson's answer was more competitive: "Big egos are not a problem if it correlates with their intelligence. The only problem is if they have a Cadillac ego and a bicycle brain."

Without question, Jackson began having a more profound effect on the Democratic party from the first debate. To hear Dick Gephardt or Mike Dukakis talk about how they would fund the African National Congress is a measure of how influential his foreign-policy views have become. And since no one among this crop of candidates has a civil-rights record like Mondale's, "Jackson's candidacy basically freezes black elected officials," according to Ron Brown, who was deputy campaign manager for Ted Kennedy. Apart from Ann Lewis and former Carter administration official Bert Lance, key Jackson advisers, he has won over almost no white leaders or elected officials. Jackson's amazing 1988 roll began with the people, and in the lily-whitest places.

Davenport, Iowa: A six-foot-nine white trucker stomps onto the podium after Jackson's speech and lifts him off his feet in a bear hug: "There's never been a candidate that really stood up for truck drivers!"

Pleasantville, Iowa: Jackson has a hundred white people praying with him. A retired farmer stuffs money in an envelope and steps up. "The way things is going, breaking all the unions, and these big mergers, corporations paying no taxes, I'm just glad you're helping, Mr. Jackson." Little old ladies lay down their canes to get close to him. "I need your autograph, Jesse," says one. "Only if I can get a hug. Trade-off." He draws the seventy-year-old under his powerful shoulder. She sighs like a schoolgirl.

Even in the cool light, away from the magnetism of his personality, it should be remembered that not only the small South Carolina city of his birth but this republic itself was defined as an exclusively white enterprise. And now Jesse Jackson threatens all of that as he moves to join poorer whites with their black and brown co-workers and fellow union members as comrades in the underclass. He has real potential among young idealists, along with the psychic wounded of the Vietnam generation, and disillusioned white farmers and non-southern blue-collar workers who have gone Republican before. He stings, nudges, needles, then adds the sweetener—what's in it for them, and for him—and leaves them feeling they hold a secret power through which they can stick it to the Establishment.

Jackson's campaign has been on the whole a cash-and-carry operation. When Jackson missed a scheduled flight from Mobile to put the finishing flourish on a speech to striking paperworkers, a plate was passed to collect money for a chartered plane. It was often unclear whether fund-raisers were meant to help meet the PUSH payroll or to collect campaign funds.

But Jackson continues to use his staggeringly effective evangelical fund-raising techniques. I watched him conjure money out of poor people in an impoverished parish house in Davenport, Iowa. He began biblically. "I often reflect on Jesus's first journey. He didn't have the budget either. If you go out amongst the people, they will feed you and clothe you." Having thus cast himself as a humble pilgrim with the same problems as the son of God, he then teased the crowd as only one who has known poverty could. "Poor folks often buy what they want and put off what they need, right?"

"Yes, sir."

"And they get a TV somehow?"

Giggles of self-recognition.

"And they get themselves a VCR?"

Their penchant for impulse spending laid bare, the audience was putty in his hands. He rolled out the heavy artillery: "If you will give or raise a thousand dollars for this campaign, stand." Two young black women rose. "Now, everyone who will give or raise five hundred dollars, come down front here." And so it went, until every soul in the room had been relieved of at least five bucks, and felt involved. From a gathering of thirty, Jackson walked away with cash or pledges of $6,000. He flew off to

Washington, first-class as always, and occupied two hotel suites for the weekend.

The advent of Jerry Austin may have institutionalized Jackson's method of fund-raising. In January, *The New York Times* reported that the Jackson campaign had distributed fliers and posters to five hundred churches of all denominations, urging parishioners to donate at the next week's services. The event was billed as "Super Sunday." Though Jackson representatives were assigned to "monitor" the collections, the effort came under attack from several quarters. "The clearest way a church can endorse someone is to raise funds," said Joseph Conn, spokesman for Americans United for Separation of Church and State. Jackson's defense was that he wanted donations from individuals, not from the churches themselves.

On one important front—Jackson's ulcerated relations with Jews—there has not been any positive change. There is some context for his apparent anti-Semitism and his association with the anti-Semitic Louis Farrakhan. When I asked how he'd heard whites refer to Jews in the South, he explained, "In Greenville I only knew black and white. There were no Jews or Poles or other distinctions in my sight. All white people's behavior toward black people was essentially legalistic."

Southern blacks quickly learned that if they were to survive and prosper they would have to rely on their own collective efforts rather than on the benevolence or goodwill of whites. Farrakhan is a black brother who provided Jesse with physical security in 1984. Jackson may also feel he will lose some power among blacks if he bows and scrapes in apology to whites—and Jews are just another block of whites. This is a man who, according to a Delta Air Lines employee, refused service from a white cabin attendant and would accept refreshments only from a black attendant. Mary Summers, Jackson's chief speechwriter during his last campaign, was disillusioned enough to write in *The Nation* in 1987 that: "For him, racial differences are so fundamental that it is perfectly natural to play to them in public and joke about them in private. . . . Jackson expects racial loyalty to be primary."

Notwithstanding the narrowness of his background, the fact remains that he has made statements derogatory to a minority, and if anyone understands the nuances of anti-Semitism, it should be one who understands racism. Yet most people reeducate themselves about their prejudices in private. Jackson has had to do it in the full glare of cameras.

Then he was asked to address the notion that he can't get elected, because he is black. "If Jesse Jackson can become president, a Jew can become president," he said. "If I can become president, anybody can."

It brought a laugh from some, offended others. Afterward, film executive Mike Medavoy and producer Robert Chartoff cornered Jackson and complained that his answers sounded phony. "Hey"—he put up his hands—"there's only so far I will go."

In every other way, however, Jackson softened his rhetoric for his second presidential bid. His issue-rich rhetoric and his refusal to join the bickering among the other Democratic candidates added stature to his already proven personal magnetism. But it wasn't until he stunned much of the nation with the clout he brought to the ballot box on Super Tuesday that everybody sat up and took notice.

The coalition Jackson had put together brought out the largest popular vote in the South for Jesse, delivered 97 percent of the black vote, and added up to more than a quarter of the primary votes cast up to that time in Democratic primaries. Even after a disappointing showing in his adopted home state of Illinois, Jackson, at the halfway point in the primary race, was out in front of every other Democrat in popular votes.

Serious people began taking seriously the possibility that *Jesse might win.* He seemed finally to have broken out of the racial box.

Some of his supporters claim that if Jesse Jackson were to wake up white tomorrow, he would be a ten-to-one favorite for the Democratic nomination. Would he? Or would he be seen as too extreme, too inexperienced, too opportunistic, and too blatantly a lover of the limelight?

In any case, that's like saying if Gorbachev weren't Russian, he might be a candidate for the American presidency. Well, if Gorbachev weren't Russian, he wouldn't be Gorbachev. And if Jackson weren't black, he wouldn't be Jesse.

It is a Catch-22 that the very qualities that evoke the sharpest criticisms of Jesse Jackson have made him the only black politician with strong enough *personal* support and a wide enough base to mount a presidential campaign. Black leaders who play by the conventional political rules, such as Representatives Charlie Rangel and Bill Gray, are still handicapped by their color but don't get the support of the protest voter.

If another politician had left the same images—Castro, Arafat, Assad, Farrakhan—in the public mind, would he or she be able to launch a serious presidential campaign? I asked Jackson.

"It depends how much kinship and credibility they had, if they could survive the attack . . . Who else challenged Gorbachev, heads up, on the question of Soviet Jewry before the whole world? No one else. Who challenged Ortega, heads up, to reopen the press and to meet with the Church? No one else. I think people call that leadership." He had to postpone finishing his answer. A plane was waiting.

What does Jesse want? The question his supporters consider patronizing was being asked with more urgency than ever as the campaign progressed.

Wyatt Tee Walker, the Harlem preacher, who knows Jackson well, says, "This may surprise you: He doesn't want to be president." For Jesse, a presidential *campaign* is Nirvana, as Calvin Morris points out. "Every day cameras following you, microphones recording your every word, Secret Service, limousines, sirens, charter planes—it's the glory he loves."

When I first began close Jesse-watching in the fall of 1987, it looked to me as though Jackson would be happy running a perpetual campaign. He had told *The Wall Street Journal*, "This isn't just a campaign. It's a mission. My future doesn't depend upon what happens in one state, or two states, or even one election. In a real sense, I'm running every day, every year." But then I began to see signs he'd been bitten by the power virus. Percy Sutton noticed it, too. On a Phil Donahue show shortly after Gary Hart's temporary departure from the scene, Jackson was asked if he would accept the vice-presidential slot. The Reverend replied imperiously, "If I were to run a successful race and did not win, the vice-presidential option would be a serious consideration because

it would be such an honor to serve our nation at that level."
A friend and government insider, who dared not be identified,
said, "Can you imagine anybody fool enough to take him as
vice-president? He must know better than anybody that he is
ill-suited to be vice-president. Therefore, he must crave power
that much."

And according to Noah junior, Jesse's focus had indeed
shifted. "It's not preaching now, it's power. The power of the
presidency. To govern the reallocation of resources, that's the
real agenda. From the White House, Jesse can go beyond all
their wildest dreams—Martin's dream, Marcus Garvey's dream,
Malcolm X's dream."

Even his campaign manager admitted to me, "If Jesse Jackson was white, he wouldn't be a candidate." Jackson has never
stood for public office, never satisfactorily performed as an
executive, never met a budget, set a legislative agenda, or ac-
commodated differences within a political body. He is not know-
ledgeable about missile systems or the international flow of
currency. He is careless about money and a dilettante when it
comes to organization. What is more, Jackson in the Oval Office
would be a caged bird. Imagine him stuck checking off budget
items when he could be walking on the Gulf of Aqaba, mediating
peace in the Middle East.

He is, however, uniquely qualified to be a historic candidate.
While Jackson himself probably carries too much baggage and
bitterness to engender the kind of confidence Americans would
need to place in their first black president or vice-president, he
can prepare the path for the next, more traditional black political leader.

The danger lies in the possible public perception that Jackson wields too much power within the party. And that could
destroy the chances for a Democrat to be elected in 1988. Not
to worry, Bert Lance assured me and many others. Jesse Jackson
is not going to allow himself to be blamed by his party for losing
the White House.

"My Jewish brethren are putting ads in magazines saying we
can't allow this man Jesse Jackson to be secretary of state,"
Jerry Austin told me. "I'm not so sure that he wants anything
like that." So, it's glory he wants?

The betting by mid-March 1988 was that no Democratic candidate would emerge at the end of the primary season with a clear majority of the delegates. Even as some Democrats were saying they now believed Jackson's indirect assurances that he will not allow himself to be blamed for a Democratic defeat in November, Jackson himself began making some muscular new demands. Forget about delegates— why shouldn't the party rally around the candidate who ends up with the most popular votes?

Jackson's suggestion that party rules be completely changed to accommodate him coincided with his grand boast, following his second-place finish in the Illinois primary: "I'm where every candidate wishes he was tonight. I'm number one in popular votes from Alaska to Alabama, Maine to Mississippi." (He was at that point sixty thousand votes ahead of Dukakis and almost half a million in front of Gore.) But exit polls in the state that presumably knows him best painted a more polarized picture. Fully 60 percent of white Illinois voters said they viewed Jackson unfavorably, as against 30 percent who said they had a favorable impression of him.

Some Democratic officials began expressing private fears that Jackson would be unable to resist pushing the party too far on behalf of himself or his ideas. The head of Senator Albert Gore's losing campaign in the South Carolina caucuses, Dwight Drake, sounded a chilling note. "White working-class people . . . are disgusted with the Democratic party because they see it as a black party." Such perceptions raise the specter of white flight from the party of Jesse Jackson, following the pattern of reaction when blacks began winning mayoralities and many whites simply abandoned the inner cities and moved to the suburbs.

It is a fact that much of the working-class white vote, once locked up by the Democrats, has simply dropped out of participation in the primaries. The pattern is seen most starkly in the South, where, since the departure of George Wallace from presidential politics fifteen years ago, overall turnout in the primaries has shrunk by half. The turnout for Democratic contests on Super Tuesday, when every southern state except South Carolina held primaries, was 27 percent black and 71 percent white (compared to a 98 percent white turnout in Republican contests across the South).

Black establishment figures who saw him after his Super Tuesday victories affirmed that Jackson wants greater involvement in the core of the party. To the speculation he might want the job of vice-president, a cabinet office, or a roving ambassadorship, Jackson replied, "I'm not looking for a job." With party insiders betting that he would arrive at the convention with as much as 25 percent of the total delegates, and that no other candidate would have the nomination sewn up, Jackson was confident he would hold the balance of power. Don't expect him to waste his power on submitting minority planks, predicted one of his closest advisers. Rather, he would make his case at the convention and get his views enshrined in minds of the voters.

Consider how Jackson might play the scene in the smoke-filled room during the bargaining period between the primaries and the convention. Mr. X and Mr. Y have two thousand delegates between them. But Jackson has racked up almost as many delegates as either, plus a huge popular vote. What can they offer him?

But wait. Jackson holds up his hands. "Friends, I'm going to make it easy for you—I don't want anything. All I ask is prime time to make the nominating speech." The nominee accepts, knowing the risk but helpless to refuse. The speech Jackson makes is a spellbinder. He pledges to spend every waking moment campaigning for Mr. Nominee, the greatest president America could have because he's committed to A, B, D, F, and G. Jesse has just burdened the Democratic candidate with the Jackson agenda.

The more important Jackson becomes in breaking down old barriers of prejudice and bringing back people who have dropped out of the electoral system in disgust or apathy, the more the opposition will try to paint him as extreme, make him angry, tear him down, distort his motives. The day after the Democratic convention, the Republican party will do just what it did the day after Fritz Mondale named Geraldine Ferraro as his running mate. It will turn its computer banks upside down and out will pour a stream of ugly leaks about a certain black preacher with a checkered past. That will be a time of severe testing for Jesse Jackson. The price of being accepted as a Democratic insider will be to take the blows, high and low, like any other political leader.

Jackson really fancies himself as American Sadat, performing the most sensitive, high-profile diplomatic missions for the president, but without the accountability of appointive office. Indeed, his odyssey as a man of color from a poor background who came up as a revolutionary, committed crazily passionate acts, waited his turn for twenty years until his moment arrived, and then seized it, is uncannily similar to Sadat's story. Sadat was one of those inspired leaders who, as the result of his own momentous passages and inner development, became the catalyst for his culture's historic movement away from ancient hatreds. Historian Arnold Toynbee pointed out this symbiosis between individuals who undergo personal transfiguration and return to the social milieu out of which they originally came with the power to transform it, citing the lives of Buddha, Jesus, Muhammad, Dante, and Machiavelli. That is the sort of historical company Jackson likes to think of himself keeping.

It is possible—by engaging in the struggle of life beyond the next proof of one's success—to reach a point of *self*-acceptance where alienation is overcome, where, as Hegel described it, one can "come home" to oneself. If Jesse Jackson reaches that point, during this election or in the future, it will be a victory of truly historic proportions, one that could transform our culture in ways now almost unimaginable.

Jackson's staff had scheduled a final phone interview for a Saturday afternoon. I had waited all weekend by the phone, to no avail. By Monday morning, I was on final deadline. At 5:30 A.M. his time, Jackson rang me up.

"Gail," the voice purred, "this is Jesse Jackson." But he had to interrupt the conversation to get on a plane. "Meet me in Mobile," he coaxed. I was exhausted, and my editors were pressing me to deliver the article. But his hypnotic voice poured through the phone. "Just tell yourself, Gail, you *must.* "

Seven hours later I was pushing a luggage cart to the gate in New Orleans when I spotted him running for the plane. "Hey,

Miss Gail." Jackson grabbed my luggage cart and started pushing it at a run. He had just spoken to several thousand health
professionals and the adrenaline was running. He had a smile
and charm-shake for the blond flight attendant; he was signing
autographs, shaking hands in pirouette; and before we knew it
we were on the Beechcraft, headed for Mobile.

Jackson picked up mid-sentence from our predawn conversation: "And you were asking me about leadership. I'm convinced people look upon political leaders much like they look
upon themselves. Reagan ran three times. He had to survive 'too
extreme,' 'married twice,' 'doesn't love his grandchildren,' 'too
old.' But his basic constituency said, 'Never mind, he represents
our point of view, he's our guy.' The same with Nixon."

In the all-white Fundamentalist Pentecostal church in deepest Alabama, Jackson was welcomed by its pastor and four
hundred locked-out paperworkers, roughly half black and half
white. The brainstorm had come to him only three days before.
He'd held forth at a rally for workers locked out by the same
company, International Paper, in Jay, Maine—a big hit. So, on
the way back from a longstanding speaking engagement in New
Orleans, he'd decided to drop by Mobile and reach out to their
brothers in the struggle.

A union man, who at first glance might be labeled a typical
redneck, introduced him: "When Brother Jackson called and
said he could come and talk to us today, I was flabbergasted.
Nobody else has come to us." The crowd warmed to Jackson
immediately. He got up and challenged "scabism." He let them
know he had reached out to their fellow strikers in Maine and
Wisconsin.

"Cudahy, Wisconsin—I called them. They said, 'You must
understand, we *white.*' I said, 'Cudahy, Wisconsin, I understand.' I said, 'I'm still comin' to help you.' They said, 'You
don't understand. The scabs are black.' I said, 'I'm still
comin'.' "

The church erupted with relieved laughter. Jackson moved
up an octave and drew them all together with his economic-
common-ground theme. "When it's dark, we must turn *to* each
other—"

"Hear ya!" shouted the audience.

"—not *on* each other."

"Right!"

People shouted out seven months of bottled-up frustration. After Jackson finished, a union man got up. "Any doubts now?" The entire audience jumped to its feet and cheered.

Jackson came out of that Pentecostal church high on his toes. He even extended his hand for me to congratulate him. "That was good for my psyche," he said.

We shared a four-seater plane to Atlanta. He settled back, stockinged feet stretched out on the seat beside me, and discussed his strategy for survival—political and personal. Jackson believes the F.B.I. and the media were engaged in character assassination of Martin Luther King, Jr. "Of course, when character-assassination attempts fail, there's physical assassination." He seems both haunted and intrigued by the very real possibility that he, too, might be martyred.

"I've had my anxious and fearful moments. But I've turned fear into a stimulus. When you seek change in a society, oftentimes you must pay the price—it's met with violence. I don't have any time to waste. Make it to Christmastime. Make it to Atlanta."

Could you ever be satisfied with elective office? I asked.

Soberly: "Yes."

Do you find yourself thinking like a president?

"More and more." His voice deepened. "You know, you really have to grow, to imagine life from that level." He began rehearsing the role, speaking comfortably in the present tense. "In the Persian Gulf, I must somehow move the Security Council from being a war council, and back in its right role. I got to do that. I got to stop the sale of arms to Iran and Iraq. Secondly, I got troops in the water. I cannot run and leave my allies exposed." He went on, obviously warming to the exercise.

I asked if he woke up in the morning and put himself in the mind of the president.

"I've done that on Central America. On South Africa. On meeting with European leaders."

How long had he been thinking that way?

"More every day, frankly, over a period of time." He gazed dead ahead, his eyes gleaming softly like running lights on a night ship. "A lot of people aspire to the presidency. But they are so preoccupied with the day-to-day adjustments and maneuvering, they don't take the time to think presidential."

That last statement says a great deal about the vision and audacity of Jesse Jackson. He doesn't play the game by the normal rules, never has. He is a man willing to give himself time to think presidentially—the hell with the mechanics and the schedule.

I tried to get him to explain the source of his vision and audacity. "We can explain the norm, and teach the norm," he told me, "but we cannot explain the abnormal. There is no rational explanation for the genius of personality." Beyond this stunning boast, there is a truth: The genius of personality *is* Jackson's power. But the very wizardry that permits him to project a symbolic persona greater than himself poses a conundrum.

Can he fill his own shoes?

FORCED CHANGE

The party didn't invite Jesse. He crashed it. But few experiences prepare one for the long, grueling, demeaning process of running for president better than growing up black and poor in America. No matter how many times he has been slapped in the face or counted out, Jesse Jackson keeps on running—the consummate political survivor. And because he has been forced by his birthright to change himself, he is brilliant at forcing change on others.

The negative identity that Robert Dole continually strives to overcome was the result not of birth or nurture but of a life accident at just the point when he was poised for the leap into adulthood. He was forced to make deep and painful changes in himself and in his life goals. For most survivors, the shock of losing what was taken for granted makes it easier to become more self-reliant in the future, but less easy to be trusting. Those who are forced to change too soon, or without someone to help preserve pieces of their former—shattered—identity, often go through all the motions of striving, even excelling, and become the most successful among us. But there may be a cold, empty space left around the heart that never quite permits the full osmosis of emotional feelings. And in such a chilly corridor the old anger and mistrust never melt.

For Senator Dole the defenses he developed, a stinging wit and an insistence on total control (since he cannot allow himself to depend on anyone else ever again), are both unique strengths and serious detriments. His story shows just how much effort, over a lifetime, is necessary to adjust to a forced change.

FOUR

The Whole Bob Dole?

Robert Dole is a survivor. Born without genealogical gloss or family wealth or social position, Robert Dole did have one obvious God-given gift: he was a natural athlete. He played basketball and football, he was tall and he could run. In fact, he ran everywhere he went, always training, lifting weights he made himself out of cement blocks and lead pipe, and he nearly broke the indoor-track record at a university he could barely afford before he went away to war, where his gift was shattered.

Granted, most people don't realize that Bob Dole is not whole. Even those closest to him often forget that he has no working right arm. So brilliantly does he compensate for his disability, even his wife will forget and say, "Will you hang that picture?" Senator Alan Simpson, another tall, blunt, irreverent wit, who has been in the trenches with Dole on deficit busting and tax reform, shakes his head in unaccustomed awe when asked about Bob Dole. "What can you do to a guy who's lain in a hospital bed for three years? You can't spook him up. He's invulnerable."

Yet not a day goes by that Dole doesn't have to prove himself. Just to tie a shoe, buckle a belt, thread a cuff link, demands the patience of the demented. And then his nemesis: pushing the tiny buttons of his shirt through the holes. Some days it takes ten minutes. If he gets flustered, fifteen. Because, you see, he hasn't enough feeling even in his good hand to pick a dime out of his pocket. Somebody asked him, "Why can't

125

Elizabeth button your buttons for you?" Because he doesn't want to get in the habit of leaning.

No. Bob Dole is dependent on nobody, never has been—well, not since that hazy, hideous gap in his life that opened up when he was twenty-one years old.

"I was all this physical-fitness, bodybuilding, da-da, da-da kind of person," he told me when we first talked, in June of 1986. Sunbathing is one of the few sensual pleasures Senator Dole permits himself, so his press secretary had set me up on a Senate veranda known as "The Beach." Then Senate majority leader, the indefatigable Dole had been up until one A.M. the night before, trying to get the tax-reform bill done. He settled back and let the sun butter his face, and talked of his passion for sports and survival.

He can remember the running and push-ups. And pumping those weights in the basement where he and his younger brother bunked together. They lived just across the tracks, in Russell, Kansas. When his father's feet hit the floor above them at five A.M., everyone else hit the floor running. Had to. His mother, Bina Dole, had to load up the old Chevy with the Singer sewing machines she sold around the county. All four kids had chores—washing and vacuuming and setting out meals—helping to keep up the standards of their perfectionist mother. Bina was the family disciplinarian, Dole remembers. "In fact, her whole life was an exercise in self-discipline. . . . Never having finished high school, she was determined that we would do better."

Shy, inturned, and given to brooding by temperament, Dole did not form close attachments to people. But he was a dutiful boy. "Bobby Dole was a good worker," recalls Bub Dawson, who with his brother Chaz used to own the drugstore where Bob worked as a soda jerk until 11:30 every night. Working at Dawson's drew out the bashful young boy. "I became kind of a wisecracker," Dole has said. "You learn a lot about people working in a public place. They used to come to our drugstore, and Bub and Chaz would insult everybody in town, and that's why people kept coming . . . they paid ya to get insulted." So Bob Dole began developing a sarcastic wit as his first line of defense: "Somebody always had a remark and you had to learn to anticipate it or get there first." These humorous put-downs served to mask his shyness and help him make contact with people—while at the same time allowing him to keep his distance.

It was only in the dark before dawn that a boy with a crush on sports had a few minutes to himself for running and push-ups, before he plastered down his hair with vanilla and raced off to school and his afternoon job delivering newspapers. The girls went for Bobby Dole, with his big sad eyes and his biceps and his shyness, but he didn't have time for girls. "If he had a girl, he'd a had to take her to the show," says his brother Kenny. "Who had that kind of money?"

Dole's father took pride in being a man who never gave in to emotion. The Western Union man would go all to pieces when he had to read the killed- or missing-in-action telegrams to families, so Doran Dole would do it for him. Cool as you please. He was not ambitious, but his wife more than made up for it. Few dared confront her. During the Depression, Bina Dole rented out their house to oil and gas people. The family moved into the boys' room in the basement. Giving up his home must have galled young Bob Dole. To this day, he appears to bear a class resentment. But rather than becoming a social reformer, he has followed his mother's pragmatic credo, *"Can't* never did anything."

Bob Dole did not seek out danger in the war. It was his duty to enlist, he felt. He was called up halfway through his sopho-more year at the University of Kansas. Time: 1943. After of-ficer-candidate school, he was sent to Italy, assigned to an infantry replacement depot near Rome. Safe. Dreams of the Olympics danced in his head when he saw athletes running around the Colosseum. "I figured the best way to get out of the army over there was to get in the sports school," he has said.

On February 25, 1945, he was assigned to the 85th Moun-tain Regiment. Bobby Dole, son of a grain-elevator manager, a boy from the dead-flat center of the States, thrown in with a bunch of Ivy League richies to an elite *ski* division—it was a bad joke. Dole had less than a month of real exposure to combat before that fogged day when he was ordered to take Hill 913.

His men scuttled from shell hole to shell hole, clinging to

what little safety they could, but when firing began from the hill, it was bad, an indecipherable, crippling rain. "I was trying to drag the radioman back into this little shell hole," he said, still puzzled. "All I remember is a sting. I must have been turning over when I was hit, because my arms were over my head. I couldn't bring them back . . ."

Sometime during the eight hours that he lay there thinking both his arms had been blown off, somebody piled them on his chest. The medic had been hit, too; in fact, almost every man in his unit was down. The orders were to leave the wounded. His platoon sergeant dipped his fingers in Dole's blood and blessed the boy's forehead with an "M" to let the litter bearers know he'd been dosed with bootlegged morphine.

When he woke up at the evacuation hospital, Dole couldn't walk, couldn't void. Whatever had hit him had crushed his most important wires. He still couldn't lift his arms. All four limbs were paralyzed. Just like that. No lead-up, no connection to his past life, no comforting sense of heroism; hell, he didn't even know the radioman's name.

"They shipped me back like a piece of furniture from Italy to Africa to Miami," he recalls. Still crated in a full-body cast, he was sent to Topeka, Kansas. Winter General Hospital. A large V.A. facility. A scrap-men dump.

A few weeks later his parents brought him home on leave for the first time. The townsfolk of Russell turned out to see his pathetic frame lifted down from the train on a stretcher. Bob Dole looked away in shame.

When he became visible as chairman of the Senate Finance Committee, in 1981, the media discovered a "new Bob Dole." Up to then he'd been best known as Gerald Ford's hatchet man, for having run around the country cutting up Democrats in the 1976 presidential election while his running mate remained, presidentially, in the Rose Garden. Suddenly Dole was being saluted for his "independent streak," for being "straight," even "warm and likable"—and funny. Much was made of these changes as Bob Dole began his first campaign for president.

There is merit to the notion of two Bob Doles. But the "new Dole" has been under reconstruction for forty years. Ever since that day at Winter General Hospital when they first got him up on his feet . . .

He had been through three stormy months, his temperature once flaring to 108.7, only hours from death. A severely infected kidney had to be removed. But the day they got Bob Dole out of bed for the first time was not a day of celebration. He heaved himself into the bathroom and looked in the mirror.

"It was a pretty awful sight, to me."

He stood before himself, this young man of twenty-two, a sucked-out, skin-and-bones invalid. His weight had dropped from 194 to 122 pounds. He'd scarcely had a chance to grow from boy into man before the gods pushed him back into infancy, and it made him bitter.

"You go through the period of self-pity," he told me.

I asked him if there was anger.

"Yeah," he said quietly. "There you are, a grown man, and you can't do anything, can't get dressed. I couldn't feed myself for a year." His voice trailed off into the ether of memory. Gratefully, he has forgotten exactly how long it took to make each step, but he admits it was an inch a day. Or less.

After languishing for six months in the V.A. hospital without rehabilitation or exercise, Dole got himself transferred to an army hospital in Battle Creek, Michigan. Doctors found his shoulder still paralyzed and deep injuries in his spine; but worse, the muscles of both upper arms had been allowed to atrophy grotesquely. His right hand was crabbed, and his left nearly as useless. Active exercises were ordered immediately. Doctors shook their heads. They did not expect Lieutenant Dole to live.

Blood clots developed in his lungs. Month after month he lay on his back, through the bleak winter days and then the nights, his mind jumping around, listening for the howl of the train whistle and the brief, tantalizing sound of motion. Not until March of 1946 was he permitted up in a chair for short periods. And the next time he looked, another year had passed.

"You think nobody could have it worse than you, why did God do it to me, I didn't do anything, it's unfair," he recalled. "I'm never going to get married, never going to amount to anything. Live off a pension. Selling pencils on the street corner." There were times he'd dream of throwing things. But precisely because the survivor does not die or give up, the self with its wanton appetite for life comes upon its true innocence.

"You change the way you measure everything," as Dole described the turning point to me. "Life becomes about learning how to use what you have left."

Kenny Dole remembers indelibly a statement his brother made in the hospital. He said he figured he'd lost ten years of his life; he swore he was going to make it up.

"And he's still trying to make it up," Kenny told me, startling himself as the revelation popped out.

"He's a man in a hurry," I said.

"It's true."

Young Dole started running around to doctors, in search of the magic operation. An immigrant Armenian surgeon by the name of Kelikian agreed to work on Dole for nothing. Still, there were other costs. So a cigar box was set up at the V.F.W. post in Russell, and the townspeople gave whatever they could. He endured three operations, believing each time that the next one would restore his shoulder. "You go through this dream period," he told me, "where you *know* it's going to be just like it was."

I asked the senator how much his disability had delayed him in starting his career. "I'm not certain I had a career before this happened," he replied. "Would I have gone back to school? Maybe not. My grades weren't all that good." He'd made a C average in high school. "This bad time actually gave me a new start."

He didn't mention his first wife—he almost never volunteers any mention of the part she played in his recovery. When I asked if she hadn't been instrumental in his new start, he seemed to resist the memory of dependence, and merely acknowledged that she had been "helpful."

I could see Dole's first wife from the door of her condo in Topeka. She had a cigarette going and she was planning folk art for Kansas Day. At the bell, she primped the gray hair piled like scissor-curled ribbons on her head.

Warm and chatty as a small-town switchboard operator, Phyllis Dole Buzick Macey told me she first saw the young Dole in the mess hall at the Battle Creek hospital. He was *not* a patient of hers. She was an occupational therapist on the psychiatric ward. "That poor Bob Dole, he has not long to live," somebody said. Such a nice-looking man, Phyllis thought, it was sad.

"I had him, probably within days, at a dance up at the officers' club," she says. When he asked her to dance, she knew to stay close so it wouldn't hurt his arm to pull. Having worked with so many shattered men, she didn't even consider Bob Dole handicapped.

Three months from the day they met, Bob married Phyllis. Shortly thereafter he was released with a "total and permanent disability," and enrolled at the University of Arizona. Phyllis went to class with Bob and took notes for him. She had to sign his checks as well. Even his good hand had no abductor and adductor control. He would have to learn to write all over again, as if holding chopsticks. Frustrated, he started running again. Sometimes he would fall. Pick himself up, fall again, pick himself up. "I learned very quickly," says Phyllis, "you don't help him unless he asks you."

Running one day, he was stopped by a pain he knew like an old friend. He'd shaken a blood clot loose. So it was back to Topeka, where he could have his blood checked weekly, and there he ran double time through his bachelor's and law degrees at Washburn University. He dragged a primitive recorder, bigger than a bread box, to every class. "Sitting there by the hour at night transcribing notes from that silly thing must have been tremendous practice for him," muses Phyllis. "I had to hide in the corner because he didn't want any noise."

Now that his body had turned incontrovertibly against him, he had a new instrument to train: his mind. Phyllis can still see him pacing the rug while she quizzed him in German. "Bob, why do you *have* to get an A?" she confronted him one day. "Why can't a C be good enough?"

He whirled with a vehemence that scared her. "You tell me how to study a C or a B's worth and I will," she remembers him saying. "I can only study until I get it."

Even as he was racking up A's in law school, he ran for the Kansas Legislature and served a term. And no sooner had he started his first job, working for "Doc" Eric Smith, an oil and gas lawyer in Russell, than he had Doc out campaigning with him. Dole was elected county prosecutor for four straight terms, augmenting his county caseload with a full private practice, and tireless campaigning for the Republican party.

"He worked harder than any man I've ever known when he was county attorney," says his aunt Gladys. The Doles produced only one child, a daughter, and Dole found time to take her to the local Methodist church each Sunday. Apart from that meager family recreation, Phyllis can vouch that his breakneck pace continued—every night until ten, every weekend—throughout their marriage.

I approached my first interview with Bob Dole having just written a book about survivors. My conclusion was that those who face and master the trauma may become almost immunized against the ill effects of future life accidents and emerge as the most successful and resilient adults. It helps if one was raised to tough it out. Bob Dole agrees, though with characteristic brevity, boils it down to "strength through adversity."

The winner against adversity emerges with what I think of as the victorious personality. Bob Dole has most of the hallmarks: the self-trust, the sense of humor, the perspective to understand that his plight is not unique. Tested again and again, a survivor develops the strength and self-directedness necessary to fix his sights and chart a course without depending on outside forces—indeed, often in spite of them.

Why did he choose to go into politics, for instance? "The one thing he really regretted about the injury, he told me, was he would no longer be able to participate in competitive sports," offered his former wife. "My feeling is that he channeled that drive to compete into politics." His brother Kenny agreed.

Yes, but why choose a profession based on glad-handing when you start with one arm tied behind your back? I speculated that perhaps the way Bob Dole defied his disability was to choose the hardest possible professional road.

"You just might have hit it on the head," chuckled Russ Townsley from Russell, the town's iconoclastic newspaper publisher. But then, Bob Dole never did talk about what he feels most deeply. Russ and his wife spent many social evenings with their neighbors Phyllis and Bob during the early career years. The two men would sit in the living room reading their newspapers.

"So," Bob might say.

"So," Russ would reply.

"Bob was in too much of a hurry to waste time chitchatting," Townsley told me.

When Bob Dole got to Washington, he again hit the ground running—first for another three terms in the House; then for "sheriff" of the Senate, to curry favor with Nixon; then for leader of his party (a job he was asked to give up to George Bush); then for leader of the Senate; and now for leader of the nation.

Few would dispute that Dole today is the fastest runner on the Hill in seizing a political opportunity and exploiting it. Survivors of extremity must return to their creature nature and rely on it to fight their way back, acting and moving much of the time by instinct. Dole doesn't have to wait and poll a dozen friends and advisers before he knows what move to take. He has the sure, silent instincts of a prairie lion.

More than ever, at the age of sixty-four, Bob Dole is a man in a hurry, a man pushing to make up for a shattered youth.

Dole still has a dark side. Given a brooding temperament to begin with, and a lifelong wound to brood over, he must struggle always not to surrender to the anger and the tendency to seek revenge for other setbacks.

It is not always easy to be a nice guy when one has to stop and work for fifteen minutes just to button one's shirt. Retested every day, in the physical mantra he must perform to dress, Dole steps out into the world hungry for action. "You'll find more decisions around Bob Dole than almost anyone else in public life," notes Senator David Durenberger.

It drives him almost crazy, when, in the newly telegenic Senate, the me-too'ers line up to offer amendments while Bob Dole is endeavoring to make a deal. The 1986 tax-reform bill was a prime example. Tempers were frayed after the second midnight session. Shouts erupted in the Republican cloakroom. "Let's stay here all night and shut 'em up!" hollered one side.

The others wanted their moment. Suddenly Dole backed off and defused it all. He suggested that they break up the night into time zones. "Let's see, we'll put the senator from Alaska on at one A.M—that's prime time where he's from." He let everybody blow off steam and then made it clear he had a plan.

"I have to keep in mind I'm the leader," Dole says. "If I start screaming and kicking, you might as well not have a leader."

His wit is described as "sharp," "biting," "cutting," "slashing"—all combative words. Just as he learned to joke away his shyness with the customers at Dawson's drugstore, he now uses his slingshot tongue to defend himself against the old feeling of helplessness. In one of his mordant moments, Dole reportedly quipped that he might vote for Pat Robertson if the evangelist could bring his arm back. He can savage more political peacocks in fewer words than anyone in public life. Here is Bob Dole at the closed Gridiron Club dinner in 1983:

"I told John Glenn it wasn't fair for him to take advantage of his hero status as an astronaut. I mentioned this to him at the unveiling of the portrait . . . showing me invading Italy."

A touch of bitterness?

He knocked off three past presidents in one blow:

"History buffs probably noted the reunion at Sadat's funeral a few weeks ago of three ex-presidents: Carter, Ford, and Nixon—*See No Evil . . . Hear No Evil . . . and Evil.*"

Then he wiped the floor with his presidential rivals:

"And my good friend George Bush can't win . . . He's the only one here tonight who will have to show an ID card to get out.

"Yes, there's Jack Kemp . . . Even as a kid, Jack wanted to play quarterback . . . because he's the only one on the field who gets to talk all the time."

It has been said that a funny man is an angry man. While Dole can swallow a rival in one bite of sarcasm, the aftertaste it leaves with voters can be sour. "I can hear him today," says his former wife, "and know it isn't funny, it's a dig."

Dole knows it, too. "I have to watch my tongue," he told me.

Given his pragmatic political style, however, Dole may be the right man for the times. As the world becomes increasingly threatening and irrational, and as it becomes harder to be reverential toward anything or anybody, Dole's lightly cynical, dead-pan humor offers a refreshing detachment. He would be a smash on *Saturday Night Live.* And in a society increasingly short on shared norms and splintered by interest groups, a master com-promiser who can play pick-up-sticks with his eyes closed could be a comfort.

When I asked his political colleagues to name Dole's most distinguishing feature, most often mentioned was his brightness. "I think Dole has the best mind in the U.S. Senate since Jacob Javits," I was told by Bush's press secretary, Pete Teeley, who once did a campaign plan for Dole. "But he's not perceived as intellectual, because of his keen wit." People mistakenly associ-ate a ready wit with being superficial, lightweight. In fact, humor is a good tool for a deal-maker. Research shows that using jokes to put people in a good mood allows them to think through problems with more creativity and ingenuity. It is also the most intellectual of defense mechanisms. Humor can serve as a bar-rier against feelings that the ego dare not let escape.

Dole's intelligence isn't book-learned. It's intuitive and se-lective. Senator Simpson swears that Dole has a four-track mind. A clutch of his colleagues will be buzzing on the floor while Dole's eyes are fixed in the middle distance—nobody thinks he's even listening. "You go back to the chambers with him and damned if he didn't hear everything in his range," says Simp-son. "His responses come so quickly, he must have a special endocrine in his head."

The private engine that drives this master deal-maker is another source of wonder to those who know about his dis-ability. "He won't quit," says his former chief of staff, Rod DeArment, not until he gets the deal done. Constantly munching on junk food as his fuel, he takes giant strides between his two offices. Everyone who has seen him campaign says that when the rest stall, Dole's engine restarts.

Yet there is no real evidence that the anger beneath Dole's bitter humor has been stilled. His tendency to disdain others and nurse his own dreams of revenge smacks of a man who believes the breaks are against him. It may be a ticking bomb that explodes with increasing force under the pressure of what is surely Bob Dole's last shot at the presidency.

Does he have compassion? I wondered. Moments of vulnerability?

His divorce was brutal. He walked into the house one night after twenty-three years of marriage—during the last year of which he and Phyllis had broken bread together twice, on Easter and Christmas—and he said, "I want out." That was it. She got no child support.

Phyllis didn't argue or confront. "You don't do that with Bob Dole," she warns. But today she says of her former husband, "He has a lot more feeling inside than he ever will let anybody know." His best male friend, Robert Ellsworth, a former N.A.T.O. ambassador and Nixon's 1968 political director, explains: "Men from the high plains of Kansas can't express feelings, especially not love for each other. We're a little bit afraid of that." But Ellsworth's feeling for Dole runs deep, and like the few others who have been allowed close to Dole, he insists this is a warm and unusually sensitive man. He volunteered several vulnerable moments.

When they came to Washington as freshman members of the House, in 1961, and were put up the first night at a motel, Dole knocked on Ellsworth's door. He shuffled a bit before he was able to ask Ellsworth to button his top button. When he looked up, his face spoke volumes of vulnerability.

And one day in 1973 he said, gruffly, "I'm seeing a lot of this girl."

"So," said Ellsworth.

"I just wanted you to know about it," said Dole.

That was it; he never talked about how he felt.

The "girl" was Elizabeth Hanford, thirty-six. She was the brainy brunette who had been sitting in his office one day to talk about . . . what was it? Anyway, he wrote her name on his blotter because she was awful pretty.

He courted far more cautiously this time—three calls before even a date. They talked about education for the handicapped. "It was really cute," says Elizabeth. He kept up the courtship at long distance during his lonely '74 campaign for reelection to the Senate in the downdraft of Nixon's tailspin.

Bob Dole is a loner who can't stand to be alone. If there aren't four people in his office pressing him at once, he'll work the phones. Elizabeth Hanford was rather taken aback when he asked for a favor. "If you don't mind my calling you kind of late in the evenings, it's just kind of something I look forward to . . ." She was a warm voice at the other end of exhausting days driving the monotonous infinities of Kansas.

Elizabeth hesitated. "These middle-of-the-night calls didn't put me in the best situation for work the next day, but I felt like that was one way I could make a contribution to his campaign."

The most revealing story Elizabeth told me was of Bob's visit to her parents in North Carolina. One morning, unbeknownst to his wife, he went downstairs while her mother was fixing breakfast. He had on bathing trunks, with a towel thrown over his shoulder.

"I want you to see my problem," he said. Then he pulled off the towel.

"It was something he felt needed to be on the table," says Elizabeth, still awed by his painful honesty. Even today, Dole admitted to me, "I purposely won't look at my shoulder in the mirror. I don't know why. It shouldn't bother me."

Finding a moment to get married in December 1975, the Doles moved into his apartment in the Watergate; six months later he was off and running again—this time on the national ticket. It was a breakneck ride. The sole survivor of Ford's vice-presidential selection process, Dole was the only Republican whose conservatism was concrete enough to please the ascendant Reagan right-wingers. Ford's people said, "Let's announce in Russell. Tomorrow."

His eye blooded with a broken vessel from all the strain, Bob Dole came home to Russell, this time in a la-di-da (as he would see it) presidential helicopter. The whole county had a population of 9,664, and yet 10,000 people were jammed in the courthouse square to see him. Stepping smartly to the speaker's stand, Dole introduced the president while his wife and his daughter, Robin, flanked Mr. Ford. But what met his eyes were the faces of the people who had filled the cigar box for his operations.

"I can recall when I needed help, the people of Russell helped . . ."

His voice broke off. His left hand came up to his head.

Elizabeth instinctively leaned forward—was he about to collapse? Ford restrained her. Russ Townsley flinched. He'd experienced that "silence" only a few times, in connection with
assassination. But then Dole's shoulders began to tremble. The
audience could see that Bobby Dole, unbelievably, was just plain
crying.

Ford broke the awkward silence by rising to his feet to lead
the applause. With scarcely a dry eye left in that sun-filled
courtyard, Townsley went back to his paper to write, "I was
relieved to see it was Bob Dole, being as human as I've ever seen
him in thirty years."

But the rough edges were still there, and under the glare
of his first national campaign, they made Bob Dole look small
and mean. He personalized his crude partisan attacks. His
charge during the debate with Walter Mondale that every war
in this century had been a "Democrat war" turned off the
nominal Democrats he needed, and incensed conservative
columnist George Will, who condemned Dole as a liar about
history who deserved to be forgotten.

Despite polls that showed he'd helped gain significant support for the Republican ticket, Dole was blamed by the press for
losing the election for Ford. It was Bob Dole's first political
defeat.

"I'd always wondered how he'd react," says Phyllis. "He
can't stand to lose control." Some say he did not react well.
"Remote" and "hostile" are two words used by old Kansas
associates from whom he remained aloof for the next four years.

During the holidays after the campaign, though he's never
sick, Dole succumbed to the flu. He gave his only comment on
the defeat. "Elizabeth," she remembers him saying, "this is a
disappointment. I'm so glad I have you." That was it. And that,
for Bob Dole, spoke volumes of appreciation. He never raised
the subject again. He told his wife, "I'm going back into the
Senate and be the best senator I can be." When Congress
reconvened, he plunged back into his work, kept busy, kept
moving forward, kept running.

In 1979 Bob Dole began a turnaround. He consulted one
of the foremost speech counselors, Dorothy Sarnoff, who ad-

vised him to stop leaning on his war-wounded arm in an effort to hide it, to stand up straight at the podium, and to take
the bite out of his humor. "Your wit is delicious," she said,
"but not when it leaves a sting." He was surprised at first,
but agreed it probably was too caustic for public consumption. The brittle remains of his old jokes, left in the detritus
of the losing campaign, he began to turn on himself. Referring to his debate with Mondale, he learned to quip, "I went
for the jugular—my own."

Some of Elizabeth's social confidence seemed to have
rubbed off on her husband as well. This was a lady not so much
as grazed by the Cinderella complex. Raised comfortably in
Salisbury, North Carolina, she distinguished herself at Duke
University and Harvard Law School, and staked out a fast-track
career path well before her time. While her friends were trading
in frat pins for wedding rings, Elizabeth slipped off to the Soviet
Union to learn at first hand about Sputnik. She made it to the
White House (as consumer-affairs adviser) by age thirty-three,
setting a record Bob Dole likes to say he can't match.

The Doles began to be in demand around Washington as a
power couple, her smiling, bubbly manner a perfect complement
to her husband's acerbic stiffness. What many miss is that she's
as disciplined as he is. Schooled in professional southern charm,
Elizabeth says nothing she doesn't intend to—with utterly convincing spontaneity. If she thought her husband's run for the
presidency in 1980 was doomed from the start, she never said
so. She appeared at joint speaking engagements with the poise
of a perfect meringue, a delicate, sugary coating over her own
raw ambition. For her, the decision to quit her prestigious job
to help her husband campaign was "all good for the career
path."

But the stakes had been raised by the time Elizabeth began
her second go-round as a presidential candidate's wife. She was
now holding a Cabinet post. In early 1987, Bob Dole announced
that if his candidacy began to take off, "She'll have to take a
look at joining up."

By that July, Liddy Dole was fielding constant questions
about the propriety of keeping a powerful job in the current
administration while her husband made his bid to head the next

one. George Bush wasn't stepping down to run, she pointed out, "So why should a spouse have to leave?" Her eventual decision to quit her Cabinet post and "stand by her man" drew both praise and disappointment.

That decision, however, was made on a very pragmatic basis: Bob Dole, if he was to take the White House, would need every bit of help he could get. And Elizabeth Dole was expected to be an asset to her husband, both as a telegenic, intelligent, and appealing surrogate—particularly in the South—and as a prop for what has been called Dole's "little-woman act."

"If you don't like me, vote because of Elizabeth," he told voters. "We'll be a team. If I get elected president, I get to make all the big decisions, and she gets to make the bed."

Joking aside, the issue has been a very real one between the Doles. Even before the senator had officially announced his candidacy, the couple met with a group of editors, one of whom raised the question of what role Elizabeth would play in a Dole presidency.

"No reason she couldn't be a Cabinet officer," Dole shot back.

Elizabeth looked startled. Her husband has never been one to speak in more than half-sentences about the most important things on his mind. When he saw the look on her face, he defended his remark:

"Well, Jack Kennedy appointed his brother attorney general."

The senator has always appeared delighted by his wife's dazzling successes. And for Liddy Dole, the decision to stand by her man was a calculated gamble. A woman who, as secretary of transportation, has commanded the equivalent of four divisions in the Reagan revolution, with 100,000 employees, would hardly be expected to find fulfillment in picking china patterns. In the event of a successful Bob Dole presidency, however, the redoubtable Elizabeth would thereafter have a unique opportunity to present herself as the first experienced female presidential candidate.

Robert Ellsworth is Dole's only confidant besides his wife. I asked him to assess how the man's character has been shaped by his life. He demurred. When I pressed, Ellsworth came up with the Germanic myth of the Ring, on which Wagner based his opera cycle: two would-be heroes, one given a head start by the father of the gods; the other, Siegfried, born an orphan without privilege. It is Siegfried who conquers all.

"Dole has not been given anything by the gods, ever, yet he's emerged from it all as truly whole, internally powerful," said the man then described as "general" in the senator's exploratory committee for the presidency. "That's what it takes."

Perhaps, but it can also create a control freak. The Doles' only child was born fat, according to her mother. Her father used to needle Robin with mean nicknames, and he bugged Phyllis about *her* weight, too. Called her "Bones." As she analyzes it, "He had to fight to get control, and I think he can't understand when other people can't control."

Dole seems to hold on tightly to control because he deeply distrusts anyone's judgment but his own. When he was helpless to manage his own life, army doctors left him to wither and he almost died. That is the last time anyone remembers seeing Bob Dole let go. He hires sassy and aggressive subordinates and demands they give 100 percent, then often turns around and undercuts them. He can fire people as coolly as his father read the war telegrams. Jo-Anne Coe, for twenty-one years his faithful office manager, cannot remember hearing a word of praise. Behind his back his young Senate staffers once nicknamed him the "Aya-Dole-Ah."

The bright side of his need to control is how proficient he has made himself at so many things. Dole operates as his own chief of staff. He has become as good a speechwriter as any of the pros who used to work for him. And he is known around Washington as his own best press secretary. Dole became virtually the designated hitter for Republicans during the Iran-contra crisis. He didn't miss a Sunday on a major news show for six weeks. Other Republican leaders watched in awe. Almost daily he came up to bat and threw out another suggestion for what Reagan should do to save his presidency.

But, alone among Republican leaders, Dole never called for the obvious: Donald Regan's resignation. Why? Because Bob Dole learns from past mistakes. During Watergate the

C.R.E.E.P. people had hung him out to dry. There he was, taking heavy flak as G.O.P. chairman, and Haldeman and Ehrlichman wouldn't take his phone calls. When the Iran-contra scandal exploded, Dole cultivated his former enemy, Regan, and was cut in on the loop of phone calls when everyone else was on the outside. He went out of his way on *Face the Nation* to praise the president's dissembling chief of staff. As a result, Dole was able to separate himself from a tar-baby president, collect praise from all quarters as a voice of reason, even knock Reagan on the op-ed page of *The Washington Post*, and simultaneously—just short of miraculously—earn a pat on the back from Reagan through Regan.

"Sitting next to his office door is like watching George Brett take batting practice every day," says his chief of staff, Walt Riker. "Dole is a Political Hall of Famer."

But what does he stand for? What is Bob Dole's vision of America's future?

Dole's brand of conservatism stands apart from the triumphant economic ideology of the Reagan era that has brought us record-busting deficits straight through a prolonged recovery. And he remains aloof from the Ramboesque interventionism on foreign policy. His innate sense of fairness has prompted him to back such conservative bugaboos as protecting voting rights for blacks, the 1982 tax increase, and the food-stamp program he helped to start with George McGovern. When reporters feed back to him criticism from conservatives who want a true believer, his anger flashes: "That's too bad. There's a need."

Dole still has a sound enough conservative voting record to earn a zero rating from the liberal Americans for Democratic Action. He has consistently voted with the president on defense, S.D.I., and funding the contras; with the pro-life forces on abortion; with the National Rifle Association on looser gun control. He has called for constitutional amendments that would mandate a balanced budget and allow for organized school prayer. And on arms control he has repulsed efforts in the Democrat-controlled Congress to force the administration to comply with the unratified SALT II treaty.

But the pragmatist in him keeps muddling the scorecard. He

was instrumental in putting together the 1985 farm bill, which reduced farm supports from $26 billion in 1986 to $23 billion in 1987, with a projection as low as $16 billion for 1988. The folks in Kansas and Iowa were not happy (although, according to Mrs. Dole, some now acknowledge the reductions have helped to settle land values and improve their net income). So, to woo farm states before the 1986 congressional elections, Dole urged the administration to offer a bonus to the Soviet Union for buying grain from U.S. government-subsidized surplus. If selling grain to the Russians had been a red flag for movement conservatives, raising taxes on Ronald Reagan's watch was a desecration. Yet Dole got it done.

While David Stockman was jumping up and down, shouting about a $100,000 billion deficit and getting nowhere, it was Senate Finance Chairman Dole, more than anyone, who slipped the blinders over President Reagan's eyes to get him to sign off on a revenue-raising measure in 1982. As a result of the bill, which raised taxes and closed loopholes on bankers and insurance fat cats, Dole now claims to have engineered a $100 billion reduction in the deficit. (The federal budget deficit ballooned to $150 billion by the end of fiscal 1987 anyway.) Dole also deputized himself as the man Reagan needed to help get Senate ratification of the arms-control treaty concluded by the president and Gorbachev at the end of 1987.

But does this add up to the sort of coherent political philosophy that projects a clear image to voters? Bob Dole grew up with hardworking people who were all broke at one time or another. In that isolated state of mind called western Kansas, hotbed of populism a hundred years ago, the paradox that inflamed passions then is echoed loud and clear today: That for all his industriousness, intelligence, machinery, and ability to feed the Western world, the American farmer is being driven into peasantry. Although they have been long and generously endowed out of the public coffers, Kansas farmers—just like Bobby Dole as a boy—like to think of themselves as long-suffering but never *dependent* on government. Yet not long after he formed his first tentative hypotheses of how the world worked, Dole's own control was kicked out from under him. He felt in his gut what it is to be helpless through no fault of one's own.

So one would have to get up awfully early to pigeonhole Bob Dole. He is the perfect example of a leader to whom ideological and even party labels just don't adhere.

"Dole has a gift for phrasing that sometimes allows him to have it both ways," said political analyst Richard Reeves. Who else can warm the cockles of conservative hearts by slamming Democrats even as he collects praise from the likes of Mondale, McGovern, and Bill Bradley for having grown beyond narrow partisan politics?

Campaign adviser Robert Ellsworth told me he believes that in this election "the issue is character, strength, integrity." For some, the fact that Dole is not identified with any specific ideological viewpoint works in his favor. "It's no particular political philosophy that draws me to Bob Dole as a presidential candidate," says Republican Senator David Durenberger, echoing other moderates in both parties. "But for the period of fragmented interests we'll be in at least until 1993, he would be a good decision-maker."

Most Democrats, liberals, and media people I've asked about the notion of Bob Dole for president have said essentially the same thing: "I could live with Bob Dole." That would be a strong plus in a general election. But it's traditionally been the poison pill for Republican primaries.

Dole had no shame in admitting to me, "I'm not an ideologue." But even many of his supporters felt that Dole came across to voters as too preoccupied with legislative details, and needed to project an overall vision. As his former adviser David Keene told me, "You can't be elected president by giving a legislative briefing."

When he was first recruited by the Republicans, Dole told *The Wall Street Journal* that "it was just sort of a game . . . you ran, and you didn't get into any philosophical discussions." He has since been trying to think about issues on an executive, rather than a legislative, level, but he is not in the habit of reading books and has had very little intellectual grounding in political theory.

William E. Brock, his belatedly hired campaign director, remembers Dole admonishing himself as late as the summer before the '88 primary season: "When you've been in Congress this long, you tend to—somebody mentions education—you tend to think of what amendment can I offer to move the thing or shape it. I've got to start thinking about what does education mean in terms of this country's future—jobs, our ability to compete internationally—to look at it in the larger context. I really am working on that, but it requires a good bit of discipline."

I asked Elizabeth Dole whether she saw her husband going through this process. "Are we talking 'vision' now?" she asked. "I think vision is very much where you've been, where your roots are. His roots are deep in the small-town value system: people helping one another, people being there for the tough times as well as the joys."

But that was during the Depression and in the Midwest, I pointed out, and people aren't like that in most parts of the country now.

She disagreed, mentioning her own experiences on the campaign trail: "As I talk about this sort of thing, I'm seeing heads nod and the message seems to be taking very well in terms of Bob being one of the people."

Dole's message to the American people is also that they will have to turn away from economic illusions, and take "the bitter medicine" of pay-as-you-go in order to make the country strong again. He speaks as a survivor who suffered through long years of just that bitter medicine and discipline to put himself back together again. But Dole's character strengths may not be mirrored by most Americans, who have become accustomed to the self-indulgent values of buy-now pay-later.

A more serious campaign handicap has been the loner problem.

A candidate can't raise his own money, write his own speeches, be his own press secretary, and still shake a thousand hands after every appearance. And so, when the political handlers looked over Bob Dole's chances for 1988, they saw his fierce independence as a liability. During his 1980 bid for the presidency, he had fired his campaign manager and several consultants, hurtling himself toward a humiliating defeat.

Early in the 1988 race, Ellsworth, then chairman of Dole's

exploratory committee, took him to the woodshed on the subject. The senator assured him, "If we're going to do this, we're going to do it right." But Dole did not name a permanent campaign chairman until weeks before the primary season began, allowing most of 1987 to slip by in drifting and indecision. Dole's new campaign team managed to build a strong organization in Iowa, but had a hard job making up for lost time in the rest of the country.

William Brock, a former labor secretary and Tennessee senator, with a similar instinct for going for the jugular of his rivals, signed on only after Dole assured him categorically that he wanted somebody to really manage the campaign. "In effect, it was a complete delegation," Brock told me. It wasn't long before Brock, frustrated by Dole's continued habit of calling all the shots, put it on the line: "There are two jobs in this campaign— candidate and campaign manager. You can have one."

As the campaign progressed, it became clearer that Bob Dole's bête noire was George Bush, and the privileged world he represented. Dole began to take more and more frequent jabs at the vice-president during debates. In his stump speeches he has repeatedly emphasized the fact that *Bob Dole* is not from a background of privilege, that *he* understands the plight of the struggling American farmer. Indeed, when he was county attorney in the 1950s, Dole had to approve welfare benefits for his own grandparents.

The Bush campaign seemed to be trying to push Dole into just the kind of slashing attacks that had hurt him with voters during his 1976 vice-presidential bid. They began to needle him in his tenderest spot—impugning the integrity of his wife.

His beautiful Elizabeth, with her part-pedigreed southern background, her debutante's poise and independent wealth, is a keystone of the new Bob Dole's self-image, important proof of his wholeness and his own success. He became surly when Bush's staff circulated a newspaper clipping raising questions about the management of a blind trust that had been set up to handle Liddy Dole's assets. At a press conference Dole heatedly told Michael Kramer, "I resent [Bush] passing around these little things implicating Elizabeth. They can take me on, but Elizabeth has lots of friends in this country."

His fury increased after the Bush campaign released a second statement, in the week before the Iowa caucuses—"a very personal attack on me and my wife, Elizabeth." The release said that "Dole tells campaign audiences of his childhood struggles in western Kansas. He fails, however, to mention that he and his wife now are millionaires . . . live in Washington's posh Watergate apartment complex and vacation regularly at a Florida condominium purchased by them with the help of wealthy agribusinessman Dwayne Andreas." It also charged Dole with being "mean-spirited" and bringing down the Republican national ticket in 1976.

The New York Times reported a tense confrontation on the floor of the Senate, during which Dole pounded the presiding officer's desk, and demanded that the vice-president apologize. Bush refused to talk about the encounter, but his campaign manager, Lee Atwater, responded that Dole had been behaving "like a schoolyard bully"—that he could dish it out, but couldn't take it. Two days later, in a statement that could not have been more bitter, Dole snapped that "I expect the next shot from the Bush campaign will be that Bob Dole shot himself— that I wasn't really wounded in the war."

Whenever the bad times came along in his '88 campaign, the old pattern of dark moods and outbursts of temper repeated itself. He rolled over George Bush so badly in the opening contest in Iowa that pundits began chiseling the vice-president's political headstone. Yet Dole could not sustain the momentum of his Iowa win even for the eight days until the New Hampshire primary. Despite the fact that Dole had made dozens of visits to that state, his inability to trust or depend on others had allowed no organization to grow and flourish there: As late as nine months before the primary, Dole's campaign in New Hampshire consisted of one desk, one person, and sixty-two names in a box.

Then, the setback. A more optimistic person might have shrugged off his nine-point loss in New Hampshire, or put it down to bad luck, and gone on to make the most of the Iowa victory. Not Bob Dole. He fell into a ferocious sulk and pulled away from everyone who was trying to help him. For days he isolated himself in the front of his campaign plane, not a single political associate invited to accompany him, and traveled aimlessly while he brooded about how to get even with his bête noire. The traveling press reported that Dole felt the presidential nomination slipping from his grasp; his speeches became halting and disjointed, and he was snappish and defensive in response to questions. He seemed to be fighting within himself about whether to keep the gloves on, for fear of raising criticism—*there goes Bob Dole being nasty again*—or to strike out against what he perceived, characteristically, as another unfair blow. Less than two weeks before Super Tuesday, as reported by *The New York Times,* Dole gathered a group of aides in a hotel room in Sioux Falls, South Dakota.

"What's the strategy?" he asked, then gave his own answer. "We don't have one."

And then the firings began. By inviting two secondary consultants to travel with him, Dole upset his campaign chairman, who felt undercut. The consultants were summarily sacked by Bill Brock and ordered off the campaign plane. Dole switched advertising agencies only a week before Super Tuesday. Serious speculation was raised anew about the ability of this loner to delegate enough responsibility to put together a coherent national campaign. Its byword, coined by staffers and picked up by the traveling press, was *chaos.*

Elizabeth Dole herself has struggled against a lifelong compulsion to do everything right, foresee every pitfall, turn every key twice, check and recheck. Anything less than perfection in her performance could upset her. Her fixation on work left her little time to be a friend. Even after pausing to admit a husband into her tightly constructed world, she began to realize, as she writes in their joint autobiography, *Unlimited Partners,* that "though I was blessed with a beautiful marriage and a challenging career, my life was close to spiritual starvation."

Secretary of Transportation Dole began to slip off one evening a week to a spiritual growth group. And there she learned to redefine perfectionism. "Some people define strength as independence, self-reliance, and resourcefulness," she writes—precisely the way Bob Dole defines it—"but I have learned that real strength, inner strength, comes from a dependence on the one source who can replenish life with the power that comes from above."

She became a born-again Christian. This is not a description Mrs. Dole uses in public, however. She was counseled by speech adviser Dorothy Sarnoff back in 1979 that to identify herself as belonging to a small group would limit her appeal.

Asked on TV in early 1988 what his wife has helped him with most in their marital partnership, Bob Dole was caught by surprise and stumbled through a response. Elizabeth, like many wives, looked impatient as her husband failed to come up with the right answer. When *she* was asked, Liddy hit the word like a keynote: perfectionism.

Looking toward the likely character of a Dole presidency, he might run it like an autocrat. It would certainly have an unquestioned leader. But a man can't be president by himself. He must be able to share control, delegate, depend, and accept less than perfection from his vast army of officers and advisers and day-to-day staffers—as well as from himself. In early 1988, I asked Mrs. Dole whether there was anything, even the smallest thing, that she could do now for Senator Dole that he wouldn't allow her to do when they first married. She thought awhile. "I don't see it as changing," she said. "The role I'm playing in his campaign is basically being out carrying his story. He's not going to come and seek help necessarily."

Queried in January about this fierce guardedness against dependence on anyone for anything, Dole replied, "Fifteen years ago that would have been right on, but I'm getting better." Still, he immediately went on to point out that he has his own good head for politics, never mentioning the name of his campaign director or anyone else working with him.

The senator was riding high in the polls and political columns when he dropped in for a down-home reception in Russell in early 1987.

The original campaigners—doctor, broker, oilman, farmer—mostly hung back in the kitchen, a bit awed by this talking head they see on TV who looks ten years younger than any of them. Tanned from a typically two-day vacation at Elizabeth's now-controversial condo in Miami, Dole presented his glamorous fifty-year-old wife. Svelte since she started pedaling on a new stationary bike, Elizabeth had stopped going to Nancy

Reagan's hairdresser, and switched to a somewhat younger, looser style. At that point she was still secretary of transportation, and the Doles normally communicated by check-off memos that flew between their offices. Some weeks the closest the secretary got to the senator was to sip from the banquet glass he'd just left. Liddy was happy to have a day with her husband.

The talk among Dole's core constituents was of hard times and extreme solutions. "I'd like to see about three Arab heads of state go boom boom," seethed an oilman. "Thing that bums me out is they're supposed to be Christian countries," said another. "All's I say," chimed in a farmer, "there's no way to get ahead of Russia unless you destroy it."

One could almost hear Dole's mind racing, the laser beam in his brain illuminating problems too far ahead for him to find solutions, yet. The people of Russell are still in Bob Dole, but he has grown beyond them. As he told me later, "I can see it coming in rural America—'It's either me or them'—farmers who are making it who don't want to be dragged under by interest payments to keep their neighbor afloat."

But what he gave them was a quick legislative briefing and a pep talk. "We will be coming to Kansas quite often, entertaining people who might be looking for stories. Be sure to keep telling them all those lies."

After a second stop in Kansas and a standing ovation, Senator Dole stood outside the snug six-seat charter he likes to commandeer around the country. The wind snorted across the Kansas plains and bit into his shoulder. Elizabeth was already inside, buried in briefing papers. The Doles began with their usual campaign-plane appetizer—Dunkin' Donuts—and finished off with a doggie bag of barbecued beef. There was no small talk. She read. He read. Once, he chuckled and read aloud a newspaper item: " 'The only thing George Bush has left to run for is the Best-Dressed List.' "

Forty minutes outside of Washington, Dole caught me napping. He grunted and pushed a cup of coffee at me. He wanted to talk, to use the time.

Dole had been a hawk on Vietnam. I asked if he had had second thoughts. "I voted for the Cooper-Church amendment [to withdraw U.S. troops] after defending the Nixon White House," he admitted. "I think Nixon did the right thing in getting us out of there."

It took him an awfully long time, I mentioned.

"Yeah. And there was never any American support." His voice suddenly became more intimate. "Every day you had a body count. How many did we kill today? How many did they kill? I mean, it's sort of sick. Not a very good period in American history."

After a pause, he added that if he was ever in a position where he had to retaliate militarily, he'd do it "as quickly and as painlessly as possible. It wouldn't be a game with me."

I recalled our first talk. Dole had mentioned an insight he has that he thinks no other candidate has. "You're sort of sensitive to people around you, whether they're poor, hungry, cold, old, sick, disabled. If I were whole, I'd be embarrassed to go into a paralyzed veterans' association." The self-revelatory words "If I were whole" had stopped me.

"Do you think you've ever fully accepted the loss of your arm?" I asked him quietly.

"Oh, I hope not," he said. "Not that I have any self-pity. But I still fantasize sometimes of raising my arm. . . ." He even dreams, still, of himself shooting a basketball.

"I think it makes you try harder. Sort of like Avis, you're number two. I push and push and push. Not because I'm disabled. I like to be a player."

Still running, still overcoming, Dole may not have accepted his handicap, but he makes it work for him. But he can't quite connect the funny bone to the shoulder bone, or make the emotions move the muscles so that strangers can *feel* the sincerity and compassion of this complex man. As with so many of us, his story goes on to repeat itself. Even as he anticipated the grim results for his candidacy on Super Tuesday, it was clear that Bob Dole's struggle to be whole was not over: "I'm going to start my road to recovery again in Illinois, just like I did forty years ago."

PASSIVE CHANGE

None of us goes out of our way to change unless we are pressed to do so. The circumstances of our birth may have an abrasive effect: some of us chafe against humble origins and stretch and bend and struggle to distinguish ourselves in spite of that start. Others are born insulated by wealth or position, and can be more relaxed and choosy about how much they want to change.

The strongest contrast in this regard, among the leaders I've followed, exists between Robert Dole and George Bush. If Dole has exerted the greatest *inner-*directed effort to change and improve himself, Bush has gone to the other extreme, bending to *outer-*directed cues as to what will please those in power. Whereas Bobby Dole had to scramble and fight to get himself into a position to make a difference, "Poppy" Bush assumed that making a difference was his heritage, indeed, his duty.

Dole has used this disparity in backgrounds to identify with average Americans—"He's one of us"—implicitly challenging his archrival's character credentials on a class basis. "Few of Russell's people think that bloodlines or bank accounts are valid tests of character," he wrote in his recent autobiography. "We tolerate anything but snobs." Dole knows his own class animosity resonates with what many Americans feel, although they seldom feel comfortable about openly expressing it.

Bush admits he is grateful for his privileged background, and says it inspired an obligation to serve. But sometimes he slips and identifies himself with too rarefied a world. Asked why he thought he didn't draw big crowds in Michigan last September, he remarked, "Everybody must be playing golf or going to coming-out parties." One Michigan man was quoted as saying, "I don't think we've had a debutante ball in this state for years."

Unlike Dole, George Bush was born with a positive identity and a solid family destiny to follow. He is the antithesis of a loner. Accustomed to having a large, prosperous, and supportive family behind him, and having built strong party alliances all over the country, his confidence is so well bolstered that he can go out of his way to make others feel comfortable.

These engravings on a candidate's character by virtue of his background can be discerned in his philosophy of government. In Bob Dole's exhortation that the direction of the country must be changed—to remove the monkey of the deficit from our children's backs and extend government aid to the helpless— one can feel the sensibility of a man who has been forced to change to improve his lot. George Bush promises relief from change. Satisfied with his personal status quo, he projects a similar conviction that all is right with his country.

FIVE

George Bush: Born to Please

Character is often colored by childhood heroes. In all of his baseball-crazed boyhood, George Bush had only one hero, and it wasn't Babe Ruth. It was the man who played in his shadow, Lou Gehrig. Why the Iron Horse and not the star? Because, as Bush's son George remembers the message, Lou Gehrig was consistently good at his job, never tried to steal the limelight, and was humble enough to wait until the end of his life to be recognized. Like his model, Bush takes the stingers and keeps on playing.

George Bush's habit of a lifetime is to avoid at virtually any cost confronting anyone. And never a person in authority or power. He placates, he pleases, and somehow, when the going gets tough, when less careful men pound tables and choose sides and leave no middle ground, he vaporizes.

Just about everyone has tried to get Bush to stand up for himself, to engage conflict. His aunt, a Common Cause liberal, stands on her head to provoke him. Nothing. His sister, Nancy, will say, "Dammit, George, why won't you say what you really think!" George junior says sympathetically, "Dad's instinct is always for the thoughtful thing, and that's probably to his detriment in the world of cutthroat politics."

I asked the vice-president's younger brother, Jonathan, if he had ever seen Bush tackle anyone head on. "No, and I don't see him tackle head on now. I've never seen George tackle head on. You just can't get him in there fighting."

Of the forty people I interviewed in the fall of 1986 for this portrait, only two could come up with an instance where George Bush had challenged someone. He once made a retort to his close friend Nick Brady, when Brady pushed him on a point. "Then how come I'm vice-president and you're not?" demanded Bush. This was in private, and Brady can't remember the point.

Senator Alan Simpson was privy to the other occasion. It was at a private dinner for six at Simpson's home in December 1985, with George and his wife, Bar, and Rosalee and David— David being McCullough, the eminent historian, like Bush a Yale man and an initiate of the elite Skull and Bones society.

"I want to ask you if my perception of this administration is wrong," McCullough began, as Simpson recalls the scene. The historian made a measured challenge of its attitude toward the poor, the homeless, and minorities, an attitude he felt was thoughtless and obnoxious. Since the president and vice-president serve as models, McCullough argued, their sense of fairness ought to be apparent in whom they associate with and what they say.

"How do you defend that?" McCullough wound up.

George Bush, according to one account, was courteous but emphatic in responding to the challenge. By another account he was inadequate and often insensitive, insisting that everyone knows the homeless are all crazy. He did not respond by articulating the wisdom of the president's actions or ideas, but only with a defense of Ronald Reagan as a caring person. He never rose above the personal to engage the debate on a policy level.

"He keeps devil's advocates out of his life," according to an old friend, Lud Ashley. "He has a way of listening—and being nice about it—without really hearing."

Not surprisingly, Bush's reluctance to confront others has made him an extremely likable and popular man. His two thousand closest friends, five children, four siblings, wife, present staff, and former aides and servants, from the U.N. to China, are all eager to say nice things about him. "George is a truster." "Dad is thoughtful to a fault." "He was a very, very impressive big brother." "He was beautiful when I met him at sixteen; he still is—without those darn glasses." "A good soldier." "Fun guy, lovely man, great friend."

But in his campaign for the presidency, this same quality has left the vice-president open to attack. Conservative political analyst George Will summed him up in an unforgettable phrase as a "lapdog" who emitted "a thin tinny arf." In his response to this attack, Bush revealed another vulnerability: He is remarkably thin-skinned for a politician. He refused to have lunch with the columnist, which Will found astonishing. "If a single newspaper column can rattle a professional politician, the man is not at ease with himself."

Trying to overcome the labels of "wimp" and "lapdog," Bush has several times departed from his lifetime habit of attempting to please. After his 1984 debate with Geraldine Ferraro, he boasted that he'd "kicked a little ass." In the 1988 campaign, he increased his attempts to appear assertive. During a debate in Iowa in mid-January, a fifteen-year-old girl questioned Bush about whether he'd flip-flopped on the abortion issue. Noticing that the girl was reading from a Kemp campaign flier, Bush ripped the leaflet into pieces, exclaiming, "Finis!" Then, a week later, he took on a tougher questioner, CBS's Dan Rather, on a tougher question: the Iran-contra scandal.

It seemed unimaginable that any vice-president could elude scrutiny or partial blame for the greatest policy blunder of his administration. But George Bush had pulled it off for more than a year after the Iran-contra debacle dragged Reagan's presidency through the depths of distrust and disenchantment. When the scandal hit the front pages in November 1986, Bush hid out for weeks, then couched his defense of the president in terms of personal affection and gratitude: "There's no pulling away from support for a president who has been so fantastically good to Barbara and me."

But once the president's coattails began wearing thin in his last term, Bush was left with no identity of his own to fall back on.

So he leaned on the loyalty defense. When the long-simmering arms scandal appeared to be damaging his presidential hopes, Bush declared: "In my family, loyalty is not considered a character defect, it is considered a strength." His focus-group responses shot up. His campaign advisers told him to stick with that line.

Most Americans would agree that loyalty is a sterling trait. Indeed, it is the life's blood of the original old-boy network. Among the great WASP Brobdingnags of the Eastern Establishment, loyalty meant they took care of their own: They opened the doors of their banks and brokerage houses and law firms to the sons of their friends, and protected them throughout their careers.

But the vice-president's emphasis on his loyalty was more than a truthful statement of George Herbert Walker Bush's family values. It was also a calculated political strategy intended to capitalize on his main advantage over his Republican rivals: seven years of putting "no daylight" between himself and Ronald Reagan. Lee Atwater, the vice-president's chief political adviser, prophesied at the time that by 1988, "Reagan will be a deity with Republican-primary voters. People will see who were Reagan's fair-weather friends, and Bush's loyalty will look better than ever."

The vice-president's public approval rating does rise and fall in direct relation to the president's popularity. But, as Steven Roberts pointed out in *The New York Times*, "If Mr. Reagan makes what is viewed as a political mistake, such as pardoning former aides implicated in the Iran-contra affair, he could bring his loyal partner down with him."

But will Bush ever be able to project the powerful image that has served Ronald Reagan so well? Comparisons of style between the vice-president and his boss are difficult for Bush. His voice is the squeaky piccolo to Reagan's mellow cello. Reagan is western boots and chopping wood to Bush's Lacoste shirts and tennis shoes. Reagan never permits a photograph to show him in his reading glasses; Bush is constantly nagged about his prissy spectacles. (George has tried contacts, says his wife, but his eyes are too square.) Reagan has used his origins— born to ordinary working people in a banal midwestern town— to play to conservatives' preference for an anti-intellectual, macho style of administration with a middle-to-lowbrow western orientation. He makes all those in the lumpen electorate who also went to a mediocre college feel better. Then along comes George Bush, who is everything they're not—Greenwich, Andover, Yale, captain of the Yale baseball team, Skull and Bones—and because he cannot be identified with any issue, people focus on the manners of his class.

Can the man help it if he was shaped until the age of eighteen to conform to the Eastern WASP Patrician Sensibility? The mold is old and solid. It has gone to Exeter/Andover and Harvard/Yale; it has studied Proust (albeit punctuated by paddle tennis and table puzzles), cut its teeth on competition, and developed a fetish about fairness. It has learned to read stock tables at "Ganny's" knee and to navigate steadfastly through Atlantic squalls in small boats. It has trudged uncomplainingly through the Pitti Palace in the hammering heat of Florence in August. It is unfailingly polite.

Yet no one gave F.D.R. a hard time for Groton and Harvard, and John Kennedy made New England prep schools and Harvard national emblems of glamour. So it is more than a problem of background or style.

I think of it as the Tinker Bell problem. Ronald Reagan is a dreamer, a true believer. He talks about his "visions," about the "miracle" that is America. Bush gave a revealing look into his concept of Reagan's miracles in an ad-lib to a speech: "Ronald Reagan and I believe in the miracle that is America. But the funny thing is, when you look at miracles, they're nothing. It's hard work."

Reagan made Americans believe that *he* believes what he reads off the TelePrompTer. When he invoked his magic to sell us an economic fantasy or something called a nuclear shield, before you knew it, he'd clapped his hands and Tinker Bell appeared.

But what happens when you clap your hands for Tinker Bell and you don't believe? You look like George Bush—as if you had strings attached.

What's more, Bush can't act. And he refuses to make himself over for the television age into a performer. Bush wouldn't know a photo opportunity if it hit him over the head, according to his own staff photographer, David Valdez. If Valdez had a dollar for every time he's caught the vice-president with his shirt out or handed him a comb before he made an appearance, Valdez could probably afford Andover, too. Of course, the mismatched, mussed-hair, mothy-blue-sweater look is the essence of old-style preppiness; i.e. one must never appear to be trying too hard. Bush would rather die than use hair spray, say his aides. His supporters once deputized a Bush family member to lobby George about persuading Bar to dye her hair. Bush threw the relative out of his office.

If even the master actor-president couldn't find a way to make Irangate play and give it a happy ending, how can the man in his shadow? George Bush may have adopted many of the Reagan tricks—the tough talk, the clever ducking of sticky questions—but he lacks the conviction to make them work for him. His muddle-headed explanations, meant to deflect attention, actually stimulated the drip-drip-drip of Chinese water torture, as more memos and recollections from Iran-contra participants came out, and as high-school students kept raising questions the press could not get satisfactorily answered.

The deeper mystery surrounding this man, who has assiduously cultivated private access to the president, is *why* he failed to protect his boss from making so many mistakes. Did Bush's need for approval from the man in authority keep him from confronting Reagan on his more dangerous daydreams?

Over and over, he has maintained that "I'm for Mr. Reagan—blindly," which may eventually lead the American public to question if this relationship wasn't a case of the blind leading the intentionally blind.

One thing should be clear about George Bush: The need for approval is a pattern that has been revealed throughout his life. It is the central defining mark of his character.

I asked everyone I interviewed if they knew of a gut issue with George Bush, something for which he has consistently stood. Most answered like the late Malcolm Baldrige, then secretary of commerce, who said, "I dunno. He probes everybody about what they think before he makes up his own mind." Neither his present nor his past speechwriters could think of an issue that consistently excites him. James E. Baker, secretary of the treasury, who is Bush's unofficial campaign manager, suggested it was fairness. Barbara Bush said "equality." George Bush, speaking for himself, thought a moment and said "peace."

Presumably no living American is opposed to fairness, equality, and peace, so I pressed for specifics. Barbara Bush thought about it, and described one time when Bush *did* stand up for something specific. As a congressman in 1968, he was the only member of the Texas delegation to vote for open housing. Racist anger among his constituents erupted in hate mail and crank calls. The rich whites who had elected him, who belonged to the same exclusively white private clubs of Houston that he did, couldn't believe this was *their* George Bush. Finally, faced at a G.O.P. rally with booing and hissing, he stood firm on the grounds that black servicemen were fighting for freedom in Southeast Asia.

"Somehow it seems fundamental that a man—if he has the money and the good character—should not have a door slammed in his face if he is a Negro or if he speaks with a Latin American accent."

His feisty performance carried the day, turning catcalls into a standing ovation. Yet in these conservative times, Bush himself never mentions that chapter from his political life. And Mrs. Bush writes it off: "Did it change anybody's life? I'd have to be honest and say absolutely not."

For all his superior education, George Bush cannot remember a single book that influenced him. He told me he vaguely recalls reading *The Robe*, a biblical potboiler. Nor does he project that easy, self-confident mellifluousness common to Ivy Leaguers. He rarely uses a word with more than three syllables, scrambles his syntax, speaks in fits and starts. Clearly, Bush is not fired up by ideas.

"Service to country underlies everything," offered Malcolm Baldrige. An old buddy from Greenwich, Barrington Boardman, explains that George Bush goes from one job to another because it's a logical extension of his desire to serve. It's all part of the eastern patrician tradition among families who don't have to worry about getting and spending the way others do. It is the noble obligation of George Bush.

But his noble ideals of service, while endearing him to party officials, have failed to win him widespread popular respect. Barbara Bush begins to turn blue when she hears the word "wimp." She can't wait to retort, "Did you ever risk your life for your country? Did you ever build a business? Churches? Y.M.C.A.'s?" She says the answer is always no.

Lee Atwater blames many of Bush's problems on the fact that he's vice-president—a job that is traditionally a national joke. But Bush had a life before the vice-presidency, several lives: He's the plucky lad from Yale who fought a war and lost an offshore rig in the wild and woolly oil business; he tangled with the Texas electorate as county chairman, congressman, and senatorial candidate; he served under three presidents—as U.N. ambassador, G.O.P. chairman, envoy to China, and director of the C.I.A.

Bush has, in fact, the perfect résumé for someone seeking *appointive* office. He has always been an ideal Number Two: He does what he is trained to do, never challenges, never initiates. Why take such jobs if one's game plan is to run for president? "There are small jobs which may seem beneath your dignity," acknowledges his friend Nicholas Brady, chairman of Wall Street's Dillon, Read, and himself once appointed to serve out a Senate term, "but if you're learning, it's not so damn important if you're rewarded or not. It's an interesting look at George's character." Perhaps Bush is now getting exactly the reward he was looking for: the support of his party for playing good soldier without the risks of criticism or failure that come with big jobs. If he reaches the White House in 1989, it will not be through the process of political combat and conquest, but by polite succession to the throne. And so, in search of the origins of his inflexible amiability, I went back to the childhood of "Poppy" Bush.

His father was austere, a towering man who invited no argument. "As children, we were all afraid of Dad," says Jonathan Bush, "every one of us." The vice-president affirmed that "Dad was really scary."

Prescott Bush, a financier who followed his father-in-law into the investment bank that became Brown Brothers Harriman, presided over a breakfast table where children were to be seen and not heard. A maid silently ferried robust meals made by a cook. At the dinner table, the father turned his booming voice like a cannon to confront one child after the other, demanding to know what they had done with their day. They dutifully reported.

"Remember Teddy Roosevelt's speak softly and carry a big stick?" Bush told David Frost. "My dad spoke *loudly* and carried the same big stick. He got our attention pretty quick."

George was the most submissive of the three sons. His older brother, Pressy, did argue with their father, and even ran away a few times. But George, according to the youngest brother, Jonathan, never. Nor was George ever a bully. "Too little," he told me. Nicknamed "Poppy," he carried a big name—George Herbert Walker Bush—for the littlest guy in his class, and was "a real, real teacher's pet," remembers Jonathan.

Always sensitive to others, George developed a disarming style very early and defused tense situations by being funny. In church he could get his mother giggling so uncontrollably the whole family would have to leave. He was also naturally athletic. Although he shot up in ninth or tenth grade, he never used his newfound stature to press his advantage in the schoolyard. And when the boys brought home their report cards, George never failed to get "Excellent" in one rating by which his mother set great store: *Claims no more than his fair share of time and attention.* Then, as now, Bush did not seize the initiative or stick his neck out. He gladly forfeited the limelight in exchange for never being in a position to be blamed for things going wrong. It became a family joke—George always did best in "Claims no more."

Money was something the Bushes never worried about, never talked about either. To discuss the filthy lucre that came from trading stocks and bonds would have been unseemly. Before eight every morning, Alec the chauffeur would have the car purring and ready to drop Mr. Bush at the station before taking George and Pressy on to the private Greenwich Country Day School. The Depression was nowhere in evidence as the Bushes' tasteful black Oldsmobile glided past the stone fences and stables and swimming pools of one of the wealthiest communities in America.

It nettles Bush to be criticized as a rich man's kid. "Life has been good to me," he readily concedes, "some of it by virtue of our birth, and I hope a lot of it by working for a living and trying to do your best." His father set the example. Everyone else's dad would come out on the tired commute from New York, head home, and gulp down a couple of drinks. Prescott Bush would go directly to run the town meeting of Greenwich, or the hospital board, or the church board. He instructed his boys never to look down on others; to be kind, serve their country, and give something back.

His mother came from an even more prominent family and one with the added pizzaz of a champion polo-playing member, George Herbert Walker—the Uncle Herbie who later opened the pipeline of Eastern Establishment money that would smooth young George's entry into the Texas oil business. Exacting in her own way, "Mum" was a petite drill sergeant who always exhorted her children in games: "You can do it, you'll get it." But unlike her husband, she exuded a warm, blithe spirit—"very much the inspiration of our family," says Bush. He was amazed when one of his friends in eighth grade told George he wished he had a mother like that. "I just thought everybody loved his mother as we Bush kids did." And as children usually do, he just thought everybody's kids had the advantages the Bush kids did—servants to light the bedroom fireplaces on bitter mornings, the winter shooting lodge in the South, the summer house on the Maine seacoast. "Other kids had a lot more," says Jonathan Bush.

George Bush's first cousin, Ray Walker, Uncle Herbie's son, told the *Los Angeles Times*'s Barry Bearak that the Bushes and Walkers never made the leap from their sense of noblesse oblige to genuine empathy. "Does anyone from the family understand what it is to be poor? No . . . And the bigger question is: Do they understand their own ignorance?" Bush's cousin grew up within the same charmed Greenwich circle and spent the same halcyon summers in Kennebunkport, Maine, but bolted from the clan after finishing Yale. A psychoanalyst, he makes the observation that Bush, like the rest of the family, misses the point that all this altruistic public service "gives you power and a sense of goodness. . . . That's the complexity of the thing. God help us from people who think they are going around exercising their goodness!"

Poppy's life as an adult began like some wonderful Frank Capra movie: It is 1944, and so many American boys are still fighting "over there." Our dashing naval pilot arrives home on Christmas Eve, painfully handsome, and stands in his sweetheart's doorway, a light snow melting on his nose.

It has been written that Barbara Pierce first saw George at a dance when she was sixteen and made up her mind to marry him. "No," she snaps, "he saw me," and proceeds to give Barbara's version, which will, from this moment on, be the official version. George, gorgeous in a tuxedo, asked another boy if he knew the girl in the red and green dress. They were engaged before George went off to war. Bar returned to Smith College, where her dream for their marriage was simply "Oh, God, let him come home."

Barbara had grown up in Rye, New York. While not superrich (her father had started as a messenger and ended up president of the McCall Corporation), she, like George, had been insulated from hands-on work and raw language.

"Don't you think it was a shock for us to see *their* homes?" says Mrs. Bush about the mind-boggling six months she and George spent traveling across the country as a navy couple, staying in people's basements. But it was the destruction of her entire trousseau of silk lingerie that really got to her. A woman they were staying with showed Barbara how to use the washing machine, then marched upstairs to crow over the telephone, "I wish you could have seen her; she put all those handmade beautiful things into the machine and ruined them, every one!"

To his credit, George Bush's pleasing, sensitive, submissive nature has won him affection from many quarters.

As a father, George Bush belongs to the sink-or-swim school of child rearing. He would compete with his kids at anything—checkers, tennis, bat-and-ball games, fishing, video games—but always Bush spoon-fed his children with confidence. He shoved his four sons off into the world without big trust funds, but with splendid educations. He reserves a special tenderness for his only living daughter, Dorothy, who never did compete academically with the boys. "Dad is the most sensitive human being I know," says his oldest son, George junior.

He is no less a model son. Dorothy Walker Bush abhors arrogance and demands honesty. She also expresses concern about the morality of certain government policies. When, as president of the Senate, Bush had to cast the deciding vote in favor of preserving nerve gas as part of the U.S. arsenal, he asked Ronald Reagan to call his mother and explain why his Number Two was doing the nation a service.

He is a storybook grandfather. When his second son, Jeb, took off on an Andover School program to do good works in Mexico and came home in love with a Mexican woman who could barely speak English, Bush was stunned. "I'm not going to lie to you and say we were thrilled," admits Barbara Bush. But anyone who has heard George Bush speak of the grandson from that union, anyone who has watched the two of them spinning fantasies of sailing the coast of Maine as they sit on a rock "boat" at high tide, would sense that more important to the vice-president than any presidential primary is the duty of protecting that little Hispanic boy's future.

Is there anyone who wouldn't want to be George Bush's friend? "I've come to know George well," says Senator Alan Simpson, who enjoys the informality of weekends at Bush's place of recreation and re-creation in Kennebunkport. Simpson describes a round of stories after dinner, then padding into the living room with a piano player and half a dozen couples to beat the devil out of the rug. Some of the world's unfunniest people suddenly feel, in Bush's presence, like true wits. The secret to his sense of humor is that he plants the punch line in someone else's mouth.

He may be the most amiable pol ever to work a rope line, and he loves "mix 'n' mingles": "Bar and I will never forget how we got where we're at—it's because of people like you." If there's one wallflower left after he's squeezed four hundred hands and posed for dozens of pictures, he'll dive over to draw her out: "I haven't met *you* yet, glad to see you." And he is. After the last gasp on a campaign trip, Bush will always make time to go up to local staff headquarters and shake the hand of every lowly volunteer. George Bush genuinely likes people, and he wants everyone to like him back.

He is the kind of guy who would step out in his pin-striped suit in the middle of a downpour to help his chauffeur fix a flat. The kind who stays in Washington on Christmas Eve so that his Secret Service men can go home to their families. The kind who saw a friend, Jim Baker, in despair after his wife's death and brought the Democrat into politics. Until Bob Dole poked him in the eye for twenty days straight before the Iowa caucuses, Bush had always practiced what Reagan dubbed the "Eleventh Commandment": the refusal to say a nasty word about his Republican opponents.

His wife says, "George Bush, and maybe this is a fault, but George Bush looks for the best in everybody. He doesn't question motives."

Sometimes his amicability borders on the ridiculous. In 1981, for instance, he stood up at a state dinner in the Philippines and troweled on a toast to Ferdinand and Imelda Marcos: "I *love* your adherence to democracy."

"There is a Christian innocence to George," says his cousin Ray Walker, the psychoanalyst. "His life has been without moral ambiguity . . . without introspection. George plays it safe. He plays for the status quo."

It seems apparent that George relies on the motherly figure of Barbara to protect him from his boyishly ebullient faith in the fairness of others. She is tough and smart and strongly opinionated. Indeed, Bar is one of those wives about whom associates of the couple routinely say, "She's the smart one."

Another Yale contemporary who grew up near the Bushes in Greenwich sees a striking parallel between George's mother and his wife. "His mother was his conscience. The real backbone of that family was Dotty Walker Bush. Barbara has inherited the role—she is in many ways his mother."

Barbara concedes that she loses no chance to let George Bush know what she thinks about the issues. "But when I disagree with him," she tells the press, "I'll never tell you."

Though she commands great respect, Barbara Bush can be a terror with his staff. "If something negative appears about her

George in the media with your name on it, you're dead," says a staffer who shall remain nameless. Mrs. Bush admits, "I can always find a tricky reason someone did something, because I could have done it *myself*. George can't."

What is never mentioned in comparisons between the president and the vice-president is the disparity in how they actually live. Bush has been married to the same woman for forty-two years; Reagan has been divorced. Bush says the proudest accomplishment of his life is that his kids still come home; only one of Reagan's children bothered to show up at his seventy-fifth birthday party. Bush spends weekends in Kennebunkport urging his grandchildren to row across the pond and giving them the confidence to do it; Reagan never sees his grandchild and takes no one with him for weekends at Camp David except Nancy and the dog. George Bush was a genuine hero in World War II; Ronald Reagan was in Culver City making movies about it. The irony is that Bush really lives the eternal values so dear to conservatives' hearts, while Reagan mouths them and winks.

When I first interviewed the vice-president in September 1986, on Air Force Two, he looked relaxed and remarkably virile for a man of sixty-two. He had changed after a day of campaigning into his Autry jogging shoes, a polo shirt, and baggy sweatpants. I was not prepared for how familiar he feels on first meeting. There is no fanfare, no invoked aura. George Bush is halfway through greeting you before you notice he's there.

"So, this is gonna be a deal on where I'm coming from, a psychiatric layout?" he asked. He told me that he's terrible at telling stories about his past, and that there are some sacred family moments he cannot share; if that makes him dull as a candidate, if that's the price of being president, well, then, it isn't worth it. So I got him talking about his war experiences.

What went on in his mind, I wondered, when he, an eighteen-year-old string bean of a pampered suburban boy, the youngest pilot in the U.S. Navy, climbed into his barrel-chested bomber and sat on top of two thousand pounds of TNT? In seconds he'd rev up his single engine, then reach over to signal

the tower and push forward on the throttle and—*swoooock*—
he'd be catapulted into the Pacific mist. Minutes later he'd be
grinding through heavy antiaircraft fire.

"I thought I was kind of a macho pilot," he says. "You were
trained, you knew what to do. There wasn't any 'wonder if it's
going to work this time' feeling to it." He flew torpedo bombers
over the Pacific, 58 missions, 126 carrier landings.

On the morning of September 2, 1944, the young fliers on
the *San Jacinto* were readied to hit Japanese installations on
Chichi-shima. They were warned that their ship wouldn't be
around to pick up anyone who went down: It was turning south.
Bush was in the second pair of Avengers to go in. He looked
out and saw fluffy little clouds all around, but they were black,
not white, and he knew there was an American plane incinerat-
ing inside each one. "I was aware the antiaircraft fire would be
heavy, but I was not afraid. I wasn't thinking, This next one's
going to hit me."

But it did. Suddenly the plane slammed forward. Black, oily
smoke belched out of the engines and fumed through the cock-
pit, and for the first time George Bush was scared. "We were
going down. I never saw what hit me, but I felt this thing. I had
to finish my bombing run."

Bush continued his dive and hit his target. Pulling out over
the ocean, he saw flames chewing the wing folds, right over the
gas tanks. "This damned thing is going to blow up any minute,"
he shouted, and he tried to talk to the two men in his crew. One
jumped out ahead of him, one was slumped over.

"My God, get your own ass out of here," Bush remembers
thinking. He bailed out, but pulled the ripcord too early. The
slipstream caught his body, all 152 pounds of it, and flung it at
the tail of the plane. He hit his head. His chute tore, then pulled
free. Sheer luck. He was falling fast. But he managed to get out
of his harness before his boots smacked the water. He climbed
into his tiny life raft and began paddling like crazy, but the wind
was carrying him toward the enemy island. He began vomiting
violently. "I was scared. I didn't know whether I'd survive,
didn't know what happened to my friends . . . It seemed like
the end of the world."

Bush is at his best talking like this, spontaneously, emotionally. But for a "claims no more" man, it came hard to learn how to brag about his manliness. This was one of the first times he had spoken of his war experiences. The story eventually became a campaign staple, although Bush still worries: "I get in trouble with my mother if I talk about being in combat."

We talked about his faith. Raised as a country-club Episcopalian, he'd prayed only by rote before that day in the life raft. "But this was the occasion to pray to God to save you," he said. He had hope—he knew a submarine was out there. He whipped out a .38-caliber pistol, a bit dramatically, he admits, and just kept paddling. After a few hours he saw a submarine periscope break the monotony of the sea. For a moment he feared it was the Japanese. But suddenly American sailors swarmed over the deck, and the frightened flier was fished up onto the *Finback*. Six weeks later, although he had the option of rotating home, Bush elected to return to combat.

I had to ask Barbara Bush to describe the other great test, the year their third child suddenly became ill. The Bushes live in the gracious vice-presidential residence behind whitewashed anchors at the U.S. Naval Observatory in Washington. Barbara was arranged prettily in a big flowered skirt on a brocade sofa, with a book open before her. It was, appropriately, *The Path to Power*, Robert Caro's biography of Lyndon Johnson. She exudes confidence from every pore, this rock of a woman with the nimbus of white hair who still wears White Shoulders perfume. As we talked above the purr of lawn sprinklers, her deeply grooved face moved easily between game smiles and a grave determination.

In March 1953, George had just started a new oil business in Midland, Texas, he and Barbara weren't yet thirty, and they had three children—it was a spring full of promise. One morning their three-year-old, Robin, woke up and said, "I'm either going to lie on the grass and watch the cars go by or lie in bed and read a book." Thinking these were the symptoms of spring fever, her mother took the child to a woman doctor who did a few tests. She said, "I think you'd better come back this afternoon and bring your husband with you." When the couple returned, the doctor dabbed her eyes and said a word neither of them had ever heard: leukemia.

"Well, do something about it," demanded George.

The doctor said, "George, you can't do anything about leukemia."

With all the certainty of a privileged young man, George fired back, "There's nothing you can't do something about!"

The doctor told them Robin had the highest white count she had ever seen. "My advice to you would be, don't tell a living human, take her home, and live a normal life. She'll be dead in two weeks."

Bar was speechless. George muttered, "No way," and before they reached home, he had stopped the car and was out calling on their friends to say they needed help. By the time their minister arrived that night, the house was filled with friends having cocktails. The next day, they flew Robin to New York's Memorial Hospital, where Bush's uncle was a doctor.

"I hated the chemotherapy, for her," Mrs. Bush said, forcing herself to recollect that important period, "but it was very good for us. We had a chance to work out, to"—her eyes trickled tears—"tell her we loved her."

Over the next eight agonizing months, the little blond, blue-eyed, pug-nosed angel of a girl became a pincushion for blood transfusions, and still the blue smudges under her skin kept multiplying. Barbara Bush made a rule that no one could cry in front of Robin. "George and his mother are so softhearted, I had to order them out of the hospital room most of the time," she remembers. George Bush, nervous about keeping his new investors happy, went right on taking the night plane to be by his daughter for several days at a time. He bent over her bed and helped her to blow her nose. He watched, helplessly, while she died inch by inch.

The morning after his daughter died, George Bush went over to Memorial Hospital to find everyone who had worked on his child's case and thank them. He waited until he returned home to Midland before he broke down. "It brought us much closer," Mrs. Bush says fervently, pointing out that the majority of families are shattered by the same experience. "Afterwards, George Bush was unbelievable. So strong. He held me in his arms a lot. Let me weep away, and not be so nice to people."

She knew she was being overprotective the day she heard her little boy, George junior, tell a friend he couldn't come over because he had to go home and play with his mother. A year later, her son Neil was born and Barbara Bush came back to normal. "All of our children were planned," she admits. "By me."

I asked Bush what spiritual lesson he had drawn from his war experience. "I consider it God's will that I'm alive," he said. He wondered aloud why his friends were killed and he wasn't. "It gives you a perspective of war and peace, what the world is like. I don't know what the message is . . ." His voice trailed off.

About his second confrontation with devastating loss, Bush expressed the same philosophical tentativeness. "We couldn't understand why this child—" he told me, breaking off. "I mean, what's God's message? Why?" He says it would have been the greatest experience of his life if the ending had been different.

Bush apparently can't synthesize the episodes of highest drama in his life and assign them meaning. If he had been able to see his war experiences as a test of strength, they might have allowed him to perceive himself as strong and manly. If he had been able to find a deeper spiritual or philosophical message in his daughter's death, he might be able to feel good about the courage his wife says he showed.

Around the time the Reverend Jerry Falwell endorsed him, Bush began to describe his religious convictions in terms more charismatic than Episcopalian: "For me, born again, and this gets awful personal, is knowing that in my case, Jesus Christ is my personal saviour." But once his political handlers concluded that the religious Right had lost its leverage, Bush stopped trying to please them with such protestations.

After the war, everyone was in a hurry. George had been a mediocre student in high school, but finishing Yale in two and a half years was common in 1945 as veterans were ground through the degree mill year round. Neither an activist nor an intellectual, "he wasn't terribly well informed," says Lud Ashley, who became his friend, "but he was such a congenial guy."

He earned a B.A. in economics, and didn't consider going to graduate school. "I didn't even have a career dream then," Bush told me.

His dad and his uncle Herbie Walker both offered him jobs as an investment banker, but George, so goes the story, was looking for a way to get out from under the shadow of his awesome father. "I want something I can see, something I can feel," he used to tell Bar.

Bush could easily have stayed with the soft life in Connecticut, gone to work at Brown Brothers Harriman, and spent weekends at the exclusive Round Hill Club. His older brother did remain in Greenwich, living essentially that life. His younger brother wanted passionately to be an actor, and went off for several years with touring companies in musicals. But pressure from the family eventually won out, and Jonathan Bush returned to take up a career as an investment banker.

As a result, much has been made in George Bush's biography of his next move—breaking away from Wall Street and his father to seek his fortune the hard way, in the Texas oil fields. But the old-boy network has an arm as long as a transcontinental pipeline. Prescott Bush served on the board of an oil conglomerate, Dresser Industries, and its chairman was an old friend. All it took was a few phone calls between the old-line banker and the new-wealth corporate speculator, and Poppy Bush was off to Texas, "breaking away" in a fine new car his father had bought for him. "You'll have a chance to run the company someday," the chairman told George even before he started at Dresser, according to Bush's older brother, Prescott.

George and Barbara set up in Odessa, near Midland, on a street of what she called "Easter-egg houses," and shared a common wall with a hooker.

"Didja go to college, Bush?" asked his boss, Bill Nelson, a tough old oil-field worker, figuring the new trainee with baby-smooth hands would last about a week.

"Yes, I went to Yale," said Bush.

"Too bad."

The Bushes laughed a lot and worked hard and lived simply, on his income. Still, "George and I never thought we were poor," Barbara has said. "We knew if something terrible happened to us, we had family."

In fact, something nice happened. Bush left Dresser in 1950, succumbing to the fever for making a quick oil fortune, and he and a neighbor set themselves up as oil-deal promoters. In 1953 he threw in his lot with Hugh and George Liedtke, sons of a Prussian immigrant who had come to Texas to avoid conscription in the Russian army, and they formed Zapata Petroleum. "They were capitalized at a million dollars, a lot of money in those days for a few young guys," says Baine Kerr, the attorney who represented prospective underwriters for the Zapata stock issue. "George's backers were friends or acquaintances of his father or his uncle Herbie Walker. The other half of the money came from Texas and Oklahoma oil people brought in by the Liedtkes, whose boys had both gone to Amherst and Harvard Business School." Kerr's first impression of Bush was "very open, but naïve." But the young easterners were lucky; leasing some land with two oil wells on it, they scored 128 hits.

Bush had had no political ambitions as a young man. Barbara says all that stuff one reads about George wanting to be president from the time he was a boy is bunk. It was only after his father was elected to the Senate in 1952 that George began to take any interest in politics. For the next ten years, however, he was swept up in the high-stakes oil business.

Offshore-oil drilling was pure adventure, and Bush had always loved the sea. But when he lost a multimillion-dollar oil rig and couldn't meet his payroll, he got bleeding ulcers, and realized he couldn't live with the risks of being an entrepreneur. Hugh Liedtke wanted to build a huge oil company (and did—today it's Pennzoil). Bush had never been driven to amass an enormous fortune, and now that he had the solid family connection in politics to back him up, he thought about starting another career, one perhaps better suited to his temperament. In 1959 he dissolved the partnership with Liedtke, sold his stock at a low for $1.1 million, and moved the family to Houston. By 1963 Bush was Harris County G.O.P. chairman. Politics was a game in which he could glad-hand and enjoy constant affirmation, but also follow Dad's commandment to give something back.

The first time he stood up to his father was in 1970. Bush had reached the middle of his life—age forty-six—and perhaps needed to declare himself his own man. Against his father's advice, having been defeated in his first Senate race in Texas in 1964, Bush gave up his congressional seat to try again. "It was a long shot, but he wanted to get into position to run for president," says Jonathan Bush.

By now George had a mentor more powerful even than his father: The president of the United States. Nixon not only encouraged him to reach for the Senate seat, but promised him a cushy landing if he didn't make it. Again, the skids on the fast track were greased by money; Nixon dispensed more than $100,000 to Bush, mostly in cash, from a secret White House fund for his favorite candidates. Bush returned the favor by tailoring his views to fit Nixon's model. Despite his father's strong conviction that American involvement in Vietnam was a terrible mistake, George played the hawk on Vietnam and opposed civil-rights legislation as well. He lost.

Bush later told an Episcopal Church official that he regretted having gone so far right, and would never do it again. "The implication was he had to do it to get elected," the Reverend John F. Stevens has said. As if to get back in his father's good graces, Bush grew so quiet about the Vietnam War in the early seventies that family members don't know what he thought about it. "But I don't think you'd have heard George opposing Dad," says Jonathan.

After a decade in electoral politics, trying and failing, succeeding modestly, and failing again, Bush found his whole game plan had been knocked into a cocked hat. He was farther from the line of accession to the presidency than when he started. And he took it hard. There were times he'd say to Bar, "I could have made seven million dollars if I'd held on to that stock!"

Listlessly, he accepted the job of ambassador to the United Nations in 1970. The way he figured, according to Jonathan, "Run those Senate races, drop back three spaces; move to the U.N., advance one space."

George Bush's experiences in taking charge as a Number One, whether as an entrepreneur or a candidate, had been mostly losing ones. After being defeated twice in electoral battles, he stopped running for office and started being the good soldier who would take any job, stick up for the party, collect political IOUs, and wait his chance to get back in line for the presidency.

A significant shift seems to have taken place in the Bushes' marriage in the seventies. The story came out when I asked Mrs. Bush about her hair. It is snow white, and people constantly remark that she looks like the vice-president's mother. The fact is, she went gray very young.

"My mother-in-law, whom I love more than life, asked me to dye it." Dutifully, Bar did. Every time she swam, the brown turned green, but she kept it up. I asked her when she finally stopped dyeing it. She spat out the date precisely, as one does only with significant events.

"I remember the day, in the summer of 1970. We were in Maine. And we were going to the U.N."

But why then, in her mid-forties, I wondered aloud, at a time when many women step up their efforts to remain sexually attractive?

"George Bush never noticed," she said almost bitterly. "So why had I gone through those years of agony?"

As ambassador to the U.N., Bush was once again tirelessly social and spectacularly popular. One of his predecessors there says he was not regarded as a heavyweight, or seen as someone who could get things done in Washington for small countries. He was basically a party-giver. Presumably bored, he was spotted having frequent tête-à-têtes at the Palm Restaurant with young women. He often went out with Bo Polk, a notorious bachelor. *New York* magazine voted Bush one of the Ten Most Overrated New Yorkers. Stylishly, he threw a party for the snubbed ten, but Bar nailed the editor at the door and scathingly chewed him out.

Nor was she happy when Nixon summoned him to Camp David; she had heard a rumor that the president was looking for a good soldier to head the Republican National Committee.

"Do anything but that!" she exhorted him.

But Bush came home wriggling like a puppy. "Boy, you can't turn a president down."

Watergate ruined everything. As he would later do for Reagan, Bush blindly carried the flag for Nixon. Five months before Nixon was forced to resign, Bush cheerily assured a Young Republicans audience: "The relation between the party and the president is excellent in every respect." Four months before the end he stated, "I remain convinced the president is telling the truth." And, three months before Nixon's surrender: "You close the windows tight, and you think you're pretty safe. You don't see how anything can get in there. But you wake up the next morning, and the house is full of dirt anyway."

Privately, according to the R.N.C.'s political director, Eddie Mahe, Jr., Bush would whine, "What is going *on*?" During the last three days of Nixon's going, going, gone—August 7 to 9—Bush was conspicuously unavailable for comment. R. W. Apple of *The New York Times* reported that he was palavering with Gerald Ford, hoping to become his vice-president. In the last Nixon Cabinet meeting, as reconstructed by Henry Kissinger for Robert Woodward and Carl Bernstein, Bush was described as "petty and insensitive," scurrying about like a "courtier" to improve his own position, concerned with himself rather than his country.

"This is very naïve, I realize, but Nixon really fooled us," Barbara told the *Los Angeles Times.*

It was about time for a reward, Bush let the party leaders know. And so a new job was created for him—the first U.S. envoy to the People's Republic of China—but this was going even farther out into the bush leagues. Nicholas Brady, who has known Bush socially for the last ten years, remembers getting a note from Bush in Beijing urging Brady to stop by and talk: "I'm sitting out here trying to figure out what to do with my life," wrote Bush. He also wrote to President Ford asking to come home.

After only a year, Ford found George a new job where his bland affability could be useful. In 1975 Bush returned from China to head the C.I.A. The agency needed a clean-jeans person to repair its tarnished image and morale. Bush seldom talks about the year he spent as C.I.A. director, nor does Bar. It seemed to have left no mark on him, nor he on it.

But it did give him a pass to the major leagues and made him a player. The next level of the game was the big time. Presidential politics. Did the Lou Gehrig of politics have what it took to be a heavy hitter?

What he did have were friends in Republican precincts all over the country, the legacy of his R.N.C. period. He cultivated those contacts over the next three years, traveling tirelessly and scattering around hand-written thank-you notes as ubiquitously as a ballplayer giving autographs.

By 1980, poised to come out of the dugout in great form, Bush soon gained enough momentum to brag about having "the Big Mo." He told an aide he thought "the age thing" would knock out Ronald Reagan. Then he came face-to-face with the aging actor in Nashua, New Hampshire. Backstage, a squabble broke out over whether all the Republican candidates would participate in the debate, or just front-runners Bush and Reagan. Moving away from confrontation as usual, Bush walked onstage by himself and sat down. Reagan followed angrily.

"George, stand up!"

From the moment the cannon of that commanding voice went off, the psychic turf between Ronald Reagan and George Bush shifted incontrovertibly. Bush obeyed. And when the furious debate sponsor pulled the plug on Reagan's mike, while Bush fidgeted in his chair, Reagan seized control with his famous declaration, "I'm paying for this microphone, Mr. Green!"

After that, although Bush won six primaries, he never established in voters' minds what he stood for; with Reagan, there was little doubt. Bush's campaign manager, Jim Baker, knew his man had earned Reagan's contempt in Nashua. Reagan thought Bush had lacked "spunk" in allowing an opponent to steal center stage. "He just melts under pressure," Reagan sneered after Bush backed down a second time during the Texas primary.

If Bush was to have any chance of getting on the Reagan ticket, he would have to work at making himself acceptable to his rival. Yet Baker had a hard time trying to get him off the mound; Bush is nothing if not a stubborn competitor. He didn't quit until June.

Now let's draw the thread of George Bush's character pattern through his seven years of service as vice-president.

Bush's transformation from the contender who'd made the most memorable case against "voodoo economics" into a born-again supply-sider occurred virtually overnight. In a pre-inauguration meeting of the president-elect's senior officials on January 7, 1981, Reagan began by telling stories to illustrate the point that they were there to remake the fiscal world. He repeated the rosy generalizations he had espoused throughout the campaign. Then he turned to Bush to ask if he had anything to add.

"Bush replied with a firm negative," wrote David Stockman in *The Triumph of Politics.* "Then he proceeded to rephrase every single one of the generalizations the President had just made."

For the first six months Bush was frozen out by Reagan's inner circle of Californians. But they praise the day he showed his true colors, the day the president was shot. Instinctively, Bush made the judgment, as he flew back from Texas, *not* to land on the White House lawn. Instead, he went home and took a limo to the White House, where he said only a few words and left. While Alexander Haig was grandstanding—"I'm in charge here"—Bush charmed the Cabinet and showed he was not a man to be afraid of. Result: Haig was axed, while Bush was given command of the Special Situations Group, to operate whenever the president was away during an emergency. It may have sounded like a job that carried a great deal of authority, but when the Korean Air plane was shot down by the Soviets, and Bush called his group together because Reagan was in Santa Barbara, Secretary of Defense Weinberger didn't even bother to show up.

"George Bush isn't going to make any decisions," scoffed Weinberger, according to Seymour M. Hersh's book *"The Target Is Destroyed."*

Bush's finest moments, say his aides, have gone mostly unseen by the public. He is said to be superb at delivering tough messages in a diplomatic manner. Not only does he know most of the world's leaders, asserts Bush's national security adviser, Donald Gregg, "He knows what their sensitivities are, and he does not inadvertently twang those sensitivities, as a great many Americans do."

So, when Bush made a swing through Western Europe in the fall of '87, major leaders in West Germany, France, Britain, and Belgium eagerly awaited signals about the upcoming Soviet-American summit and the Persian Gulf crisis. At the very least, they expected to learn from his own lips Bush's ideas about leading the American superpower in the future.

"Nothing, nothing, and nothing," as a West German official summed up the substance of their meetings. Another European official told Jim Hoagland of *The Washington Post*, "When he did speak, it was almost as if he were reading from index cards, rather than telling us anything he thought."

As everyone knows, Bush set great store by his weekly tête-à-têtes with the president. Much of the time was spent swapping jokes, according to those in the know. Some considered this as nothing more than good therapy for the president. Others say that in playing to the president's view of himself as a world-class communicator, Bush deserves some of the credit for softening Reagan's cold-war rhetoric.

But sooner or later it had become clear to all those surrounding the new president that either one allied oneself with Reagan's daydreams and fantasies, or one was out of the loop. Bush had to figure out, *How can I get approval from an unrealistic optimist? By cheerleading for him!* And so, from then until now, throughout his attendance at hundreds of meetings, and despite his access to all of the president's briefing papers, he submitted to Reagan's unreality.

As the public's incredulity turned to revulsion in the first weeks of the Iran-contra revelations, Bush was constantly on the phone, reacting as he always does when pushed to the wall—getting advice from everybody. I asked Donald Gregg at the time whether Bush would have supported Oliver North's secret diversion of money and arms to the contras. Gregg, a former C.I.A. officer operating out of the vice-president's office, selected and supervised the whole cast of American operatives in Nicaragua and has been accused of knowing about North's activities all along. He gave an intriguing answer:

"The vice-president would not have taken a position without looking into the laws that might apply. And I personally," says the man who advises Bush on such matters, "think he wouldn't have found North was breaking any law."

Bush's main status within the Reagan administration, as the man who claims the most foreign-policy savvy, was undercut when it came out that the key Israeli official in the three-way arms dealing, Amiran Nir, had told Bush plainly in Jerusalem in July 1986 that they were "dealing only with the most radical elements" in Iran. "We've learned they can deliver and the moderates can't," Nir told the vice-president. But did Bush introduce this vital piece of reality into Reagan's fantasy? Did he privately try to disabuse the president of the notion he was sending TOW missiles to some nice clean freedom fighters just hiding under their turbans, waiting to spring on the Ayatollah and bring him down with a cake and a Bible?

The most telling of Bush's Iran-contra rationalizations has been this one: "In Ronald Reagan's *mind* it was not arms for hostages. And it was the same for me." If Reagan had said, "I stand for facing the tough choices, let's expose our problems in getting the hostages out to the American people," presumably Bush would have encouraged him to tell all. But since Reagan is a daydreamer, Bush simply endorsed the fantasy.

Bush has not spent seven years as an understudy to the master performer in the White House for naught. Fresh questions were waiting to trip him up in January '88—on the very day of the big Republican debate before the Iowa caucuses. A Republican member of the Iran-contra committee, Warren Rudman, then New Hampshire campaign chairman for Senator Robert Dole, had released an overlooked computer note in which John Poindexter, former national security adviser, said Bush was "solid" in support of a "risky operation" to sell arms to Iran to gain release of American hostages—back in February 1986.

This conflicted with Bush's statements, up to the week before, that if he'd known all the facts he would have told Reagan, "Don't do this."

"Mr. Vice-president," a reporter shouted as Bush stepped out of his plane at Des Moines, "did you know in advance about Bud McFarlane's trip to Teheran?"

With a helicopter buzzing conveniently overhead, Bush cupped his ear, shrugged, and ducked the embarrassing question. It was an exact replay of the stage business used by Reagan hundreds of times as he strode to the helicopter that would take him away, in the middle of Friday afternoon, to relax at Camp David: "What's that? Can't hear. They tell me I've got to go."

Bush has also learned the art of press agentry from his boss. Reagan demonstrated that even in a democracy the president can both avoid the press and control it to his own best advantage. Bush grants one-on-one interviews so rarely, his staff begs him to set aside even two hours a *month* to honor requests that have been waiting for half a year. The only candidate in either party to turn down Marvin Kalb's request to appear on his highly respected *Candidate '88* series was George Bush. I asked Kalb if he saw intimations of another Reagan-style presidency, with Bush insulated from the American press and therefore the public.

"When they tell me it's not going to advance his candidacy to talk to me for an hour," said Kalb, "that in itself confirms the implication of your question."

But despite all the judicious tactics, questions about Bush's role in the Iran-contra affair continued to dog the vice-president. So, under the expert guidance of media adviser Roger Ailes, Bush tried to dispel the issue by going head to head with CBS's Dan Rather. Rather walked right into the trap. The point of the exercise was to paint Bush as the slayer of what movement conservatives see as their archenemy in the media: CBS News in general and Dan Rather in particular. It was a brilliant, if risky, stroke.

The tension mounted as Rather introduced the five-minute taped report that was to precede a live interview with the vice-president. Suddenly, CBS producer Tom Bettag, a phone on each ear, was alarmed to hear the vice-president complaining over the open line from Washington: "Iran-contra affair? . . . I didn't know this was about the Iran-contra affair. Nobody told me. . . . They aren't going to talk to me about Iran-contra, are they? If he talks to me about the Iran-contra affair, they're going to see a seven-minute walkout on their hands."

Then the interview began—and so did the fireworks.

Bush had insisted upon a live interview and that meant limited time. So the vice-president started right off filibustering, eating up the minutes with his usual evasive explanations. Rather managed to point out that a recently uncovered memo indicated Bush had been at the meeting during which Secretary George Shultz made forceful arguments against the arms-for-hostages plan, "and then you said you never heard anybody register objections."

"I've heard George Shultz be very forceful and if I were there and he was very very forceful at that meeting, I would have remembered that. I don't remember that."

"How do you explain that you can't remember it and the other people at the meeting saying he was apoplectic?" Rather persisted.

"Maybe I wasn't there at *that* point."

"You weren't—you weren't in the meeting?"

"I'm not suggesting. I'm just saying I don't remember."

Ailes's theory is that you can win a debate with a sharp line or two, since that's the sound bite most of the electorate will see. He had coached Bush on Rather's weak spot, and now Bush threw his hardball: "How would you like it if I judged your career by those seven minutes when you walked off the set in New York?" he asked the newsman. Rather was indeed thrown off stride.

The sparring continued, pushing the interview way past the time allotted, until Rather's producer finally screamed into his ear, "Cut! Cut! Cut! You gotta cut!"

Rather ended the interview, and many thought he cut the vice-president off somewhat rudely. Bush looked miffed.

Bush campaign manager Lee Atwater was smug the morning after when asked if he had put the vice-president up to the sandbagging of the sandbagger. "We never talk about how we make sausage," Atwater told me. "I am always in favor of going on the offensive, and staying on the offensive."

Bush, campaigning in Wyoming the next day, was all bluster. Chest out, arms high over his head, he walked up the main street as if to say, "Look at me, the new, tough, take-no-prisoners George Bush." He was asked how he'd felt during the interview with Rather.

"It's kinda like combat, isn't it?" he said and giggled.

Well, no. No matter how heated is an exchange with a member of the media, it's not a blood sport. And if the second-ranked man in America can be rattled by a nine-minute TV interview, how does he stand up to Gorbachev, or the obstinate leaders of Israel, or Margaret Thatcher for that matter?

In the immediate aftermath of the tussle, Bush gained some favor with Republican voters. "So much for the wimp factor," crowed his supporters. But the news blitz following the interview would serve only to highlight the fact that serious questions still remained about the vice-president's role in Iran-contra. As one Republican consultant, Douglas Bailey, put it, "The Rather thing was a short-term plus for him. . . . What is a problem for Bush is that somewhere there is a character issue for him."

Furthermore, Bush didn't have the cool to confront Rather successfully. He sounded whiny. And in open-mike remarks following the live broadcast, the vice-president made a few vulgar references to Rather. "That guy makes Lesley Stahl look like a pussy," he said. "The bastard didn't lay a glove on me." His locker-room language smacked of the bluster young adolescent boys engage in to mask the fact that they feel overpowered.

Until February 1988, Reagan had not displayed much interest in the election or in Bush's fate. One G.O.P. leader who tried to talk politics with Reagan received the distinct impression that the president does not much care who his successor will be, and "is just not engaged in 1988 politics one iota." But Reagan did go on record after Bush's confrontation with Rather as saying that the vice-president had been "exactly right" in maintaining silence about any advice he might have given the president. He also reportedly told an aide, "I didn't see any wimp in that." Columnist Lou Cannon suggested that the president had gained a new respect for his second-in-command. But it is also possible that Reagan realizes that the only surefire way to seal permanently the record on Iran-contra is to help Bush into the White House.

Reagan and Bush have echoed each other in hailing a man who lied to Congress, destroyed government documents, and made a mockery of leadership in the White House with his rogue operation: Both have called Ollie North "a national hero." Bush invited Oliver North and John Poindexter to his 1987 Christmas party, three months before criminal indictments closed in on them.

Reagan, when asked whether Bush had been at the meeting when Shultz became "apoplectic" about the prospect of selling arms to a terrorist government, chuckled and covered for Bush: "No, he was not present." Thus Reagan and Bush have stonewalled against White House records, as well as four of the most powerful members of their own administration—Shultz, Weinberger, Meese, and Regan—who have all said in sworn testimony that the vice-president was present at the meeting.

By never having spoken up in all the meetings on the secret Iran dealings where other members of the administration were present, Bush has joined himself at the hip to the president. What they know about how the Iran-contra policy was really made and carried out neither Reagan nor Bush will ever tell. They cover up for each other.

Is it any wonder that Reagan has said, "George Bush is the finest vice-president I ever have any recollection of"?

George Bush's need for Reagan's approval came through loud and clear in the interviews I had with the vice-president. On one such occasion he put his stocking feet up on the couch in the private cabin of Air Force Two and spoke emotionally of the president and the "closeness we have." I asked him how he had cultivated such trust from Reagan. "It took a while, but the president knows now, which he probably didn't know, that I'm not going to betray him. I know that this is the right way to approach this relationship." I asked if he had regrets about remaining steadfastly in Ronald Reagan's shadow. He wrapped one arm in another and rubbed it. "I know I'm right. Even if it wasn't the right way to approach the relationship, the respect and the affection I have from Ronald Reagan would"—his voice was deep and flooded now with feeling—"would dictate to me that I couldn't do it any other way if I wanted to."

The parallel between his relationships with his father and with Reagan seems palpable. To put it in an archetypal context, George Bush will do anything to keep from making the father angry.

Something changed in George Bush since the '80 and '84 presidential seasons. For one thing, he turned sixty. When we spoke in the autumn of 1986, I suggested that is a stage where many people feel a new detachment from goals about which they may have felt intensely only a few years before. "I think there's something to that, yeah," said Bush. "The things that are important aren't how you get from point A to point B, but your values, what's gonna happen to this little kid that I love so much, what's his life gonna be like? It's more than 'Now I gotta really get near the end here, and in this primary plot this and do that.' I mean, I'm past all that."

Bruised by the criticism he took in '84 even as Reagan's running mate, he was not at all enthusiastic about stumping on his own again. Neither was Bar, according to their friend Barry Boardman. "She knows he doesn't need to tack on any more for his *Who's Who* listing."

And it's been twenty years since he won an election on his own.

Was George Bush running, I wondered, only because it was a game to be played, and everyone expected it of him? There was no doubt he would work hard at it; he always does. Whether it's tiddlywinks or a presidential race, once Bush gets in, it's hard to pull him off. He loves to win.

He headed into the primary season with a commanding lead in the polls over his Republican rivals, which made the drubbing he took by Dole in Iowa even more humiliating. But Bush quickly bounced back and settled in with his superior organization for the long ride. After all, he had been campaigning for nine years straight, the past six with all the pomp of a procession from *Aida*—twin helicopters always hovering above Air Force Two, sleek limousines at the ready, roughly two hundred campaign staffers, and a court photographer to record him smiling, always smiling, next to another one among his thousands of instant best friends who will receive an autographed photo as a souvenir—Vice-president Bush could hardly have a more formidable organizational procession in the long effort to reach the White House. The Lou Gehrig seems to have become the Ho Chi Minh of American politics.

But can George Bush lead?

He has always appeared to be driven by two primary needs—to do an A-plus job at every game he plays *and* to make everybody keep on liking him. These are quite compatible goals for a vice-president. They are an oxymoron for a president.

"Niceness shouldn't be a disqualifier for the presidency," Jim Baker insists. "It certainly wasn't for Reagan." Yes, but. There is a dramatic difference between Bush niceness and Reagan niceness. Reagan, while always amiable, keeps his distance from everyone. He knows he is the star, the others merely directors and stagehands. People who mistakenly think his amiability means he needs their approval challenge him at their peril. "Reagan's a really tough politician," says Bush's press secretary, Pete Teeley. "He'll leave them hanging."

A 1977 study by psychologists David Winter and Abigail Stewart, comparing presidents who had a conspicuous need to win social approval with presidents whose primary needs were power and achievement, reached a clear conclusion: "A politician who is obsessed with getting along with others is likely to become a blank spot in the pages of American history." If George Bush becomes the nation's leader, at age sixty-four, he cannot be expected to change a lifelong pattern of deferring to, and needing to please, those more powerful in position or personality.

Furthermore, as a family friend of the Bushes points out, "You could make a case that the worst possible training for the presidency is seven years as vice-president. Seven years of perfecting the habit of never making decisions or speaking up—something has to atrophy."

In sum, what we have in George Bush is a person whose most consistent characteristic is the effort to avoid confrontation, to evade taking charge so he cannot be blamed for things that go wrong.

What happens if this man who has gone out of his way to avoid accepting responsibility for authority becomes the highest political authority in the land? Do his advisers battle among themselves until the strongest personality in his administration emerges to dominate him? More likely, Bush himself would again find a person to play the role of father, a stronger personality who is not afraid to assert himself and be confrontational, so Bush could yield to him.

Who, then, would become the unelected president behind the president? Jim Baker? Barbara Bush? Or a clone of Ollie North, the man whose "passion for what he believes in" Bush extols at length in interviews? As one close observer notes, "You don't see people around Bush who challenge one another, who let intellectual sparks fly. The people around him seem mainly to be staff, not people of the substance or stature of a Kissinger or Cy Vance or McGeorge Bundy. The only two are Jim Baker, who is a heavyweight, and Nick Brady—not a broad-gauge guy." Alternatively, Bush might seek to create a brotherhood of gentlemen through whom assertion, authority, and leadership could be exercised by *committee*. He would be convinced they were all true-blue "nice guys" because, as we know, George Bush cannot believe ill of anybody.

In a world where our closest allies sometimes need the strongest reprimand, where terrorism tests the mettle of every president, where we've all seen how a new Soviet leader can switch effortlessly from charming the crowds on Pennsylvania Avenue to intimidating our opinion leaders in intellectual confrontations, we know one thing for certain. We need a leader who is tough. If George Bush cannot bear to offend people, if he hasn't got the outer strength to pursue a lonely course, if he feels wholly comfortable only when being liked, might he not, as a president, become paralyzed?

ACCELERATED CHANGE

Albert Gore, Jr., like George Bush, was born with a compliant temperament, rarely gets angry, and impresses people as the kind of guy who gets along with everybody. When push comes to shove, Gore would rather be an ambassador than a military man. He, too, has been nurtured and nudged by his family members and a series of mentors. Both men have been shaped by strong mothers and raised in the shadow of dominant fathers who were United States senators.

And Gore is *perceived* as having the same unfair advantage as Bush: an inside track. Isn't he cut from the same Old Guard East Coast mold?

Indeed, Gore was polished at St. Alban's, the elite Episcopalian boys' prep school in Washington, D.C., where the sons of mayors and diplomats, members of Congress and star journalists, are trained to take their places in the political Establishment. English classes at St. Alban's are probably the only ones in America that train boys to write speeches in the formal style, using the "rhetorical triad" and "elevated diction," with references such as Churchill's Dunkirk speech.

One day a random group of St. Alban's students agreed to stay after lunch to talk to me. One was Korean, one black; the rest had princely blond locks and hairless faces. Moustaches and beards are forbidden, and as for earrings—well! this is a Right Stuff school. After all, two of the first astronauts graduated from St. Alban's. And so, buttoned down in de rigeur jackets and ties, the boys dine in the atmosphere of a private men's club, with servers hovering over them whilst they speak in paragraphs. Yet all the while they know they are historical errors.

"We all understand the environment we're growing up in," said William and John. "It detracts from Gore in our perspective." They all acknowledged it was the best education one could find, but, well, "in terms of the real world . . . ," and then they blurted it out: "You really have to respect someone like Jackson. He started in the real world and then elevated himself." John summed up the feeling in this quarter. "When you hear Jackson, you think of civil rights, when you hear Bush, you think of experience. When you hear Gore, you really don't think of anything."

It is a measure of the discomfort all Americans feel around blatant evidences of class privilege that even those who have it knock it. But Gore is not another Bush. Whereas Bush chose the path of passivity and conformity to social class, committing himself to being liked and preserving the status quo, Gore began as compliant by temperament but chose an active path. Over the last ten years Gore has shown feistiness—both to win elections and to set himself apart from his rivals by confronting them on serious issues—at the risk of being branded by his party a disruptive brat.

What makes Gore an accelerated changer, rather than a passive changer, may be the result of a very important distinction between his father's background and the long, prosperous history of the Bush family.

Albert Gore, Sr., did know what it was to be poor, and was restricted in education because of his family's sorry condition during the Depression. Compensating for the limitations he himself had faced, the elder Gore started pushing his son's development very early and pushed him very hard. He is still pushing his son, with even more urgency, as the end of his own life approaches.

Neither Bush nor Gore, therefore, has the luxury of listening to a clear inner voice that tells them when and how to make the critical moves in their lives. The voice of an inner guardian-censor, implanted by their powerful fathers, probably always will be difficult to tune out in order to hear their own.

But Al Gore's inner voice, when it *does* make itself heard—which may be only in his dreams—does *not* necessarily echo his father's.

"Hey, Al, are you going to move the tree?" was the question Leon Wieseltier, a friend from the *New Republic* crowd, kept asking. It was code for: Are you going to run for president? At dinner one sweltering night in the summer of '86, Gore had confided a dream. He was working the land and came upon a tree that needing moving. But he decided in the dream to put it off.

He told Wieseltier he was convinced that moving the tree symbolized running for president.

Yet in 1988 Gore came on like a presidential fetus—one could almost see the cells stretching, pulling, pop!—dividing at double the normal speed. Even as he labors to sound older and wiser than his years, candidate Gore today likes to point to evidence of his accelerated spurts of growth.

SIX

Al Gore:
The Son Also Rises

So young.

Albert Gore, Jr., was conceived after D day and born into the first generation to grow up under the shadow of nuclear war, with television and spaceships as companions. He was barely toilet-trained when he met President Truman, and just starting school at the time of *Brown* v. *Board of Education.* Vice-president Nixon sat the boy on his lap on the podium high above the U.S. Senate and gave him the gavel to play with. He was in high school when John Kennedy was assassinated. Too young to join the great civil-rights marches in the South. But he was old enough to volunteer for Vietnam and to come home with scars on his soul, belly-sick of his country's politics run amok.

So young. His face was pale and his lower lids red and puffy the first time I met Al Gore, in the lobby of a Holiday Inn in New Hampshire. It was ten at night and he'd just finished a long debate. "So, where do we go now?" he asked his staffers. "No plants we can visit?"

Hearing I was a jogger, he asked if I'd like to join him in the morning. "What's our drive time to the first stop tomorrow?" Five minutes, said a staffer. "I've got to leave more time than that for my hair to dry," said Gore. "See you at five forty-five?"

The knock came at exactly that ungodly hour. Friday, the thirteenth of November. Outside, New Hampshire was lightless, 35 degrees, groaning under an ice cap from a freakish storm.

Gore stood barelegged in the motel corridor, clad in a T-shirt, shorts, and cap. Not a crease or ripple or age spot. And his hands! No wormy veins, the knuckles without a single pucker. He looked so preposterously young I couldn't suppress a smile. He stared back gravely. So off I went, running with this thirty-nine-year-old colt of a country boy who was running for president of the United States.

He looks like a boy. As he warms to his subject in a speech, his ears often turn red and waxy, and somehow he always seems to be just growing out of the dumb blue suits he wears. He walks like a boy, head thrown back and feet f ping sideways. He eats like a boy, chomping down on a roll oozing barbecue behind the banquet speaker in the few minutes they give him between speeches. But he never, ever, talks like a boy.

On the contrary, he can often appear dry and wooden, stiff and stuffy—"an old person's idea of a young person," in columnist Michael Kinsley's memorable phrase. His handsome face looks as if it had been planed, and the eyes have that too-close-together Harvard squint. His father says he has the hardest time persuading Gore to use his sense of humor in public speeches. His mother despairs of getting him to smile.

In a New Hampshire high-school gym in January 1988, he came across like a superintendent of schools. His answers appealed to reason, unlike Jesse Jackson's, which are fired like shoulder-held missiles straight at the brain's emotional silo. Only when he was hounded by a rabid little right-to-lifer, who wanted him to send women who commit abortions away to the federal pen, did Gore's passion for fairness punch through the rhetoric. "I think abortion is wrong, but I don't think the federal government knows enough to go in and tell a woman who is pregnant against her will, 'Look, we don't care whether you want to go through with it or not, we don't care whether it's a result of circumstances you didn't want, we're going to force you to go through with a pregnancy.' "

The audience—20 percent strongly opposed to abortion—erupted with applause. Gore's straight-ahead, candid answers are his most attractive quality on the stump, often winning people even when they don't agree with him. But even his most

ardent supporters admit that his speaking style oscillates between banal and brilliant.

Politeness characterizes Gore's opening to any speech anywhere—"Distinguished guests, ladies and gentlemen . . ."—but
the formality seems misplaced when he stands before only
twenty or so mug-grippers at a luncheonette. After some gentle
down-home stories, his voice suddenly jumps register and lands
on the word "leadership," as if a bad D.J. had cut in on a
Tennessee waltz with a Sousa march by simply dropping the
needle. To convey emotion, he has but one technique, like the
rock 'n' roll stars of his youth: Turn up the volume.

But something happens when Gore goes south.

The instant he stepped into the limpid embrace of the Carolina air, he started warming up. Formality melted into informality. The academic turned into the anecdotalist. Shut your eyes
and you could almost tell how deep into Dixie we had gone by
his accent. "We *cain't* have that." "We share *tobaccah* . . ."
"The farmer's *vee-hick-ul.*" It was not a put-on; it was a thawing
out in this softer environment that suits the genteel liberalism
Albert Gore, Jr., inherited from his father, Senator Albert Gore,
Sr., whose fourteen years in the House and three terms in the
Senate were ennobled by his refusal to sign Strom Thurmond's
segregationist Southern Manifesto and by his early and unrelenting opposition to the Vietnam War.

Gore Jr. talked to his greater-kinfolk network, black and
white, about how "we, as southerners, have a special bond."
Striking deep into Jesse country, he showed up in New Orleans
for the powerful Conference of Southern Black Democrats. Com-
bining presidential sincerity and a lung-belting Baptist
preacher's passion, he had the all-black audience moaning responses. "Come on, Preacher." "Come on now, lay it on."

Gore's cultural affinity for Dixie is obviously something he
can taste. He was thrilled by walking into a fund-raiser in
Fayetteville at the luxurious home of Larry Shaw, a black entrepreneur, and feeling the comfort of a roomful of black southerners listening to and laughing with a white politician. "That
couldn't have happened fifteen years ago." The turnover in
marrow that Gore has experienced as a progressive white south-

erner renders his commitment to civil-rights issues less conflicted than that of many northerners who fancy themselves
liberals. As he puts it, "I've been thinkin' about this issue since
I been thinkin'."

It shows in his rapport with Jesse Jackson. The two southern
candidates were often seated next to each other at the endless
Democratic debates, where they traded sotto-voce jokes. At one
such gathering, Richard Gephardt was trying to sell the oil-
import tax by using an analogy from his childhood. "When I was
a child," Gephardt intoned, "my mother gave me cod-liver oil
every day, every day." "Jesse," Gore whispered to Jackson,
"did your mother give you cod-liver oil every day when you were
growing up?" "No," Jesse said. A beat. "But I wasn't full of shit
either."

Soaring back from New Orleans after his stem-winding
speech, Gore was positively giddy with good humor. Popping
M & M's and crooning country tunes—"Awall my exes live in
Texas, that's whaaa I hang my hat in Tinnissee"—guzzling
Coke and doing imitations, he even tried card tricks, flopped,
threw up his hands, and turned to burlesquing a black Baptist
minister.

Yet for all his lighter moments, the ancestral occupation is
never far from his mind. His progenitors, mustered out of the
Revolutionary War, were given a land grant in Livingston,
Tennessee, and by 1907 a blind Oklahoma cousin had become
the first southern Senator Gore. When Al was twelve, his father
took him to Jamestown to see a plaque with the names of the
original settlers. There was Brinton—MASON. And somebody
named Cassen—LABORER. When they came to the name Gore—
GENTLEMAN, his father remembers, he watched for young Al's
reaction.

"We've slipped a little, haven't we, Dad?"

So young. And yet so worldly-wise.

Albert Gore, Jr., has always lived two lives in one. Political
articles kept trying to pigeonhole him. "He's either a smoothy
from St. Alban's and Harvard or a down-home farmer-politician
from the hills of rural Tennessee," proclaimed *Regardie's* magazine. But what is intriguing about Gore is that he is both. There

is the country boy inside Gentleman Gore. There is also the young man inside the old man. He is a divided man from a divided generation.

When I asked him to tell me his life story, Gore's first words were "I've always lived two places, two lives." There were two homes (Washington, D.C., and Carthage, Tennessee), two schools (St. Alban's prep school and a rural southern public school), two families (the farm manager and his wife, with whom young Gore often lived, and the peripatetic father and mother they referred to as "Miz Gore and them"). There were two sets of friends, two sweethearts. Every Sunday he went to a different church: Mother was Church of Christ and Father a Baptist. As a teenager Gore chose to join a one-room, plain-board country Baptist church in Carthage with pews lumpy from hundreds of coats of paint and equipped with paper fans, the image of Jesus Christ on one side and a funeral-home ad on the other. Then there was Washington's National Cathedral, with its Gothic stone spires and one-tenth-of-a-mile walk up to the high altar where one's knees sank into needlepoint cushions. This is where St. Alban's boys attended important services and where, in 1970, Private Gore would be married to his picture-book-pretty wife with a full choir resounding through the Gloria in Excelsis tower.

Gore's natural dividedness explains a lot about the double image he projects. "Everybody thinks he's a put-on," says Steve Armistead, his best friend throughout childhood. "But Al's always been both ways—stiff-looking when he's around new people, but when he gets close in with people he knows well, he lets loose and there's always a lot of laughs."

Today, as his redoubtable wife, Tipper, continues her crusade against rock 'n' roll smut-and-violence peddlers, Al Gore still loves to go to raunchy comedy clubs. He sings rock 'n' roll whenever there are no tape recorders around, even likes Frank Zappa, who has branded his bride a "cultural terrorist." But he prefers country-and-western tunes. One of his favorites is apt: "I Got My Feet in Dixie but My Head in the Cold Cold North."

Non-southerners think of Gore as a younger Jimmy Carter. The two are decidedly different. Carter is a southerner from the South, with all the problems of parochial insecurity that implies.

Gore is a southerner educated in the North. Not for him any of the complexes about Harvard that bedeviled both Lyndon Johnson and Jimmy Carter. And growing up in the Fairfax Hotel on Embassy Row gave him an insider's confidence in the game of Washington politics.

Still, on the last day of every term at his Washington school, Al was already packed and raring for the all-night drive to Tennessee. It was an easy choice for a young boy, as Gore describes it, "between a small hotel room on the eighth floor in a big, impersonal city, and a two-hundred-fifty-acre farm with horses and canoes and all the outdoors, where you knew everybody and everybody knew you." When I asked Gore where he felt most at home, he answered, "Carthage. Always."

Passing Salt Lick Creek, an hour outside of Nashville, one sees a sign: ENTERING BIG AL COUNTRY. The farms of Albert Gore Sr. and Jr. spread over several hundred acres of loafy hills on either side. The population of Carthage, roughly 2,700, has hardly changed since the late forties and fifties, when the family spent every school holiday, summer, and congressional recess here.

The way the sign dominates Carthage, Al's father dominated his childhood. Several times in thirty-two years, the senior Gore was among those mentioned in the Democratic presidential field. "I looked in the mirror each time and thought I might be seeing a president," Big Al has said. "I found it was a hallucination." He saved up those grander visions for his son.

There was a compelling reason why young Al was sent to be polished at one of the best schools. Gore Sr., born in Possum Hollow, in the country outside Carthage, in a home without running water or electricity, came of age just as the Depression hit. After working his way through Murfreesboro State Teachers College, he had to commute to the Nashville Y.M.C.A. to take night classes in law after teaching school all day. Decades later, when President Kennedy sent him to nuclear-weapons-test conferences, Gore Sr. was painfully aware, amid the multilingual delegates, that the only other tongue he knew was Tennessee hillbilly. One can almost hear his silent vow: *I'm not going to allow my boy to be a southern hick. I'm going to make him the perfect version of me, so that he can be unbeatable.* "If I may be a little proud," father can say aloud of son today, "his grammar is as near perfect in extemporaneous speeches as you can come by. You can just see the commas falling in."

But the senator was not going to have his son alienated from his southern heritage either. "Mr. Gore always had him to get up early just like the farmhands," said Mattie Lucy Payne, who worked for the Gores. Mrs. Gore pleaded mercy for the boy. Pauline Gore is no slouch herself, being one of the first women graduates of Vanderbilt Law School and a practicing corporate lawyer early on. She has long been seen as even keener than her husband, always interjecting common sense into his lofty rhetoric. But Al senior laid down the law: "I'm not going to have a boy who lays up in the bed!"

Steve Armistead, a boy from a poor holler up the road, became young Al's best friend. "He didn't have any privileges," recalls Armistead, who spent many a twelve-hour day hoeing and weeding the Gores' tobacco fields right beside their son. "I guess I was a little severe," reflects Al senior today, "but I didn't want my son to have the easy tasks."

The elder Gore brought his son into the world of politics almost as soon as the boy could walk. After attending his first nuclear-weapons conference at the age of four, young Al would follow his father anywhere. At six, Al took a bus by himself to Nashville to hear Senator Gore speak. Having traveled back and forth with his father between Carthage and Washington on tiny, twisting Tennessee roads, young Al was all ears when he attended the Senate hearings on the interstate highway system his father proposed. They had their first debate. Al wanted to know why his father opposed billboards—how would anybody know where to stop for ice cream?

At the dinner table Al listened to his two professional parents wrestle with the issues of the day. As a pre-adolescent, he would be brought into all his father's most important confabs with the Kennedys, House Speaker Sam Rayburn, William Fulbright. "My father encouraged that. 'Son, we need some iced tea,' he would say, then motion to me. 'Sit right here, son, right here.' " Gore Sr. let him eavesdrop, at fourteen, on a particularly heated phone conference with the president. Little Al's ears turned crimson on hearing J.F.K.'s scatalogical saltiness.

But when young Al was called upon to speak on his father's behalf for the first time, in a black church, he found himself tongue-tied. To stand in the giant footsteps of his father was awesome. "What the boy's trying to say," belted out the black preacher once Al had finished, "is, come Election Day, git out and vote for his daddy!"

Gore's temperament did not render him a natural politician, any more than he was born a champion athlete. But from infancy, Al was ever agreeable, the ideal clay for his father to mold. "Always a sweet baby, an easy baby," hums Mattie Lucy, who filled his childhood with fudge and fried chicken. "Just most anything you did for him he loved." His mother found him agreeable almost to a fault. "He was very active," says Pauline Gore, "but we weren't ever sure just what he was thinking about."

One Christmas his parents gave him a pony. Ecstatic, he told them, "Every wish I ever made, I wanted a pony."

"I wanted to cry," remembers his mother. "He'd never said a word about wanting a pony. He never pushed for things, never rebelled when he was young." Their daughter, Nancy, ten years older than Al, was the opposite. "I always said Al wanted to find out what you wanted to do and do it," says Mrs. Gore. "Nancy wanted to find out what you wanted to do and do something else—a total nonconformist."

He attended the local country school for a few weeks at the end of every summer and when his folks were away on long trips, leaving young Al on the farm. Miss Eleanor Smotherman, a dedicated spinster teacher who to this day takes her own bread into the coffee shop to be toasted so as to confine her expenses to coffee, had Al Gore in her second-grade class. She set him to tutoring the rural kids, who trucked in with their runny viruses and poor corpuscles from hollers that weren't even places, only near places. "When I conversed with him," recalls Miss Smotherman today, "I almost had to look at him to see whether he was a child or an adult."

"He always seemed older," affirms Alota Thompson, wife of the farm manager and a kind of second mother to Al. "He was always doing things that, well, he wasn't hardly old enough for," such as sitting on her husband's tractor at age seven or eight, "wanting to guide it."

But there was also the natural, ultracompetitive, all-male young boy inside the sage little Gentleman Gore. He and Steve Armistead matched up too well as athletes, so their competition carried over to daredevil tricks on water skis. One day Al told Steve he was going to get up holding the tow rope behind his back. He hooked a life cushion over his back, but when Armistead jackknifed the boat out of the shallows, Al catapulted into a capsule of water so high and dense, Steve shouted, "Are you drowned?" From somewhere inside the water capsule, a voice called back, "No, I'm breathing in here, keep going."

They found other ways to test their country-boy macho: diving into the icy Caney Fork River in March—a tradition Gore still maintains. Sneaking the senior Gore's car, driving like desperadoes shooting their way out of a stickup, "We'd flip rocks from the driver's side across the roof and try to hit street signs," says Armistead. "It was kinda like shooting a gun." Al hit the hay feeder and lost control on several occasions before the day he finally flipped the car altogether. He came walking home, barefoot, tail between his legs. Mrs. Gore was just glad to see him alive.

Even on the farm, however, Al had his sensitive and serious moments. He talked to Steve about being in political life. "He was enthralled by it. The big picture had been painted for him." He talked as though it was his destiny to be a United States senator, like his father, who was his hero. And, always, he wanted to bring his good country friends into the bigger world with him. "I'm fixing to do a lot of things," Al told Armistead when he got him a job as an intern in his father's office, "and I would like you to be with me."

One holiday, Gore was fixed up by Armistead with his sister Donna, one of the gang of four—along with Steve, Ed Blair, today a state trooper, and Gordon Thompson, a factory worker—who remain Al's best friends in Tennessee. "I thought he was going to be kind of immature and smarty," says Donna, "like most boys of fourteen. But always he was being serious." In the backseat at the drive-in he and Donna talked politics all through the show. Before he took her home that night, Al brought Donna in to meet his mother, and for the next three years they went steady.

By now, Donna has accumulated the solidity of several grain sacks piled together; but "we're talking a hundred pounds ago, when I had a twenty-two-inch waist," she says wistfully. Sometimes, snuggled in Al's den, listening to Ray Charles purr, "I can't stop luuuhving you," they had urges they didn't know what to do about. Donna remembers his amazingly intelligent mother saying, "Hey, you kids, let's not get in trouble here. You could work out in the gym for an hour. And there's always cold showers."

Donna found Al unfailingly thoughtful and attentive. Like everyone else I interviewed, she couldn't remember his ever getting mad. "He's a country sort of gentleman." Away at school, he would write to her twice a day, like a diary, and save up seven dollars a week to phone her on Saturday night.

On the flip side of his life, at St. Alban's, Al came under the personal moral tutelage of Canon Charles Martin with his porcelain-blue Episcopalian complexion and steel-pointed eyes and bulldog underbite: "But he was always the Tennessee boy," demurs the canon. "His sense of values and liberal tendencies were developed by the time he got here, because of his tight family." Gore's temperament—always looking for what was wanted and giving it—found perfect resonance with the clear rules and sedate social life of St. Alban's. When it came to cracking heads with "less talented but scrappier" football teams, St. Alban's was simply too gentlemanly to avoid humiliating defeats. Team Captain Gore tried to make up for those losses in basketball. According to his coach, he kept staying after practice to perfect his jump shot.

In his senior yearbook Al's classmates called him "the epitome of the all-American young man," but also "frighteningly good at many things." Behind his back they gave even freer vent to their envy, calling him "Ozymandias," after the king who cried, "Look on my works, ye mighty, and despair!"

More than anyone seems to notice, Al Gore's persistence—and impatience—are what have paid off for him. Just as he worked at taming a pony and driving a tractor too big for him, he later started too slow as a journalist, but soon got up to speed and began breaking prizewinning stories. The same pattern has held in his political career. He is stiff and formal as he enters the competition at each new level of the game. But after an awkward and ridiculous start, he plugs away impatiently until he masters the key skills. Once he is good enough to relax a little, he appears so effortlessly confident that others assume he was born that way—damn him.

They fail to understand what drives him—the need to fulfill his father's dream and the fear that he may fail to do so.

Young Al did not pull up roots according to the normal timetable. He maintained close ties with his parents until his early twenties. Rather than rebelling, he was always at pains to do twice as well as expected, so as never to be seen as coasting on his father's coattails. "He would fight you if you said to him, 'You've got an easy out—your father's a U.S. senator,' " Armistead recalls. Al worried himself to death that people would say he got into Harvard on preferential treatment. In fact, Gore was a National Merit Scholar, and received a scholarship from Harvard. Because Al Gore doesn't really *have* to, he has to all the more.

He came roaring into Cambridge, Massachusetts, after Christmas on the motorcycle he'd saved up to buy secondhand, driving it straight through from Washington and turning up in Harvard Yard *blue*. Savvy boys from northern suburbs, like John Tyson, at first look chalked him up to the bad element that Harvard was attracting in its egalitarian lurch. Tyson came out of an elite, black upper-middle-class family in Montclair, New Jersey. He assumed this big, galumphing southern boy with his hick bluegrass music—one of the first white southerners he'd ever met—was some dumb slugabed and social Neanderthal.

But Al persisted in getting to know Tyson. Anticipating the need to compensate for the social confines of a place like St. Alban's and the narrowness of the segregated South, Al had wanted a black roommate. "We really came to terms with each other to the point where race did not matter at all," says Gore, acknowledging, "That's hard, surprisingly hard." Tyson says that "the most important thing I learned from Al was not to be prejudiced myself." Today an international business investor,

Tyson remains one of Gore's best friends. With Al Gore, say his intimates, once a friend, always a friend. And the choice of those friends—multiracial, from farmhands to Harvard professors—reflects a natural humanism and an openness that is never awkward or forced.

This quality was one of the things that his future wife found so appealing in Al Gore. Mary Elizabeth "Tipper" Aitcheson was a paradigm of the pretty, popular blonde. Gore first laid eyes on her at his high-school senior prom. He called the next day and Tipper soon discovered that he couldn't make cocktail-party chitchat worth a damn. "Going to debutante balls was the most important thing in the world to many of the kids I knew," says Tipper. "He was odd, he rejected all this." But this Hickory Kid on the deb circuit, with his solid country values and embarrassing polyester suits and oh-so-serious worldviews, "spoke to something in me that didn't go along with that other world, either."

Tell me the inside story of the Bay of Pigs again, she breathed.

Immediately after school ended, Gore invited her down to the family farm. "It was a bad case," smirks Big Al, who says he will never forget the next morning, at breakfast, when "she came out dressed fit to kill, her eyelashes done up, every hair in place, ready to go before the footlights! A doll, just as pretty as a doll."

Al and Tipper stuck to each other from the start. Neither dated anyone else all through college, and they married after graduation. The counterculture peaked during their college days. All norms were dissolved. Pot was everywhere. But Al and she "wanted to be very careful," as Tipper says. "We saw the dangers, we were seeing people let everything else fall away, and we did not want that to happen. It didn't mean we didn't occasionally indulge. We did." But, Tyson asserts, "no way in the world Al was a pothead."

Radicalism never attracted the Gores, either. Al loudly resisted being mau-maued into supporting violent actions. But he still carries a menacing image in his head of the 1968 Democratic convention in Chicago. While his father was inside as a delegate, Gore was on the street when army jeeps bore down on the kids with movie cameras. "Slowly, systematically, they were taking faces. I remember when the lens came right to me, staring into it." Tipper adds, "Kent State was just like they shot us. I can remember calling home and saying, 'Hi, J. Edgar.' "

Instead of throwing bombs, Al cultivated mentors. Signing up for an independent-study program under Richard Neustadt, a political scientist often consulted by J.F.K., Gore turned himself inside out to produce a high-profile, 103-page thesis on the emerging influence of television on the presidency. Professor Martin Peretz took such a liking to Al and Tipper, he'd often invite them to his weekend place on Cape Cod. Today, as editor-in-chief of *The New Republic*, Peretz cannot publish enough praise of his former student. Older men have always naturally assumed a mentor role with young Al Gore. He is accustomed to being deferential to older pros, having fitted himself to that mold in his relationship with his father. Gore listens. Rather than coming on like a young Turk grabbing at the reins of power, he is the respectful disciple who incorporates their experience. It is one of his most attractive qualities to the men—and women—who can do him the most good.

Gore also studied with Erik Erikson, father of life-cycle theory, whose seminal work, *Identity: Youth and Crisis*, prompted Al to do a psychobiography of his father. When I asked if that research had helped him to pull away from his father and declare his own identity, Gore laughed it off. "Oh, I was beyond that by then." Then he caught himself and mused, "Well, maybe it did, a little." I asked the family's farm manager, William Thompson, how the younger Gore is different from his father. "Their ways is about alike," he replied.

The perfect progression of the perfectly groomed political heir was stopped dead in its tracks by the Vietnam War. As Tipper remembers, "You didn't think about getting on with your life, you thought about getting through the war, stopping the war." The draft was upon Al Gore, Jr., in the summer of 1969. It was a time of terrible decision. All through college, with swelling pride, he had watched his father stand tall against the war in Vietnam in the televised Senate Foreign Relations Committee hearings. But Gore Sr.'s antiwar stance placed him on the precipice of defeat in his fourth Senate race. The challenger, Bill Brock, was making hay with the fact that young Gore was a known antiwar protester. The best way for young Al to defuse the issue was to go to the war he detested.

And there were other considerations. "Hey, if you're ever going to have a career in politics, if you don't go to Vietnam, you can hang it up," homeboy Armistead told him. "The main influence on my decision was Carthage," says Gore. "My draft board was there—those people had known me all my life. If I was removed from the pool, one of my friends would have had to go in my place."

Pauline Gore reportedly told her son if he chose to go to Canada she would go with him. "I wanted to emphasize our feeling he should make up his own mind," Mrs. Gore explains, "free of any effect it would have on Albert's campaign." She also expressed her concern that he would be killed. "Oh, Mother, you don't understand," she remembers him replying. "I just don't want to be *made* to kill."

When young Al Gore volunteered to go off to war, he was unprepared for the cruel ironies that lay ahead. The Nixon administration held up his shipping-out orders until after the election, the family presumes, so that no son of Senator Gore would go getting himself killed and galvanizing a sympathy vote. And while Gore Jr. dug trenches as a private at Fort Rucker, Alabama, candy-fortune heir Bill Brock sat back and smeared Al's father, claiming the senator's antiwar statements were responsible for helping the North Vietnamese brainwash American P.O.W.'s.

Meanwhile, Al kept up his usual agreeable demeanor. Echoing friends from every stage of his life, his Mexican-American buddy at Fort Rucker, Richard Abalos, says, "Al was the kind of guy who got along with everybody, no pretensions whatsoever." Al's pride in helping make campaign commercials for his father is clear in Abalos's memory. Gore Jr. described one of them to him, "My father and I are riding across our farm, he's on a white horse and I'm on the brown horse, and just before we ride off into the sunset"—he smiled for political emphasis—"we turn left." In the voice-over, Gore Sr. said, "Son, always love your country."

A further blow was his father's brutal defeat in November 1970. "It was a bitter campaign," says the senior Gore, clenching his teeth even today against saying any more. (In one of those wry twists of fate, Bill Brock is now Bob Dole's campaign chairman.) "When he lost, it was the same feeling you have when somebody dies," recalls Tipper. The day of Gore Sr.'s defeat also raised the stakes on his son's political future. The old gray fox stood to make his concession, speaking in his rounded Tennessee tones. Suddenly turning in the direction of his son, eyes flashing in defiance, Albert Gore, Sr., rattled the saber of the father who will be avenged: *"Someday, and someday soon . . . I know that the truth . . . shall rise again . . . in Tennessee!"*

"Al was disillusioned, but not to the point of dropping out," recalls Abalos. "Not until he went to Vietnam and saw the consequences of politics."

What hit Al Gore at a gut level was seeing the atrocities that were an inevitable part of almost any tour in Vietnam. As an army reporter, "I took my turn regularly on the perimeter in these little firebases out in the boonies. Something would move, we'd fire first and ask questions later." According to his army buddy Bob Delabar, "Al and I wanted to be more ambassadors than soldiers. It really got to him to see the U.S. debasing itself by carrying on an armed conflict rather than using civilized means of resolving problems."

The toll taken by Gore's six months in Vietnam was reflected in his letters to friends who stayed behind in Alabama. Gore wrote about seeing women and children being cut in half by America's Huey helicopter gunships. Abalos remembers in particular one "eerie letter" in which Gore wrote, "When, and if, I get home from Vietnam, I'm going to divinity school to atone for my sins."

"I didn't know how hard it would be on me," Gore told me, admitting there were psychic scars he had to take time off to heal. And yet, for all the horror and revulsion he had felt there, his tour in Vietnam had been the most *intense* experience of his life. Nobody back in the land of the walking numb seemed to understand; nothing of mundane civilian life matched the livid colors of a war where young men felt they were doing something important. The crazy part, he confided, was he wanted to go back.

The final irony was that none of Gore Jr.'s old Carthage gang had had to serve. Neither had more than half of the 234 sons of senators and congressmen who became eligible; only 28 had gone to Vietnam. Back home, with his natural confidence in both himself and his government shaken to the point of bitter disillusionment, and burdened with his father's political defeat—the symbolic death of his hero—young Gore turned away from politics as if from a betrayed dream.

"He could hardly make up his mind on what he wanted to do after he came back, and then the marijuana thing" recalls Donna Armistead Rankin, who saw a different Al Gore return to Carthage. "He was truly doing some soul-searching in that period."

At this point, aged twenty-three, Gore might have chosen to remain locked in, suffering from father's-footsteps disease. Safe but stifled, the familiar men who fall into this trap are reluctant to take risks or be too different, are good at tasks but poor at self-reflection. Almost inevitably, their compulsively calm exteriors rupture later, in their forties. But Al Gore resisted being lost to conformity.

"There came a time when he had to find his own identity and be different," affirms his father. "This manifested itself after he came back from Vietnam. I encouraged him to take part in Young Democrat functions, but he was really turned off by politics."

Al had been sensitized early on to the uglier underbelly of political life. "Through a child's eyes, I felt as if I saw through a lot of the conceits and trappings of power." Having had many intimate experiences with politicians—including, at times, his father—who believed they were indispensable to a cause or constituency, Gore developed what he now calls his "hubris alarm." Yet it had been a source of wonder to see what politics could accomplish, to see his father literally move the earth, helping to launch one of the largest public-works projects in world history—an interstate highway system clear across the United States. Over the next five years, while Al attempted to fulfill his destiny outside the world of politics, his parents never pushed him. They admit to hoping he would come back, but "we didn't articulate it," says Pauline Gore, "not even to ourselves."

Tipper and Al moved out to Carthage and attempted a "back to nature" existence. They grew their own vegetables and had a baby. Al senior, then working for Armand Hammer as chairman of Island Creek Coal Company, a subsidiary of Occidental Petroleum, nudged them to start up a homebuilding business. Al junior successfully developed several tracts, but his heart wasn't in it. He broke out on his own only when he took his first job as a newspaper reporter. Tipper had sent his army-newspaper clips to editor John Seigenthaler, who hired him for the Nashville *Tennessean.* Seigenthaler became Al's first professional mentor, and one of the most influential. Gore believed he had finally found his one true course in life: not merely to be a journalist, but to work his way to a Pulitzer Prize.

"He was as enthusiastic about the police beat as he was about the metro beat," says Tipper, not without showing her own lack of enthusiasm. Her husband would become so engrossed in his job, he'd often spend the night on the couch at the newspaper office. She finally gave up on the idyllic country life and moved into town, taking a part-time job as a photojournalist. When Al got a tip-off about a city councilman taking bribes, he and the newspaper carried their investigation to the point of photographing a payoff. But a mistrial allowed the accused man to go free, and "it shocked Al," says his wife. Having "atoned" at Vanderbilt University divinity school for two years—while working the night shift at *The Tennessean,* and with no intention of being ordained—he decided to go on to study law at the university. Although he continued to write editorials for the newspaper, Gore was beginning to feel frustrated with the limitations of journalism; as he approached thirty, he wanted something more.

One day Gore got a call alerting him to a congressional seat that was unexpectedly coming vacant. He put down the phone, dropped to the floor, and started doing push-ups. The instant decision to run for political office at the age of twenty-seven reflected Gore's feeling that his life course was obedient to a higher logic. He says he found a jolt of energy like nothing he had ever felt before. All along, at a subconscious level, the family destiny seems to have guided him like a secret tiller. As Tipper notes with resignation, remembering the shock of suddenly having to give up her own nascent career, "All was right with the world."

Moments before he stood in his father's footsteps, all spiffed up, ready to announce his candidacy from the Smith County Courthouse, where four decades earlier Gore Sr. had launched his political career, Al junior went to the men's room and threw up. His first handshakes and attempts at making a political pitch were abominably stiff; he kept working at it. His need to resurrect his defeated father turned this first race into an obsession. "He felt like he had to overcome his father's beating," confirms Armistead. "He overkilled—he'd go back and go back and go back."

Yet even during that first campaign he struggled to separate himself from his father: "Hold up, Dad, this has got to be my race. I just can't run as my father's candidate." He made Big Al pledge not to campaign for him, not even one speech. When a supporter came up from a southern county to beg, "Don'cher want the boy to win?" his father stood adamant, though it almost killed him. "How 'bout his mother?" the supporter persisted.

So off went Pauline, to tell crowds about her two Alberts. "I trained both of them, and I did a better job with my son." His mother's input has always been critical. "Al really relies on her as his most sensitive barometer—they're very close," says Armistead. And Nancy, the minute her kid brother phoned, rolled up her sleeves and went to work to secure all the toughest counties for him. It was like old times, when the two had campaigned together for their father.

Once elected, determined to make up for his father's failure to stay in touch with constituents while he roamed the world taking lofty foreign-policy stands, Gore Jr. overcompensated, holding 1,200 town meetings in the next eight years. By the time Howard Baker's Senate seat came available in 1983, Gore was a shoo-in as the new Tennessee legend—almost.

For in the middle of that first Senate campaign, the cold slap of fate hit Al Gore. His beloved sister was dying. Lung cancer. Breaking away to see Nancy became more surreal each time:

that slender, green-eyed, globe-trotting girl who'd helped found the Peace Corps—how could it be? He'd always looked upon her as indestructible. Nancy did not know her illness was terminal. She suffered in the extreme, but resisted heavy medication to remain lucid. Her husband, Frank Hunger, remembers her pleasant, alert conversation the night before her final struggle. "She received medication the next morning," and as far as he knew, "she did not come to for the next twelve hours until her death."

But Al spent several hours alone that day with his gallant sister, and there came a moment—one transcendent, heart-shattering moment—when the full powerlessness of his humanity came upon him. Swimming up out of the whirlpool of drugs, his sister came to focus and fiercely searched his face. "Her eyes said it all," Gore remembers: *Is there anything I can do to save myself? Tell me and I'll do it, or tell me no.* The tears in his eyes were his only answer.

I asked Pauline Gore if her son, thirty-six when he went through that harrowing time, was moved to think about his own mortality. "Probably not," she replied candidly. "It had a tremendous impact on him—he was surprised at the devastation of death—but probably not that much."

When his wife learned on April 1, 1987, that Al Gore was deciding whether to run for president, Tipper hit the roof. "Shock therapy—you continue to do it to me," she told her husband. Sure, there had been that article in *The Washington Monthly* about Al as a long shot for the White House, but she had tried to ignore the gathering claque. "I thought, well, that's nice, his career, people telling me, 'Your husband looks wonderful,' thank you very much."

Then, in March, Al had spoken to a group of powerful Democrats known as IMPAC '88. They had interviewed all the other candidates and thrown up their hands, but this bright young man impressed them as a potential winner. The legendary Armand Hammer, a close friend of Al senior's, began making the kind of phone calls on Gore's behalf that only A-list power brokers can get returned. Clark Clifford, the consummate Washington insider, later flew up to New York to introduce Gore before his well-received address to the Foreign Policy Association. The Gores' phone began ringing off the hook, and Tipper found "it was getting harder and harder to say 'This is ridiculous.' " The final straw was finding out that her husband had had a powwow with his father the previous Christmas—"he didn't even tell me."

After Christmas dinner at the farm, the two Als had drifted back to the library. Gore Sr. stunned his son by announcing, simply, "I think the Democratic party will turn to you as its nominee in 1988." Quietly, he laid out his reasons. "The American people have a way of compensating for the inadequacies of a presidency by selecting its antithesis." The veteran senator cited Eisenhower's sleepy second term as a setup for the energetic Kennedy, and Nixon's corruption as a foil for Carter's strict morality. "The horrible mess we are in, with the oldest president we've ever had, makes me think there might be a tendency for the country to turn to a young man." Gore Sr. wound up his analysis by reminding Gore Jr. that for the last twenty years neither party had been able to elect a ticket that didn't carry the South.

"He didn't rebut it," Al senior recounts with satisfaction. "He just . . . he listened." But while his father talked in high-flown examples, the sensitive younger Gore registered a quiet, eschatological shock. His father was nearly eighty. What was never voiced, but hung between the two men as thick as the smoky haze between their beloved mountains, was the reality that there might not be another chance while his father lives for him to make good on Big Al's declaration of unfinished family business: *Someday I know that the truth . . . shall rise again . . . in Tennessee!*

When Dale Bumpers backed out of the race, and Sam Nunn looked ready to do the same, Gore Jr. felt all at once that "what I dreamed of might actually be possible." He decided to take the long shot. His announcement speech was a bomb. With chagrin and a chuckle, Al admitted that his first appearance in North Carolina, where expectations ran high for this native son, was, well, barely adequate. Same old pattern. But he worked hard on his presidential campaign, and he is a remarkably quick study.

Young Al allowed his father more input in this race than
ever before. Eighty now, with a snowy Palomino mane, Big Al
still jogs a mile a day, and he got around even faster than his
son on the campaign trail. He'd covered all ninety-nine counties
of Iowa before Richardt Gephardt did. "We've got two Gores out
there running for president!" laughed Arlie Shardt, Al junior's
press secretary. But the candidate was painfully aware that his
father can be somewhat incontinent with the press. When I
passed on his father's disclosure that the Gore strategy was to
"eliminate Gephardt," Al clapped his hands to his ears and
wagged his head in woe, wrestling with the twined emotions of
love, respect, and embarrassment.

On the campaign trail I mentioned to Al senior that his son's
name is most often raised as the likely *vice*-presidential nominee. "No, no, no. No! Wouldn't have the slightest interest. No
interest at all." It was clear from the vehemence of his reaction
that the vice-presidency just wasn't good enough for the boy he
had groomed to be the perfect political heir.

By the time Tipper faced the facts, Al's self-imposed deadline of April 10 was upon them. "It was an agonizing ten days,"
his wife admits. She found herself sitting opposite her husband
and asking silently, *Could I actually fancy you as my president?*
"I went back and forth. This may seem strange, but what
changed my mind was the state of the Democratic party. I think
we've lost our way."

As a result of her crusade against sex and violence in rock
music and videos, Tipper had been the famous name in the Gore
family. In fact, that spring saw her halfway through the publicity
tour for her first book, *Raising PG Kids in an X-Rated Society.*
I asked her whether she and her husband had discussed her
public image when making the decision about whether Al should
run for president. "No. What was talked about was that I was
going to have to cut short my book tour. Once again," meaning
that, again, her career was being cut short in deference to Al's
political needs. She said wistfully that "the book is doing fine,
about sixty thousand copies, but I could have gotten it up to two
hundred fifty thousand."

As a child, Tipper never dared speak up in class. Socialized at a proper Episcopalian girls' school in suburban Alexandria, she could walk home through the woods, swinging her long blond hair, to the castlelike house her grandparents had built. But a crack existed in the glass over this fairy-tale tableau: Her parents had been divorced when Tipper was only four, and she felt branded as different. Her mother holed up with her child in the only zone of safety left, her own parents' house, and supported them by working at a series of tedious jobs. Tipper came home from school to watch the soaps that completely absorbed her grandmother. "I was not raised to do anything except get married and have children."

She looked to Al as "a man who is going to make my life very interesting." In college, she fancied him a movie producer, and after reading Betty Friedan's *The Feminine Mystique* dreamed of collaborating with him on feminist films. Politics, while carefully absent from the young couple's career conversations during the first six years of their marriage, hovered always as a potential competitor in the back of Tipper's mind.

Even today, ensconced in the living room of the same Tudor house in which she grew up, and where she and Al now live, Tipper looks at times like a little girl playing dress-up in Grandma's high heels. With her perfect scrolls of perfectly ash-blond hair, her creamy skin and blue button eyes, she revives images from the pre–Cabbage Patch doll days when Barbie reigned, and didn't let Ken kiss her until the third date. But just as one is in danger of not taking Tipper Gore seriously, she says something bold and smart. She is certainly not an average, rubber-stamp political wife. On the contrary, her controversial crusade immediately became a liability in her husband's campaign.

"Nobody in my generation can support Tipper Gore" is the phrase commonly heard from one of Gore's most obvious constituencies, the young. Tipper knows her image is that of "a moralistic bluenose trying to Lysol the world." In fact, her perspective is a feminist one. When she describes the new genre of video rentals and the most popular heavy-metal rock lyrics being served up to eleven- and twelve-year-olds as well as rebellious teens, her concern seems more than reasonable. And it is shared by Surgeon General C. Everett Koop, who has warned against the dangerous influence on children of "a combination of senseless violence and senseless pornography to the beat of rock music."

"What's frightening," says Mrs. Gore, "is that most of the audience for heavy metal is males, twelve to nineteen. And let's say that they are not getting a lot of sex education. . . . One of the lyrics says, 'Sex and pain are the same, the same.' That women want to be forced, that they're just pretending when they say no. There's a perpetuation of the rape myth in a lot of these lyrics; they're about forcing sex." Contrary to accusations from the $4.7 billion music industry, Tipper has never advocated government intervention, merely a voluntary rating system like that used for movies.

"Is it only legitimate for conservatives or Republicans to ask questions about how we raise children in this culture?" asks her husband.

Super Tuesday, of course, meant everything to Albert Gore. For the first time, the South would dominate the twenty states that choose one third of the delegates to the Democratic convention—all on March 8. Having thrown in the towel on Iowa, and having projected tepid expectations for New Hampshire, Gore's southern strategy banked on the hope that neither contest would produce a clear front-runner.

Although most political commentators had already written him off, he managed to come close to his own exuberant prediction the night before Super Tuesday. "I'm going to do just fine!" he called me to say. Realistically? I pressed him. "Yup. I'm either going to be first or a strong second." He turned out to be one of three big winners in a suddenly narrowed and serious field.

Gore's race with time was to convince voters that this young, cool, calculating son of Dixie could grow fast enough to be adopted as a *national* candidate. Certainly, he had the intellectual capability. Every one of the people I interviewed—friends, colleagues, family—spoke of his intelligence as his most distinguishing characteristic. In the flash of a reporter's question, he can switch from relaxed repartee to laying out his philosophy of social obligation. Or drawing you a diagram of world fossil-fuel consumption overlaid with recent recessions.

"I love to tackle something and learn everything about it," says Gore. "I'm thrilled when somebody with a normal perception of the way the world works can, with determination and an unbiased approach, understand it, and communicate it."

For a man who runs three to five miles a day after a regimen of sit-ups and push-ups, and who eschews caffeine in favor of chamomile tea, I thought it surprising when he accepted the ubiquitous airline salted nuts. "I created the whole public awareness on salt," he retorted, and eagerly described getting his own subcommittee and holding hearings as a congressman. He lobbied *Time* magazine until it did a cover story on salt as the enemy.

The same seriousness of purpose struck Diane Sawyer the first time she had dinner with Gore at the Russian Tea Room in New York, totally off the record. Inhaling blinis, he never stopped talking about the ozone layer. And he got her to do a story on the subject. Unlike his father, who thinks that TV campaign commercials are beneath the dignity of a serious candidate, Gore is clearly a child of the media age. His journalist's nose for tomorrow's story, together with the maniacal appetite for learning he showed as a beat reporter, have served him well in Congress. He has been able to identify issues of new importance and concern—toxic waste, for example—and use the media to publicize the problems as well as his efforts to solve them.

Al was well liked by the House leadership: Tip O'Neill told *The Tennessean* in 1978 that Al Gore "is one of the most able and talented kids we've got here. He's an ardent student who doesn't know it all." But colleagues have accused him of seeking out "safe issues" in order to get media coverage. As the second youngest member of the Senate, Gore is a lightning rod for jealousy among his peers, who grumble that he is arrogant and too thinly prepared for such grand ambitions.

Labeled as a "progressive" and a "technocrat," the young congressman's primary areas of interest were the environment, science, and health. He spearheaded the effort to put stronger warning labels on cigarette packages and ads. "Coming from a state with a hundred thousand tobacco farmers, it was not easy leading the fight for the toughest possible health warning and measures where smoking is concerned," Gore told Marvin Kalb. But the young congressman had a personal, as well as a public-spirited, motive: the death of his sister from lung cancer. He had already stopped planting tobacco on his own farm.

Representative Gore also led the first congressional hearings on the dangers of toxic waste, and went on to play an important role in the development and passage of the 1980 "Superfund" legislation to clean up chemical spills and toxic land dumps.

It is an issue he has continued to work on. I watched him on the campaign trail, mediating between frustrated homeowners living near a waste dump and their nemesis, an Environmental Protection Agency lawyer. Gore put on his investigative reporter's hat, synthesizing the opposing arguments, and then confronted the E.P.A. stonewaller. The angry homeowners scoffed when the senator told them, "You will hear back from me," pointing to the number of politicians who had already made them such promises. But as Al Gore slid into his car, he rattled off instructions to aides. A month later, his computer-perfect staff had followed up on the problem.

It is generally agreed, however, that Al Gore's most important contribution has been in an area less amenable to legislative solutions. After tutoring himself on arms control eight hours a week for a year, Gore was able, as a mere congressman, to get the attention of the Soviets for what became the hottest arms-control proposal of the presummit eighties: de-MIRVing ballistic missiles on both sides. Since such counterforce weapons (which included America's MX missile) made it possible for either nation to knock out most of the other's nuclear force, Gore reasoned, the critical disarmament step would be removing these destabilizing MIRVed missiles from their arsenals. In an apparent contradiction, he did support research and development funds for the MX in 1983—though he explains that this was in return for the administration's promise of more flexibility on S.D.I. at the Geneva START talks (a flexibility that never materialized), and points out that as a senator he voted in 1985 to limit deployment of the missile.

Balancing national security and arms-control concerns, he

likes to say, have made him part of "the beleaguered center."
But Henry Kissinger was mightily impressed, and Paul Nitze,
doyen of arms control, says Gore is the best-informed man on
defense issues on the Hill—better even than Sam Nunn. Yet he
is truly happy only when he can push beyond the gathering of
information and *act* upon it. That—as well as living out his
father's dream—is why Gore's search for identity brought him
full circle, back to politics. He loves the action.

Still, it's not easy to get past those puckerless knuckles.
Another journalist and I, both over forty, asked Gore about his
age. "Wouldn't you be scared, at forty, with the world on your
shoulders?" pressed Mort Kondracke of *The New Republic.* "A
little thing like that?" Al goofed. He often talks about refashion-
ing American economic policy in the global context. I asked
how, faced with barnacled German bankers, he would compensate for their view of him as a brash young buck.

"I'd overreact and stomp 'em," he dead-panned.

Then, in a voice vibrant with youthful sincerity: "I honestly
and sincerely believe that I know exactly what needs to be done.
And I am impatient to do it!"

The political answer is the analysis that Gore Sr. put before
his son and that Al junior has given as the staple of his stump
speech: "In 1960, we went from the oldest president . . . to the
youngest . . . and by sheer coincidence, in 1988, we have a
chance to do that again."

It might appear that Albert Gore, Jr., is the national political figure most representative of the vanguard of the Baby
Boom. Gary Hart is really a child of the Silent Generation, and
Joseph Biden never got close to the great upheavals of his youth.
By contrast, beginning with those long, hard commutes on a
two-lane road between the nostalgia for country and the necessity of city, Gore has taken so many of the journeys of his
generation. He is part of the remarkable transformation of a
poor, backwater, segregationist South into a booming industrial
region, now more gracefully integrated than the North. Married
at the moment the women's movement emerged, he and his wife
have slogged through all the struggles of sexism and are still
trucking.

"I'm really proud of my generation," he says sincerely. "We ensured the success of the civil-rights revolution, and we will not just stand for backtracking. We are serious about changing the role of women in society. We have brought a new understanding of the environment to political awareness, and we're trying to stop the arms race. There is a source of energy in this generation that is incredibly powerful. I've had my own personal experience of feeling that energy unleashed."

The lessons he brings to foreign policy are the boldly new lessons of a generation that has borne the burdens of American empire—together with the budget-busting costs of the Cold War—without any of the glory of an older man's war. Republican front-runners George Bush and Bob Dole are classic World War II heroes. Both were unable in interviews to draw any meaningful lessons from America's war in Vietnam. And both are committed to continuing the Cold War and pursuing the overthrow of the Marxist regime in Nicaragua by military means.

Among his Democratic rivals, Gore was the only one who had served in a real war. Jesse Jackson, the strongest anti-interventionist voice, never came close to military service. Michael Dukakis went to Korea two years after the truce had been signed. Gary Hart was doing back-to-back stints in graduate school during the draft. Paul Simon, with his high-school German, was sent by the army in 1951 to do intelligence work in Bayreuth.

Gore, confronted like every male of his generation with his government's intention to send him overseas to kill people and perhaps be killed, bit the bullet and made it back, indelibly marked, but neither encased in cynicism nor permanently ambivalent about America's ability to fight foreign wars. He has been the only Democratic contender to give specific instances of when he would use military force. He favored the U.S. military actions in Grenada and Libya—both broadly popular with the American people—and has supported the Reagan policy of reflagging Kuwaiti tankers: "If we can be frightened away by a medieval despot, then why should anyone in the world rely on us?"

The age question begins to fade when one hears Gore talk like this. And that seems to be exactly what he intends. Yet he shows no early signs of binding up the ambivalence of the Vietnam generation. Whether because of their continuing dividedness over the war or their resistance to being age-identified with a man old enough to be president ("That would make me *old*"), or because Gore himself seems to have popped up like Flipper—smooth and earnest and unmarked as a baby dolphin—he received less support among Baby Boomers on Super Tuesday than among other age groups.

Gore's strategy has been to portray himself as a good ol' boy who is a natural hawk on defense. Starting last fall, he seized center stage in the candidate forums by painting his competition as out of step with the voters' desire for a strong national defense. His rivals—who'd been hoping to wriggle through the Scylla and Charybdis of the Iowa peaceniks and the southern hawks—all piled onto Gore, and Paul Simon accused him of "tearing the party apart." But this strategy separated him from the "six-pack," endeared him to swing voters, and projected an Albert Gore with strength.

The truth of the matter is, his votes in Congress have lined up with those of his liberal Democratic colleagues on major foreign policy and military issues. He has opposed funds for the Nicaraguan rebels, voted repeatedly to restrict Reagan's S.D.I. program, and backed a freeze on nuclear weapons. His philosophy is nothing like the ideology of containment that has driven U.S. policy for forty years: "The outcome of any guerrilla war is going to depend in large part on the attitudes of the people who live where that war is taking place. The simple truth is that the people of the Nicaraguan countryside are not giving much support to the contras, no matter what their feelings are toward the Sandinistas." He talks about restructuring the U.S.-Soviet relationship to enable us to redirect our resources from new ways of killing people to fighting diseases, providing education, and protecting the global environment. Those are hardly the sentiments of a southern hawk.

Gore is most passionate when he talks about how "we're between two eras. . . . We've got to speed up the maturing of our civilization. . . . We've really got to find within ourselves the capacity to create that new world." In these impatient pronouncements one can hear the inner shift of tempo characteristic of one just entering the mid-life transition. Standing on the rim of mid-life, as he looked out at the presidential race, Al Gore, Jr., saw a reflection of his own imperatives—the hurry-up feeling, the sense of time running out, the urgency to complete his destiny *now*. Forty, after all, feels like the old age of youth.

Has he been tested by enough life accidents or blows of fate to compensate for the fact that he hasn't made the passage into mid-life? No one really knows what unfinished business might come up during the deadline decade, from thirty-five to forty-five, particularly for a person who never rebelled during adolescence and who married young with little time to sow wild oats. His sister's death, while a tragic loss and a brush with the existential sense of helplessness that such an experience engenders, did not apparently strike him as the knell of his own mortality. His candidacy raised the possibility of a man going through a mid-life crisis while in the White House.

Yet Gore's intellectual and political growth has always proceeded at double time. And in this campaign, he believes, his development has been accelerated more than ever. "Frequently the candidate who learns the most and grows the fastest in a campaign wins."

Mario Cuomo was thoroughly impressed after watching Gore in the candidate forum convened by the governor in New York City at the end of 1987. As he told one journalist, "Long after people leave here or turn off their TVs, they'll remember the strong cut of his jaw, the timbre of his voice, the way he sat forward—so presidential."

The more I saw of Gore campaigning, the better he got, as if by leaps and bounds. One night, during a whirlwind tour of the Southwest, standing on an airport people-mover with his buttoned-down-gray-suit bag over his shoulder, Gore suddenly turned toward me, looking boyish and all puffed up with confidence, like—yes! zowie!—like Clark Kent in the process of metamorphosing into Superman. Challenging the champion campaigner of American politics, he called out his boast: "I promise you this. By the time this campaign is over, I'll be as good as Jesse!"

CHANGE AFTER FAILURE

Albert Gore, Jr., and Michael Dukakis are both political wunderkinder. Gore knew from the age of six he wanted to be a senator; Dukakis told a classmate in college what he wanted more than anything in the world was to be a governor. Dukakis, too, has always been seen by his contemporaries as infuriatingly good at almost everything he attempts, because he works at it until he surpasses them. And like the breathtakingly confident young challenger from Tennessee, the marathon man from Massachusetts had never tasted failure before he hit his forties.

There is no telling how any one of us will react, riding high and convinced of our own best intentions, when we hit our first serious personal or professional downfall. It is often in the course of dealing with a bitter rejection that one learns to admit mistakes and to savor what is lastingly important. Among the sixty thousand people I surveyed for my book *Pathfinders*, at least half of those who felt exceptionally good about themselves had failed. But almost every one of them found it a useful experience and said they were better off for it.

The ability—and willingness—to take criticism is not a quality with which we are born. It is an acquired strength. And it is a particularly critical strength in anyone who wants to lead others. Men who cannot admit they were wrong—and their numbers are legion among history's rulers—are dangerous. Lyndon Johnson could see his Vietnam War policy in no other terms but a final military victory. In the winter of 1968, when his White House was covered with a shroud of hatred, and he had gone to ground so as not to hear the clamor telling him he was wrong, President Johnson was having a recurrent dream. Historian James MacGregor Burns learned that the president kept dreaming he was lying in bed in the Red Room, paralyzed from the neck down. He could hear his aides next door quarreling over how to divide up his power, but he was unable to speak. Awaking in the night, he would pace the empty corridors of the White House until he came to Woodrow Wilson's portrait. Only by touching the picture of a president who had been paralyzed could he comfort himself.

"In the morning the fears would return—of paralysis of the body, paralysis of his presidency," wrote Burns. It is a classical dream of impotence, as the scholar pointed out.

Equating potency with keeping up the fight and proving himself right, Johnson, rather than accept a failure and force himself to change, preferred to step down from power, and five years later died.

Knowing that one has *survived* a failure, even made something fruitful of it, adds to the armor of resiliency needed during times of risk and uncertainty ahead—both for an individual and for a nation.

Michael Dukakis bit the dust when he was forty-four, and was humbled. He could no longer dismiss the need for introspection. It forced him to change some of his stubborn, self-defeating ways, and eventually changed the way his family, friends, colleagues, and constituents came to think about him.

SEVEN

The Metamorphosis of Mike Dukakis

Who's the grinning Greek on the platform? The man's mouth is spread so wide his teeth look like a string of taverna lights. Now he leans over to hug someone, his thick black hair flopping over his swarthy forehead, his face flushed with feeling. Then his hands go to his hips, thumbs backward and fingers splayed, the way the men do in dusty Greek villages when the dancing starts. "People ask me, 'Are you tired? Is this a grind?' " he tells his audience. "Are you kidding? My folks came over on the boat, and I'm running for president!"

"Bravo!" shouts the crowd. They have come from every corner of New Jersey to this restaurant in Edison, American-born Greeks mostly of the first generation, and he touches in them all of the chords they share: the reverence for education, the primacy of family, the communal approach to getting things done. Couples with combined incomes of $50,000 drop $500 on the plate for no more than a few spareribs, a drink, and a speech. Young men making minimum wage step up to contribute a hundred dollars in cash. "I feel like I know him," says a teary-eyed teacher, astonished at the welling up of ethnic pride his presence has evoked in her. "He's family."

The governor's speech is good, but his mother's is better. Euterpe Boukis Dukakis steps forward, ramrod-straight at the age of eighty-four, even jaunty in her bright-yellow plaid dress, and she tells the gathering in her flawless Greek, "They are calling me from Greece to claim they are related to him. They are calling me even from Australia." Everyone laughs. Then Euterpe Dukakis draws herself up in majestic, truly Athenian pride, and embraces these five hundred strangers into an extended family with her felt words: "He is not just *my* son, he is the son of all Greeks everywhere."

All at once a bouzouki throws a lasso of sound into the air. Plaintive and shrill, it pulls the crowd toward the center of the floor. Suddenly there is shouting. *"Bravo! Bravo!"* What is happening? People surge forward. "See, see, he's dancing! With his mother!"

Sure enough, in an uncharacteristic act of spontaneity, Michael Dukakis has come down from his platform to throw his arms over the shoulders of the dancers. He begins moving, slowly, sinuously, in a circle that knows no end. The white handkerchiefs come out and the crowd breaks into rhythmic clapping; a clarinet pierces the ears; people are whistling, shrieking with delight. Euterpe Dukakis, who taught him all that now, at last, he can cherish about being Greek, dances with elegance. Her Michael steps over his clunky wing tips without missing a beat, carefully, properly, executing the oldest line dance from the Peloponnesus. Zorba he isn't, but it doesn't matter—he is down on their level, dancing the old traditional steps, and he is one of them.

Who is this man? And why is he having so much fun? It couldn't be Michael Dukakis, otherwise known as Mr. Clean, whose reputation for integrity over twenty-five years in public life had frozen into caricature. With his feet flat as doorstops wedged under a small, trim frame, he was known by his Massachusetts supporters to stand as stiff as a cigar-store Indian. Honest, cool, cerebral, and dull, that was their Mike Dukakis. And cheap. His uncharismatic reputation preceded him on the presidential campaign: Look for a soup-and-stew, Neolite-and-Timex type of guy, strictly brown-bag lunches and Holiday Inns and house brands. His emotional temperature range, they'd tell you, was about that of a climate-controlled museum. No extremes of any kind. Strictly business.

Surely this could not be the same man now standing on the platform, a politician who doesn't talk politics at his audience, but who emotes about his mother: "She was the first Greek girl in Haverhill, Massachusetts, to go to college" (waves of applause); who brags about big money: "In the first three months of this campaign we raised four point two million dollars" (gasps of "ooh"); and who canonizes all of their immigrant parents: "We owe them."

When the music stops, a receiving line is called for, but the crowd is too overcome to stand in line. One by one, they press their faces close to Michael Dukakis, and coming off the line they say, one after the other, "He's so warm."

Warm? Michael Dukakis?

Yes! Loosened up, smiling, cracking jokes, dazzled by his own sudden national prominence, raking in cash contributions at a record rate, moving ahead with one of the best organizations of any Democratic candidate—why shouldn't this man be warming up?

The transformation of Michael Dukakis did not begin a year ago, but the adrenaline of a national campaign accelerated a process that began a decade earlier. Powdered overnight with the aphrodisiac of power, the hedge-browed, Mediterranean-dark, fifty-three-year-old governor from Brookline, Massachusetts, was designated in the September 1987 issue of *Playgirl* magazine as one of the ten sexiest men in America. Campaigning, he would whip out a pair of black wraparound shades that looked very Onassis or Agnelli, with a campaign bumper sticker running across the bridge (a gift from a local firm), and play his new image to the hilt: "If the news hasn't reached you yet . . ."

In an election season increasingly focused on what Representative Patricia Schroeder has called "the warm fuzzies" of family life, Dukakis was being projected also as an ideal husband—despite his wife's disclosure of a twenty-six-year diet-pill addiction. Michael and Kitty Dukakis still live on a sweetly scruffy street of clapboard triple-deckers and small apartment houses. The Dukakis residence, with its twin gables sitting like proper bonnets atop a solid, brick Victorian, shares a wall with another family. Inside, the Danish-modern furnishings have a fond, frumpy, leftover sixties look.

Kitty Dukakis would far prefer a little luxury, but she chooses her battlegrounds. She'll buy Ultrasuede dresses and drag her husband out for celebratory dinners at expensive restaurants, having arranged in advance that he be given the ladies' (unpriced) menu. The difference in their tastes and temperaments has mellowed into a burlesque. "Teasing dispels the tension," says a family friend. To Ira Jackson, the state's former tax collector, who used to baby-sit for the Dukakises, the marriage is an inspiration. "He can be stubborn, tenacious, a bull, and he doesn't concede on the basis of any personal relationship. But Kitty's commitments are equally muscular. For two such disparate personalities to find a syntax where they can be totally relaxed with each other, it's unusual." What's more, the family celebrates Kitty's heritage as well, so a Dukakis seder is followed by the Dukakis Greek Orthodox Easter celebration.

But, like even the best marriages, it isn't perfect. Although an intelligent, tough-minded woman, Kitty Dukakis seems to have more to prove than Michael Dukakis does. Some of their friends see her as the more ambitious of the two. And when they heard of her public announcement that she had finally put the amphetamine habit behind her five years ago, those who know and love Kitty had to chuckle. "Because, frankly," says one friend, "she's still so wired."

As the transformation of Michael Dukakis into presidential symbol proceeds, to the gleeful Greek, the sexy Greek, and the devoted Greek family man is now added another metamorphosis: from unemotional man to tearful ethnic. Imagine the surprise of all those Boston Irish pols, who believe that the Mediterranean man in Dukakis is packed in Yankee ice, when they read about their governor in Astoria, Queens, with thousands of Greeks screaming and hollering, "Du-*ka*-kis, Du-*ka*-kis," and a misty-eyed Michael starting off with "I wish my father could have been here tonight to see this."

Dukakis has cried at least three times in public since announcing his candidacy. For a man who has always stood somewhat removed from his emotions, be they political or personal, and who has struggled during the campaign to close what the pundits called his "passion gap," Michael Dukakis seems close to wearing his heart on his sleeve.

Cut to another restaurant, nine years before: The German Club, in South Boston. A thousand people are jammed into a board-tabled beer joint where a St. Patrick's Day political roast is under way. The Yankee lobbyists are pumping hands with the Irish pols in a profusion of interethnic fraternity, and there isn't a political figure of importance in the whole state who is missing. Except Michael Dukakis, the sitting governor. Never one to hang out with the boys, Dukakis by March 1978 is well into the last year of his first term as Massachusetts's chief executive. It is primary season, but at the moment that seems less important to the pols at The German Club than the brand of beer to order; like it or not, Dukakis's reelection seems a foregone conclusion.

Tommy McGee, a bantam rooster of a man who is then speaker of the Massachusetts House, stands up to throw his wisecracks on the fire. But something different comes out: "On the drive over here, when I thought of the possibility Michael Dukakis might be elected to a second term, I threw up in the back of my limousine."

Slack-jawed, people sit in silence, while from the speaker pours wave after wave of angry, bitter slurs about the governor he is currently serving. The mood of frivolity shrivels. By the time McGee winds up, people are almost literally picking up their feet to avoid stepping in the vitriol.

"You all know what you should do on that vote," he glowers, and sits down.

Despite McGee's reputation as a ruthless insider, his words were not discounted, according to a participant. Such uncontainable venom from another Democrat illustrated the disastrous state of relations Dukakis had allowed to develop with his legislature. People were calling Dukakis names behind his back: cold, arrogant, heartless. To all this unrest, the governor turned a deaf ear; so sure of himself, he seemed sealed behind glass. Dukakis's single goal, at least as far back as college, was to be a governor. "He had an advance man in high school," sneers classmate Beryl Cohen, who lost an election to Dukakis. "A political wunderkind," says a more charitable longtime friend, Don Lipsitt.

When he attained his goal in 1974, Dukakis bragged about leaving politics at the statehouse door so he could get on with the business of Good Government. He became such an insufferable know-it-all, according to movers and shakers in Boston who attempted from time to time to offer an opposing view, he would start his patronizing spiel with "Let me explain it to you one more time."

Blinded by his own stiff-necked self-righteousness—hubris, to use the Greek word—Mike Dukakis slammed into that 1978 primary election like a bird hitting a glass wall in full sunlight. The vote went heavily against him, and, worse, the rejection was pointedly personal. It was, for Michael Dukakis, the first failure in forty-four years. And unequivocally the lowest point of his life.

How did he get from there to here over the last decade? For a wunderkind like Dukakis, often the best thing that can happen is a major midlife crisis. That appears to be what took place as he began his passage into midlife with a major defeat and a series of heartbreaking personal losses.

John Dukakis, son of Kitty Dukakis from a former marriage, made a routine call to his folks' hotel room the night of the 1978 primary, expecting to hear whoops of victory. Instead, the governor, Kitty, and their two daughters were weeping openly as the returns came in. "When they realized it was me, a sudden hush came over the room," he recalls. "It was very much like being told a close relative had died."

An old college friend called the next morning. Dukakis didn't waste words, but those few he said took the effort of someone kicked in the stomach and short of breath. "Very tough," he said. "It hurts."

John caught the first plane to Boston. "I found my dad in his rocking chair looking out the window of his office. It was awful. Clearly, most of what was going on was internalized for him." Walking back across Boston Commons, he and his parents bumped into a former liberal supporter who had swung over to work for Dukakis's opponent, Ed King. "My mother had a hard time shaking this guy's hand." Only when the family retreated to Nantucket for a week to lick its wounds did John Dukakis realize that his normally imperturbable father was not sleeping. Dark divots appeared under his eyes. Whenever John went into his parents' bedroom, his father would be lying, mummylike, face up on the bed.

The phone never rang. Michael Dukakis began to mutter

questions. Humble questions, "What did I do wrong?" questions. Kitty, always the carrier of more flamboyant emotions for both of them, railed at the opposition for using anti-Semitism against her to bring Mike Dukakis down. She is the daughter of a talented Boston Jewish family. "That had nothing to do with it," Michael said flatly.

He began using the phrase "I blew it." He said it over and over again. Then he began to telephone the many people he'd brought into government and to handwrite notes of apology. He used the same blunt phrase, "I blew it," with all of them.

Having lost in a primary, he was stuck in limbo for the next three months, a humiliated, personally rejected lame-duck governor.

Putting one foot in front of the other, he turned up a week after his defeat for the kickoff of a progressive-referendum campaign. No one expected him to honor this prior commitment, least of all John Sasso, the fiery organizer who would go on to manage Dukakis's 1988 campaign (until his controversial release of the "attack videotape" on Senator Biden). Boston's South Station was swarming with two hundred liberals, most of whom had sat on their hands during the primary, as liberals are often wont to do, never expecting their governor's defeat but determined to send him a message. All at once a ghostly figure appeared. It was Mike Dukakis, drained but composed. He gave a little talk about the bright future for homeowners' tax reform.

People came up to him and mumbled their guilty catechism: "It's such a shock," "My God, what just happened?" and "Gee, we're really sorry."

Brookline's liberal idealists had always cleaved to Dukakis for being above politics. His own exalted expectations of himself had only been exaggerated by the special devotion and high hopes these adherents had for their indefatigable reformer. So he had practiced what they all preached: He had come into office and sealed all the cookie jars in which, historically, the hands of state-government officials had been caught. And *this* is how they rewarded him?

If Dukakis harbored any bitterness, it never showed.

That left an indelible impression on Sasso, who two years later began plotting Dukakis's return as governor. "He's a person of great strength, and the way he handled that defeat showed it."

"But he still wasn't quite getting it," says his son, John. "It took him a very long time, I'd say about six months, to really get under control."

One of his very few close friends, Dr. Nicholas T. Zervas, a neurosurgeon at Massachusetts General Hospital, has called the defeat "the single most influential thing that ever happened" to Dukakis. "He blamed it totally on himself. It took him quite a while to get through the tremendous pain and humiliation and guilt; he felt he'd let people down."

Don Lipsitt, a psychoanalyst who has known the Dukakis family for twenty-five years, observes, "I don't think Mike was ever clinically depressed." Part of that impression, he believes, has been created by Kitty's often quoted characterization of the defeat as "a public death." But a person in the depths of depression would withdraw, slow down, and not be very motivated to do productive work. "I think," says Lipsitt, "he began to examine himself in exquisite detail, in a very cognitive, intellectual way." At first, it was virtually impossible for Dukakis to believe that his high principles could have been knocked down.

"We did some real talking in those months," says Kitty, who is credited by both Michael and his mother as a tower of strength during that period. "It hurt to see him hurt. But he became more comfortable as time went on with inviting people to come in and talk."

His closest Greek friend since Harvard Law School, mild-mannered Paul Brountas, says, "He looked at the mistakes he had made, and Lord knows there were plenty of us telling him about the failure to listen, the inability to be persuaded by others, and the unwillingness to admit he might not be right on absolutely everything. He also looked at his relationships with people. And he said, 'My God, I should have spent more time with the speaker, with the president of the Senate. I fought very hard for my programs, but I wouldn't let them have theirs.'"

The Duke, as many call this cool man, addressed the rational grievances of the voters first. He had run on a promise not to raise taxes. Once in office, faced with a half-a-billion-dollar deficit, he had been forced both to hike taxes and cut services.

Dukakis had scoffed at California's Proposition 13, claiming, "Massachusetts voters are too smart for that." His undistinguished challenger, Ed King, was carried into office on the winds of property-tax reform. Why hadn't Dukakis seen the tax revolt sweeping the country? "Tunnel vision" was another one of the criticisms he hadn't stopped to hear.

Now the man who had always been in such a hurry to be ahead of everyone else had the enforced luxury of the next three years to examine the personal charges against him: that he was stubborn, holier-than-thou, and a cold, unemotional, insensitive man.

Stubbornness. This, above all, registers as the most consistent mark of Michael Dukakis's character. *Monos mou*—"by myself"—if not his first words, he admits, were certainly the watchword of the second son born to Panos and Euterpe Dukakis. Was he always stubborn? I asked his mother. "Always. Michael never gave up."

The dirty-socks wars would turn into marathon tests of will. "Those socks won't do," his mother would say. Michael would insist his choice was right. "Then go to your room and close your door," his mother would order, "and don't come out until you're ready to do what your mother tells you to do." An hour or two would pass. "He never gave up." Mrs. Dukakis shrugged.

She, too, was a formidably strong figure, however, and determined to "channel" his stubbornness into perseverance plus obedience. Euterpe Dukakis, who became the first Greek-American teacher in her town, was turned down for her first teaching job because she was of foreign birth and had an accent. The sting of rejection is still fresh. Even today, her speech is so correct it borders on the stilted, and her posture is almost a parody of prideful erectness. She never relaxed her vigilance in polishing her son's self-presentation so that he would pass as a full American. Whenever the boy mispronounced a word, Euterpe Dukakis would correct him. Later, she would find Michael standing in front of a mirror, by himself, mouthing the word over and over until he got it right.

Did young Michael ever have a failure? I asked his mother. Her smooth forehead braided in thought; no, he didn't bring his disappointments home. Finally, she remembered one occasion. His sixth-grade teacher kept scolding him for writing too small. Michael stubbornly persisted. The teacher gave him a C—the only C he ever got, and it remains today engraved on the memory of his octogenarian mother.

Then, and only then, castigated on all sides, did Michael Dukakis listen and amend his ways, a pattern that would repeat itself until it was expressed years later in the definitive failure of his life.

His father's example also made a significant imprint. When Panos Dukakis came to America from Turkey in 1912, alone, at the age of fifteen, it was with a burning desire to get an education. Panos earned entry to Harvard Medical School eight years later—by himself. A stern disciplinarian with his sons, Stelian and Michael, Dr. Dukakis had two passions in life: work and family. "My father worked a six-and-a-half-day week and then some," Michael remembers, "but there was nothing he liked better than coming home and spending time in his backyard." Panos's son, today, has the same habits.

The family had no social circle to speak of, since the Greek community was gathered in Boston, where its activities emanated from the church. The Dukakises settled in Brookline, a "just so" suburb a few bus stops from Boston. Its exclusive club is listed in the phone book under "T" (for The Country Club). The few Greeks were scattered among an affluent Jewish population, and the ethnic Irish were mostly public-service employees. Michael connected with both groups, working summers collecting garbage with working-class Irish kids and competing at Brookline High for grades and girls with rabbinically bright Jewish boys.

"Brahmin Boston just wasn't part of my life," Dukakis told me, a touch of reverse snobbery showing. "You know, big deal."

Despite his father's increasing affluence, the family paid cash for their first house and never traded up, never bought a thing on credit, never changed their living habits to keep up with the Joneses. "We were what we were, and that was it," said Mrs. Dukakis, serving iced tea and cookies on the pocket-sized, screened-in porch of the same clapboard Colonial where Michael was born.

Michael, the younger of the two sons, was designated to become a doctor. Both parents impressed upon him the responsibility to give back by serving one's fellow citizens. Dr. Dukakis exemplified those values by delivering hundreds of babies to Greek families for little or nothing. A stern man with Old World manners, Panos Dukakis was unquestionably "the master of the family" and recognized as such, says Mrs. Dukakis. According to a Brookline friend, Dolores Mitchell, "He wasn't the sort of father a sensitive young man would want to disappoint."

For the first twenty-nine years of his life, Mike Dukakis never strayed far from his parents. It wasn't until the morning of his wedding that Euterpe kissed him good-bye, instructed him to love and cherish Kitty, and let him go. Even today, he lives only two miles away.

Too good was another of the subjective beefs that even his best friends had with Michael Dukakis. "Michael had everything you'd hate in someone your age," says an admiring high-school classmate, Haskell Kassler, who, like Brountas, went on to become a prosperous Boston attorney. "He was an exceptional student, varsity in all his sports, played first trumpet, and on top of all that he dated one of the most popular girls in school." There is still controversy over whether or not Michael won the girl, Sandy Cohen, but his competition, Bob Wool, did definitively whip him for election as senior class president. Michael shunned the school's invitational boys' clubs, disapproving of their blackball powers. And that, according to "Hasky" Kassler, probably cost Michael the presidency of his class.

"Your mother doesn't remember you ever talking about any disappointments or losses," I observed in my first interview with Mike Dukakis.

"There weren't many," he came back cockily. Defeats or mistakes weren't admitted in the Dukakis household—no, he just kept putting one foot in front of the other until he had made up for his loss by winning the presidency of the student council.

"What about when you first realized you wouldn't grow up to be a giant?" I asked.

"I had myself programmed to grow three inches every year until I got up to five eleven," he told me. "I was on time until I hit about five seven. Then I started slowing down."

That was in junior high. But when a gym teacher directed, "All the tall kids line up over here for basketball," Dukakis ignored his limitations and joined the tall kids.

Besides being short, he was slow. Again, Mike Dukakis overcompensated. He disciplined himself to be a marathon runner. Telling the only lie of his life, he admits, he entered the Boston Marathon at the age of seventeen. After sprinting up the first three hills, he got a stitch near his heart. For the next twenty miles, despite his fear that he was about to have a heart attack, he kept running. Finally, a few blocks from the finish line, he shook out the pain and ran in at three and a half hours, a creditable time. The next morning at seven, he tried to get out of bed. As captain of the tennis team, he had to make that day's match. But his legs locked like a rusted-out door hinge.

"So finally," he said, laughing, "I sat on my rump and bounced down the stairs."

This extraordinarily driven boy once sighed to his mother, "Life is just hurry time—in some ways I wish time could stand still."

In college he continued to improve on his Mr. Clean credentials. Swarthmore, a Quaker school in Pennsylvania that was strong on community involvement and internationalism, opened up new worlds. "He was a bit daunting in his ability to carry on multiple activities," recalls his roommate of three years, Frank Sieverts, now spokesman for the Senate Foreign Relations Committee, "and still manage to handwrite all his papers." Dukakis was the kind of kid other people's mothers love to hold up as an example. Always a plugger, he made seventh man on the junior-varsity basketball team, second-string catcher on the baseball team, and he ran cross-country. That was one of the attractions of his small college: "I wasn't a star, but at least I could play," he says candidly.

No amount of tenacity, however, could get him through physics. He had to call home and admit he couldn't live up to his father's expectations that he would become a doctor. But young Dukakis had another goal in mind.

"Already by our freshman year, when we'd shoot the breeze about our futures, he had a lot of people talking politics," remembers Sieverts. "But all of us would think rather vaguely in terms of becoming senator or representative. Michael was the only one I ever knew who said, 'No, I think governor is the way to go. State government is the place you can really make a differ-ence.' " By the time he was close to finishing law school, his goals had become more defined, even messianic. "As a governor, you're kind of running a small country," he told Paul Brountas. "You have a lot more power than even a senator."

Between college and law school, he waived the easy college deferment taken by most of his friends and, despite his father's objections, went to Korea as a draftee. "I wasn't thrilled about sitting in a rice paddy for sixteen months," he admits, but he kept his mind occupied by learning a smattering of Korean and by traveling. Returning in 1957, Dukakis gritted his teeth and did his stint at Harvard Law School, winning a local office at the same time. Burning to get to work in public service after gradua-tion with high honors, he went into a law firm that would allow him to launch his political career.

Never one afraid to be different, Michael Dukakis found the right bride *monos mou*—by himself. Straightforwardly, he faced his mother with the facts: She's divorced, she's Jewish, and she has a child. He had known all that before he ever allowed his old girlfriend Sandy Cohen to fix him up on a blind date with Kitty Dickson.

Their first date bore the makings of a disaster. Kitty had always suffered from a stare-at-her-shoes shyness. Her father, Harry Ellis Dickson, a natural musical artist who played first violin with the Boston Symphony and later became associate conductor of the Boston Pops, used to scold her for being so shy. As a child, she played the piano, badly, gave up, tried acting, shriveled with stage fright. Not until she was eleven or twelve did she discover modern dance as a mode of self-expression. Even then, Kitty knew her limitations would not allow her to be a performer, and settled on teaching interpretive dance.

By the time she reluctantly agreed to the blind date with Michael Dukakis, Kitty felt like an old woman. Twenty-six. College dropout. One failed marriage. Several miscarriages. A three-year-old son. And a rotten body image. Swell, and here, coming up the walk to her low-rent apartment, was "that brilliant Greek kid from the more affluent side of town."

As the couple prepared to leave to see a movie, Kitty's son, John, started howling hysterically. She steeled herself and got outside to the street. With the special castigatory powers of a three-year-old, the boy pressed his nose against the glass and followed his mother from window to window. After that, Michael insisted they take the toddler with them on dates. "The most attractive thing about Michael was the gentle way he handled John," says Kitty. John, today twenty-nine, can't remember when he accepted Michael Dukakis as his father. It happened effortlessly; before he could reach the top buttons on elevators, he remembers, he was proudly campaigning for his adoptive father.

The newly married reformer had no trouble winning reelection to the state legislature for an eight-year stretch. There he made his initial splash by sponsoring the nation's first no-fault insurance law—though his colleagues had to pull him off the conference committee because his intransigence was endangering the bill's chances.

He even *looks* too good, for his age. Look at his high-school and college yearbook photos and, dammit (the expletive is barely disguised by Sieverts, who is snowy-haired, and Kassler, who must eat slowly after a recent heart attack), the man looks no different today, at age fifty-four. So clear about himself, so utterly unaware that others might be wrestling with hidden demons, Michael moved like a bullet train through the next fifteen years with a tunnel vision so complete it came as a total shock to discover, in the midst of the most important campaign of his life, that all along, unable to reach him, his wife had been an amphetamine addict.

In 1974 he found a bottle of her "diet pills." Kitty had always been thin. She took her interpretive dancing seriously and routinely performed in leotards. To the rational Dukakis, diet pills simply didn't make sense.

"I felt caught," admits Kitty. "Michael early on was just not a good listener. I'd gotten very frustrated." She later took up her own causes (Holocaust studies, refugees, environmental beautification), "but in the sixties and even the early seventies," Kitty reminds us, "I don't think women expected credit."

The couple discussed the physiological problem, and Kitty promised to go to their family doctor and break her habit. "In three or four months she was off them," says Michael, "or I kind of assumed she was." In fact, feeling depressed as she tapered off, Kitty resumed taking varieties of amphetamines. Five milligrams every day gave her a kick, she says, and everything she did well she attributed to those magic white pills.

When I asked how the body's natural tolerance of such a tiny dose would still allow her to feel a kick after all that time, Kitty Dukakis said, "There might have been times when I took more than one pill, but they were very few." The natural volatility of her temperament became more pronounced. And, to mask the constant drain on her already watered-down confidence, she developed a loud, aggressive surface.

Michael turned back to his first campaign for governor and just kept putting one foot in front of the other. The opposition laughed him off, as usual underestimating him. He won.

The elixir of victory evaporated quickly. Although he had campaigned against the profligate ways of the previous administration, the new governor had no concept of the grave depths of the state's deficit. One bitter day in February 1975, John Buckley, the secretary of finance Dukakis had brought in with him, broke the news to the governor and his staff.

"We're three quarters of a billion dollars in debt," a staffer remembers Buckley saying. "The state's bonds are going to be rerated downward. We'll have to borrow to pay off the debts." In fact, Massachusetts was tottering on the brink of default.

"No one breathed a word," recalls Dolores Mitchell, then coordinator of the state cabinet. "We were too stunned." With a constitutional amendment requiring the governor to balance the budget, Dukakis faced either fiscal disaster or probable political suicide. He froze.

Over the next eight months of his term, bills literally piled up in shoe boxes. Governor Dukakis, a man who had never bought so much as a car on credit, drilled from childhood to pay as he went, would not, could not, comprehend the catastrophe waiting to happen.

When he did start to slash the budget, he included a series of symbolic razor cuts to state employees that never quite healed: "Foolish things, like stationery, newsletters, cars for cabinet officers, drove everybody wild," says Mitchell.

Kane economia, "economize"—his father's motto—eventually became the emblem of the values Dukakis imposed on state government from top to bottom. He didn't need perks, why should others? His own needs had been pared down long ago to a minimalist art. When Dukakis walked into his $40,000-a-year job as governor, his income had never exceeded $25,000. It was in that first term that he earned his reputation as a skinflint.

He cut $300 million in human services. His liberal supporters were aghast: How could a progressive Democrat be so utterly soulless? It was the cool, aloof, accountant-like manner in which he delivered them, as much as the cuts themselves, that really turned his core constituency against Dukakis. Day after day, protesters picketed outside the governor's home in Brookline. "We had almost daily bomb threats," his son has told the *Los Angeles Times*. "Those were tough times." Dukakis also antagonized the "techies" who had been laying the very roadbed—Route 128, Boston's answer to Silicon Valley—for the economic turnaround in Massachusetts. "There's no question he was perceived as a major impediment to business during his first term," says Mort Zuckerman, a major Boston real-estate developer, now owner of *U.S. News & World Report.*

But the real blind spot for Dukakis lay in operating as a politician too principled to practice politics. The Massachusetts legislature had always operated on patronage, but the concept of political favors was alien to Michael Dukakis. According to one close friend and former colleague, "He saw all of us as working for the common good, not working for Michael Dukakis. He sometimes had to be reminded to say thank you."

No one could talk to the new governor about an appointment for a friend, regardless of how qualified. Dukakis even refused to hire his own campaign workers, and would not meet with lobbyists. His lieutenant governor was Tommy O'Neill, son of the congenitally charming Irish politician Tip O'Neill. "I was the battering ram for everyone else," says O'Neill. "Kitty and I."

Kevin Harrington, the towering Irishman who presided over

the state senate during Dukakis's first term, swears that Kitty entered into a thousand conspiracies with him to get things done politically that Michael was too "good" to do. Harrington describes her marching into the chamber, during session, and striding up to the president's rostrum to whisper in his ear.

"Why can't you get this vote through?" she demanded, according to Harrington. "Michael really needs this program."

"We can't get the vote through, Kitty, because your husband is alienating a third of my senate."

Kitty maintains that she rarely entered the senate chamber and doesn't remember any "conspiracies." But according to Peter Pond, an advocate for Cambodian refugees who has often been on the barricades with Kitty Dukakis, "She goes to the top and says, 'Do it.' And she often pulls off something spectacular. Of course, she has also gotten people angry, because she has no patience with bureaucracy."

The charge that Dukakis is henpecked, launched in the nastily personal Ed King campaign, still lurks among some of the colorfully chauvinistic characters who inhabit the Massachusetts statehouse. But those closest to the Dukakis family assert that Michael Dukakis wears a full set of pants. His much-touted involvement in domestic chores is a matter of choice, predates feminism, and in fact reflects his traditional Greek reverence for family. It was very much his idea to walk his two daughters to school every morning before hopping the subway to the statehouse. And it was he who would look at the schedule and bark, "I will *not* go out four nights this week—I want to see my kids!" Heartfelt encomiums come from women who worked for Governor Dukakis. His example allowed them, too, to meet their obligations to their families.

"You have to make choices in public life between best friends and a family that is close to you," says his son, John.

But family closeness could not salve all the wounds of that postdefeat reflection period. One loss seemed to follow another. The death of Michael's mentor, Allan Sidd, an avuncular liberal who had tutored Michael like a Jewish uncle, was a blow. And the year following his defeat saw the death of his father. The day of that funeral was a cruelly sad one.

No one came. Well, not exactly no one, but the usual full

court of legislators and old appointees whom a politician can count on at such times was noticeably thin. "It must have been devastating for him," says a co-worker who attended the funeral. But Michael Dukakis drew his pain deep inside and expressed not a word of mourning to his friends.

The Duke had already started to teach at Harvard's Kennedy School of Government. He was not looking forward to an involuntary midlife career change that, for all he knew, might be permanent. "But Dad was up within the first week after the defeat," reports his son. "I could hear the excitement in his voice." Kitty, too, picked up on work toward her master's degree, having graduated from Lesley College. Michael studied hard to prepare himself for the course, as he always does. And very soon he became good at teaching, drawing openly on his own mistakes to supplement the case-study method. "I blew it," he would say, "too management-oriented and politically naïve." "The thing that stands out," recalls Chris Evangel, today a Wall Street bond analyst, "is he never said a word of self-pity." Dukakis accepted blame for failure just as he had pursued success—*monos mou,* by himself.

Cold, unemotional, insensitive. These, above all, were the perceived personality traits that seemed to be getting in Dukakis's way. Kitty told him so.

Dukakis has always been something of a bystander, keeping his distance from emotional politics, from demonstrations, protests, and passionate campaigns for all-but-lost causes. Although he credits John F. Kennedy with being his inspiration to enter politics, he never worked in his campaign, nor for Bobby Kennedy or Eugene McCarthy. When Martin Luther King, Jr., came to Boston to march in 1965, Dukakis wasn't among the marchers. He never took part in antiwar protests during the Vietnam years. And when I asked how he had participated in the busing crisis that almost tore Boston apart ten years ago, he couldn't remember.

His battles have all been bloodless. He gets indignant about meat-and-potatoes issues—the need for cheaper insurance, tougher tax collection, a more efficient welfare system—but has steered clear of the great history-shaking confrontations of our times. According to one consultant who worked with him on the reelection campaign against Ed King, his sins are those of omission: "He's the kind of leader you can imagine standing by while the guard orders Christ's feet crossed because they only have one more nail." If it isn't his issue, he doesn't blink.

Those closest to the Duke, however, say he is not without emotional range. He can blow up at the kids and Kitty. He gets choked up over tragedies that befall friends. When it comes to conflicts between pursuing his own goals and dropping everything to close ranks with his family at inconvenient moments of crisis or ceremony, the family comes first. But you'll never hear him *talk* about his wounds. Evelyn Murphy, his lieutenant governor, says, "You'll never see where Michael hurts."

"The notion that things don't reach him on an emotional level is a misconception," explains his psychoanalyst friend, Don Lipsitt. "I think in his family culture whatever they felt was to be kept contained. Michael is not a person who shares his innermost feelings."

"I'm not a neutral guy, and I never was," Dukakis insists. "I always loved what I was doing."

But in his presidential race he has had to fight the public perception that Michael Dukakis "appeals to the head, not the heart," as a Des Moines paper put it. Democrats have always wanted their candidates to be warm and sweaty, to emote, and some Iowans found Dukakis lackluster and vague. He has since worked to bring some of his passions to the surface and frame them in emotional images. In a more recent interview with the governor, I asked him what he would most like to project about himself, to counteract the "lackluster" charge. The intensity that came through in his reply caught me by surprise.

"When I talk about the homeless in the most affluent nation on the face of the earth, Gail, I mean, that comes right out of my gut! I'm just outraged. I'm outraged at what's going on in Central America."

He then rehearsed the images he would use for Iowa audiences, drawing on the description by Steven Kinzer, a *New York Times* reporter who once worked for Dukakis, of the horrors he'd seen in a Managua hospital.

"I read about how it's so important to keep the pressure on the Sandinistas," he tells audiences. "You know what pressure is? Pressure is a kid with his hands, with his arms blown off. That's what pressure is. Pressure is a pregnant woman raped and killed in a contra raid. And that's why I say: Not one dollar of contra aid. Not one. Not one!"

One Iowa woman told columnist David Broder it was a side of Dukakis she'd never seen before: "I could feel his rage."

For the man who, like Dukakis, starts out "running for president," or playing to win rather than playing not to lose, the dividing line between work and private life is blurred early. Work is his fix. He works even at play. Seldom introspective, the wunderkind rarely shares his private thoughts, fears, and hurts. They are locked up because he is afraid to admit he is not all-knowing, afraid to let anyone come too close and see his soft underbelly. Somewhere, back in the deep recesses of boyhood, each wunderkind I have studied recalled a figure who made him feel helpless or insecure. It may have been an overbearing mother or a father who withheld his blessing, or a parent who meant to be of goodwill but locked in the chosen offspring to fulfill a family destiny—"You have the chance I never had to become a doctor," and, as in the Dukakis case, "You must enhance the family name by reaching the highest levels of public service."

The most important legacy of such a dictate is the last and implied part: *or you'll be nothing.*

Many wunderkinder have a midlife crisis—a screeching inner halt that forces them to take stock. Jimmy Carter, for example, after being defeated in his first race for governor, went into a profound period of despair and penance, seeking rebirth through religious commitment. Once his mental balance was restored, and the defeat assimilated, he went on to run again and win.

I asked Dukakis about my theory, and whether it had been his mother or his father who had pushed him to be good, better, best—to carry out the dream.

"I think it was a mix of the two," he replied. "It's interesting, the older I get, the more I think in some ways I'm like my father, and yet I'm very much like my mother. The fact that my family, my home, my community are very important to me, that material possessions aren't really, that what I'm doing is the thing that I love the most, the being of service to others, so on—that's my dad."

To me, the real question is, did a transformation of character take place in Mike Dukakis at a deep inner level during those exile years? Or did he do a rational makeover of his political style in order to *appear* more open and accessible, more caring and compassionate?

His successful second race against Ed King was a grudge match. There was clear evidence that Michael Dukakis had learned to play politics, even hardball politics. He authorized the leaking of stories that revealed King had been using state funds for his own personal expenses. Dukakis had decided, as he recently told the *Los Angeles Times*, that "if King started the negative stuff, I was gonna have to come back."

And, according to one adviser on that campaign, both Mike Dukakis and his wife had heard a tape prepared by John Sasso—and subsequently played by Sasso to several report-ers—which distorted an Ed King public-service announcement about sensitivity to the handicapped. King had talked about his wife's polio, but the doctored tape made it sound as if he were complaining because he didn't get enough sex from his crippled wife. In the ensuing flap over Sasso's "dirty tactics," Dukakis again played the part of bystander, acting as though it had nothing to do with him.

In the aftermath of that first loss, he had gone about building bridges to those he had offended, one by one. Over Labor Day weekend in 1980, for example, he followed State Representative Philip Johnston around, to see the improvements that Johnston had made in the former governor's failed workfare program. "He was trying to tell me in his own way, 'Look, I know I didn't listen enough.' I appreciated *on a personal level* that he was reaching out to me. I didn't think it was phony, either." John-ston, who led demonstrations against Dukakis during his first term, and is now secretary of human services, believes the governor is a different man today. "He went through agony. He came out of that with more of a sense of how people suffer."

So, when Mike Dukakis was returned to the state capitol, his new watchword was consensus. Lobbyists, demonstrators, people affected by his policies were given a share in the decision-making process. Mitch Kapor, the whiz kid in the Hawaiian shirt who founded Lotus, the world's largest developer of personal-computer software, is one of the many entrepreneurs spawned by M.I.T. and Harvard who have helped create what Dukakis calls "the Massachusetts miracle." Kapor says it would be simpleminded and wrong to give the governor credit for the boom. "But he's grown to appreciate the absolute importance of high tech to Massachusetts. He's been able to see the big picture."

Traveling in his state, one hears the governor praised repeatedly for innovative public-private partnerships and for spreading the new wealth around to formerly depressed areas. The already impressive figures keep improving. Unemployment had dropped, as of August 1987, to 2.5 percent—the lowest of any industrial state in America. Dukakis has cut taxes five times in four years. More than thirty thousand families have been taken off welfare and provided with the training, day care, and transportation to keep the jobs that make them taxpayers.

Mort Zuckerman sees Dukakis as having grown into a skilled orchestrater of government and business. Even his most garrulous detractor, Kevin Harrington, admits with grudging respect that "the man has done a 180-degree turnaround." One still hears grousing around the statehouse, though, when leaders are asked if Dukakis would make a good president. "A good president, maybe," says one. "A good buddy, no."

His close friend Paul Brountas hasn't seen much change: "The Michael Dukakis of the first administration is not substantially different from the Michael Dukakis of today."

This is a short man from a small state who is easy to underestimate. But mark this well about Mike Dukakis: He will always overcompensate. Despite the fact that his immigrant Greek family provided an airtight upper-middle-class home from the time he was born, that he took political root in an affluent suburb, was polished at Harvard Law School, that he later taught at the Kennedy School of Government, and that he can speak six languages, there isn't a trace of Haaahvad snootiness about Michael Dukakis. He consciously avoided dropping his *r*'s in Des Moines. Plunging into steak houses and Greek pizza parlors across Iowa, he was the swarthy ethnic in rolled-up blue shirtsleeves who talked straight to the voters. They didn't have to be Greek to appreciate his unpretentiousness. A retired farmer who took Dukakis around southern Iowa said the rural Iowans were impressed that he talked to them for forty-five minutes *before* his speech, and he listened. "Mike is one of us. He isn't the kind of guy who'd have fourteen forks at his dinner table."

Racing through airports, he was rarely recognized and scarcely even seen. But one could always tell where he was because there would be a ripple in the crowd and a hole in its center. And that was where, five feet eight without his thick Neolites, one could always find Mike Dukakis—putting one foot in front of the other. But that played well with short people. "He'd be the first president to be shorter than me," said a Tampa man approvingly.

He has discreetly compensated for his height by having a riser slipped behind his podium, but size is not a problem on the tube because his face is as broad as a billboard and his features chiseled like a prewar automobile hood ornament. To subdue his dark beard, Dukakis travels with a compact of pancake makeup and a pocket shaver, and always makes up before his plane lands if TV cameras are going to be around. And with four years as a moderator of public television's *The Advocates* under his belt, he has learned how to speak in sound bites.

What is more unusual for a politician, he genuinely seems to like the press. After interviewing the governor twice, I still had some personal questions to ask. His then press secretary, the highly independent Pat O'Brien, approached the governor's van on my behalf. "Sure, c'mon, Gail, jump in," Dukakis called jauntily. "I could get used to this," he told me, settling back against a cushion embroidered with the presidential seal. "I can see a whole fleet, Van Force One, Train Force One . . ."

Cautiously, I broached the awkward subject of his brother. "No brothers were ever closer," he said of Stelian Dukakis. "He was my leader." Three years Michael's senior, Stelian had entered Bates College and was itching to get into politics himself. "And suddenly, bang, for no apparent reason . . ." Dukakis's voice trailed off.

His brother had a mental breakdown. Thereafter, although he had lucid periods, Stelian never fully regained stability. He got a master's degree from Boston University, held a full-time job as local town manager, and even announced as a congressional candidate, though he never ran. But his mood and weight swung wildly. He'd pull childish pranks, such as hiding in closets and then jumping out to scare people. Some of Stelian's more embarrassing escapades took place while Michael was a Brookline representative. The disturbed man would collect his brother's campaign fliers off the town's stoops and substitute his own, ill-conceived literature. Friends suggest he resented his more successful younger brother, particularly in light of the high expectations of their parents. People would talk. "Isn't it a shame?" "It must be terribly upsetting when you're running for office, having a brother who's, well . . ."

Michael Dukakis swiveled to face me, eyeball-to-eyeball, the way he must have with his brother's detractors then. "You've got to be supportive and as understanding as you know how. I can't tell you what great shape he was in, the best two-miler in the state," and the recollections poured forth, putting his brother only in the best light.

"Mike never did try to distance himself from Stelian," Dr. Lipsitt had told me. "He dealt with it the way I've seen him deal with other disappointments. He showed extraordinary tolerance and never said anything negative. For a man so politically ambitious, that was very impressive."

Further heartbreak came when Stelian was knocked off his bicycle by a hit-and-run driver. He was hospitalized and remained comatose for four months. Michael, then thirty-nine and running for governor, kept a daily vigil at his bedside, "hoping he would move a hand, or respond at all. It was a terrible experience for my parents, for me, for all of us."

When Euterpe Dukakis told me about that tragedy, she indicated that a decision had had to be made about whether to keep her son alive on support systems. Michael Dukakis said, simply, "We lost him."

This life accident, as tragedies so often do, came at a very difficult time for Dukakis. The emotional control that allowed him to run a campaign for high office while standing vigil at a loved one's deathbed, and the tunnel vision that allowed him to ignore his wife's twenty-six-year-long drug addiction, are two interconnected sides of Michael Dukakis's character.

I asked him if he disciplines himself not to show the things that hurt. "Not consciously," he replied slowly. "I've never been terribly introspective."

Is he consciously trying to let go and show his emotions a little more these days, to offset the image of coolness? I asked.

"I think I've gotten more relaxed these days," he said. "The defeat did a lot of that for me. It made me more philosophical." He smiled, and mocked his tendency to self-righteousness. "I'm less sure today that I have the revealed truth."

When Michael Dukakis began his campaign for president, he found he was enjoying himself. Peter Bassett, a fellow Greek and longtime friend who has worked on the campaign, described those first few days: "We were joking from the very beginning. We were all very excited. I remember answering the phone at my house—'Dukakis headquarters.' I was laughing, and he said, 'This is going to be fun.'"

The fun stopped abruptly in late September when Dukakis's campaign manager, John Sasso, admitted that he had leaked a videotape highlighting the similarities between Senator Joseph Biden's speeches and those of British politician Neil Kinnock. The resulting plagiarism charges were the beginning of the end of Biden's campaign.

When *Time* magazine named the Dukakis campaign as the source of the "attack video," the governor called a press conference and flatly denied it. Sasso, listening to a tape of the press conference, realized, "I've got to tell the Duke. I can't let him continue to lie." He made an immediate political calculation: Anybody can take one day of negative questioning by the networks. A well-known candidate can take two days. But a candidate who is unknown can't survive three or four days of damning press.

That Monday night Sasso went home and told Paul Tully, Dukakis's Number Two on the campaign. He talked to his wife. First thing the next morning he tried to talk to Dukakis but was told he could only be squeezed in for five minutes. Sasso knew this would not be a five-minute conversation, so he waited until four P.M., when he'd have more time with the governor. Pat O'Brien remembers he was "quite desolate. He had prepared a resignation letter that he intended to present to the governor."

When Dukakis heard Sasso's story, he knew what he'd have to do—and why.

I later asked Dukakis why he hadn't simply told the press, This is politics, this is the way it's played. He answered, "I had made it very clear from the beginning that I wanted to run a campaign that was for the office and not against others. Look, I want to win this nomination, Gail. But I want to win it in a way that has members of my party saying, 'Hey, whether we're with this guy or not, we like him, we like the way he's campaigned, he treated our candidate with respect and friendship.' "

Then why didn't he ask for Sasso's resignation right away?

"Look, he's as close to me as a brother and having gone through a very painful situation myself, I'm very sensitive to others. And families, and what they're going through. And here was a guy who really probably is the best person I've ever worked with. Bar none."

Dukakis wanted to give his manager some time to prepare himself and his family for what was to come. On Wednesday morning he gathered a few members of his staff together, including Sasso. The governor looked very sad, according to one participant. "He was at one end of the table and John was at the other, and John—poor John's eyes—to this day when I remember him looking down that table at the governor, it was very sad." Dukakis had put in a call to Biden, and he outlined for the staffers what he would say to the press later that morning. "I am going to express my deep regret and anger over this," he told them, and announce that "my campaign manager is going to take a leave of absence of several weeks."

With television cameras and reporters converging on the campaign, which had skated along happily for five months, the next few days were described by one Dukakis aide as if "somebody had poured grease all over the floor, and you're trying to get on your feet." Giving Sasso twenty-four hours to put his world in order, Dukakis finally accepted his resignation.

The incident was a mini character test. Dukakis was under

a great deal of pressure, and uncertain about the outcome of the revelations. In the first heated hours after the news broke, the conventional wisdom that the Duke was the Democratic party's biggest hope shifted dramatically. A week later, reports had the Dukakis campaign completely eviscerated by the departures of Sasso and aide Paul Tully. It was "the political equivalent of a lobotomy," wrote one analyst. "Dukakis has eliminated the part of his brain that understood politics." The smooth, cigar-smoking Sasso had long been regarded as the governor's dark alter ego, the tough guy who could play the game while Mr. Clean stood aloof from the less admirable side of politics.

But Mike Dukakis just kept on campaigning, putting one foot in front of the other. The night he formally accepted Sasso's resignation, he went through with his scheduled interview for David Frost's TV series *The Next President.* Frost's producer was impressed by the fact that Dukakis kept excusing himself to take calls from frightened lieutenants around the country, calmly reassuring them.

Although Dukakis never faltered outwardly during that period, he was less than impressive on the stump, his tone always modulated, the words crisply formed and clipped, but no emotional buttons pushed, no spiritual uplift. Nick Metropolis, his close aide, says it took him about a month to recover. "He was off his game, until one night in Iowa when Joe Kennedy, Jr., was introducing him, and he loosened up and began to have a good time."

John Sasso has had only one criticism of the campaign since he left it. He worries that Dukakis is not being aggressive enough: "You can't be elected president without taking some risks."

I told the governor this, reminding him that he'd effectively dismembered Richard Gephardt in Iowa the previous August with one line—"That's the difference between you and me, Dick. You're a legislator, and I'm an executive."

His response echoed the rationale he gave for leaking negative material in the race against King. "The only reason I did it was because the guy was coming after me. When somebody starts attacking you, you have to—just once!—that's all." Sure enough, later in the campaign when Gephardt ridiculed him as a "yuppie" candidate supported by Establishment "elites," Dukakis fired back with both barrels, calling Gephardt a "flip-flopper" and a "prince of darkness." Indeed, he hired Sasso's advertising firm, Hill, Holliday, to do the TV commercial that animated Gephardt's flip-flops. And he pulled out in front of all his rivals on Super Tuesday.

I asked the governor whether, as the nominee, he'd take on George Bush directly, and challenge him on his Iran-contra story. "I certainly would have no hesitation in saying, the guy with the longest foreign-policy résumé in this race is a fellow that sat there and approved or just went along with swapping of arms for hostages. Went to the Philippines, told Marcos, 'We love your commitment to democracy.' If that's experience, count me out."

Running on character is Mike Dukakis's best issue, and he knows it. His blunt phrase "I believe we can make a real difference in real people's lives" comes across as sincere. With an incumbent president believed by 60 percent of the American people to be a liar, the prospect of being led by a man who seems congenitally incapable of lying is refreshing. His stubbornness, however, is a trait to be weighed from both sides. Channeled into the perseverance needed to run a long, hard campaign, it can be both admirable and formidable. But a stubborn, self-righteous president, dug in against Congress, evokes the prospect of an irresistible force meeting an immovable object. The example of Ronald Reagan's intransigence on the budget is instructive.

Dukakis has learned to inspire loyalty, and that is another great asset, both on the campaign trail and in the White House. The same man who had to be reminded to say thank you to his gubernatorial staff now goes out of his way to make phone calls to people, according to Hale Champion, his chief of staff. "If somebody is not going to get an appointment that they wanted, he'll say, 'Make sure I talk to that person who has done good work,' " says Champion. "On that personal aspect he's enormously careful and involved."

Hitching a ride up to a debate in New Hampshire on the governor's charter, I had been curious when the first stop by his van was outside a small wooden college building. Nick Metropolis told me, "He's stopping here to do staff interviews." Staff interviews? "He interviews every person who wants to work for him—he may be the only candidate who does. It's what he believes in most strongly—the grass-roots level of a campaign."

Governor Dukakis says that any political leader who wants to be president must be a cheerleader for the highest ethics. Like John Kennedy. Yes, but, I interject in one of our interviews, in the twenty-five years since J.F.K., Americans have learned situational ethics.

"What are situational ethics?" he asks.

To such dark thoughts Mike Dukakis seems all but impervious. He has a real capacity for incredulity. Gary Hart's behavior was as far from his comprehension as Reagan's invasion of Grenada. "What kind of craziness is that?" he will say. Friends like Lipsitt, expecting a more sophisticated analysis, have to remind themselves, "When it violates his deeply held values, it hits a gut, emotional response."

While his responses on domestic issues are often detailed, with an underpinning of experience, Mike Dukakis's pronouncements on foreign policy sound like liberal bumper stickers. He is an internationalist. As a result of growing up in a household that was bilingual and had another tradition, he says, "I think you have a kind of world view almost automatically." But he seems to favor a *MacNeil/Lehrer Newshour* format for settling the world's problems: In a perfect world, reasonable people would sit down and make Costa Rican President Arias's peace plan work in Central America. And we wouldn't be "wandering around in the Persian Gulf bumping into mines." Let Kuwait ask the Russians to run interference for them in the Gulf, Dukakis says.

His message restates Reagan's appealing ends, but calls for very different means: a national comeback to optimism, energy, innovation, sacrifice for country, and social utopianism. It is the sort of call to revitalization on which political cycles have turned, every seventeen years or so, away from the retreat into privatization, denial of social problems, and old-time religions. The question is, can Mike Dukakis transmit his personal discipline and unswerving confidence to a nation sliding into the twilight of its supremacy?

The team he might assemble in the White House would surely draw on Massachusetts's competitive edge in advanced education and its cottage industry of raising prize politicos. One can imagine a beehive of idealistic young postgraduates. Unlike Jimmy Carter, to whom Dukakis is often compared, this small man is not threatened by larger-than-life experts or political appointees who get more press than he does—as long as they get the job done. And Kitty Dukakis would unquestionably bring a new dimension to the job of First Lady; she'd be a fiery activist with a love of the arts who knows, from experience, that it's not enough simply to tell 'em, "Just say no."

In a sense, his candidacy has been a release for Michael Dukakis. As a boy, he searched for Greek-American role models, but it is a relatively small ethnic group and he soon stopped looking for a hero and started trying to become one. The Greek-American community has certainly rewarded his efforts, with spectacular financial contributions as well as political support. As his friend Peter Bassett explains it, "There's a very active Greek press, and when a guy like Mike Dukakis becomes governor of a major state, they follow his career avidly, they know what his accomplishments are, and then, perfect, he's running for president—let's go!"

Dukakis has returned this enthusiasm manyfold. One of the things that has made him most happy has been taking the wraps off his heritage—tentatively at first, then enthusiastically—and now, every day, being affirmed for it. To first-generation Americans of any origin, not to mention the new class of refugees, Mike Dukakis is the living, breathing restoration of the American Dream. He has certainly met the highest expectations of Euterpe and Panos Dukakis. All their efforts to give their Michael every advantage and push him into the mainstream of American culture have produced a son who is conducting a successful and respected run for the presidency of the United States. Having come about as far as he can, he is just now able to return to his roots, to relax, to have fun.

In January he told me, "I want to be president, but not so badly; I mean, it's an incredible experience, for all of us. And I'm running to win. But if it isn't there, I'm still going to be a happy guy."

REFUSAL TO CHANGE

Ronald Reagan in 1984 was a giant among men, "The Emperor of the West," as political columnist Joseph Kraft dubbed him. His reelection campaign was a pageant of symbolism from start to finish. And as if by extension of his patriotic magic, the opening ceremonies of the summer 1984 Olympics in Los Angeles satisfied the eternal need for ceremony like no other spectacle in recent memory. The athletes who marched, nation by nation, through the living rooms of two billion people connected by television sets around the world, were men and women so strong and splendid in form that everyone wanted to live up to them. The Games over which President Reagan presided symbolized nothing less than the triumph of human beings over mortal limitations.

By the time Ronald and Nancy Reagan were ready to star in the Republican-convention spectacular in Dallas, theirs was a closed, self-congratulatory world. They had come to Washington as Hollywood stars, and now they were in a position of power to fuse their "real" life in Washington with a movie life that had always been more real to them. Gigantized images of the convention speakers were thrown up on a screen behind them in the huge Dallas arena. We saw a movie of Nancy in which footage from Ronnie and Nancy's last Hollywood film, *Hellcats of the Navy*, was juxtaposed with sentimental images of the couple strolling, arm in arm, across their ranch. When the screen behind the real Nancy suddenly switched to an image of her husband—monitored from his hotel room—the audience wouldn't rest until he had seen her, and she had seen him seeing her. NBC's Tom Brokaw drily observed that this was a giant version of *The Dating Game*.

In that vast arena I watched young men, with buzz-cut hair and button-down shirts and yellow silk ties, who looked like Secret Service agents but were really college students, and their female counterparts, who were wearing sweet summer dresses but strictly for success. These were not the radical-right fringe. They were, many of them, sons and daughters of Democrats and independents. And they were all fired up by Ronald Reagan.

They belonged to what was suddenly the most conservative age group in the country—eighteen to twenty-four. How had these kids made such a sharp right turn? The first political image to sear itself into their teenage consciousness was of dozens of blindfolded, stumbling, powerless prisoners—surrogates for Uncle Sam suddenly stripped of all dignity—being marched before the eyes of the world by a bunch of bearded young Iranian thugs. They had come of age under a president who seemed helpless to effect the release of the American hostages in Iran. In the transition from the teens to the twenties, the drives toward independence and a positive self-image are always in high gear, and these kids were desperate for something, anything, of which to feel proud. They had been denied even an Olympic team to root for when Carter pulled out to protest the Russian invasion of Afghanistan. And if they were able to start college, they could hardly indulge themselves in liberal-artsy courses like Comp. Lit. or History. Many went into accounting or business school, or some hard-nosed curriculum that might "give them an edge" in a world of double-digit inflation and double-gender competition.

The first president for whom many of them voted had immediately rewarded them with a very different visual symbol—hostages coming home to an outpouring of bottled-up patriotism. Reagan appealed directly to them, as a leader who personified the innocence and virtues of a nation that feared itself lost. Churchill at the withdrawal from Dunkirk, Napoleon in the Alps, Roosevelt during the long night of the Great Depression, Ronald Reagan presiding over the liberation of American hostages on his Inauguration Day—they all exuded this charismatic quality of leadership possessed by a rare few and used effectively only by those who have mastered the communications medium of their age.

But the watershed was Grenada. These kids identified with the "day of freedom," when American medical students were carried across a hostile beach by U.S. Marines in full battle gear, as if it were Okinawa or Normandy. It was a perfect war—no bigger than a TV set, no longer than a mini-series, no casualties to speak of, and we knocked over a Marxist dictatorship, so there! Somehow, these images wiped away the ghastly bombing of a marine barracks in Beirut where 241 Americans were killed while they slept—only three days before the invasion of Grenada. The kids, like their president, lived by a selective reality. Ronald Reagan was a winner. And they were determined to win with Ron and Nancy.

Le tout Dallas turned out for the Republican party of parties during that convention week. It was a white-tie Arabian Nights theme party held at the Willow Bend Polo Club. Staged with extravagant sets and fabulous scenes with costumes meant to make everybody part of the production, it was a fitting tableau for the whole Reagan presidency. The evening was all about status. People discussed how it really wasn't *that* expensive to keep a couple of polo ponies. Or about selling off the old homestead for "five point nine." "And what business are *you* in?" asked a breathy matron, as offhandedly as Blanche Dubois. Her seat partner smiled and made a big O with his lips. For oil. A fifth-generation Texan exclaimed over the women's gowns with a little puff of excitement, "Why, they're just like the dresses we wore for my deb party in 1933." No one talked about issues or the convention or the campaign or even the Democrats. They talked about how fabulous they were.

Standing by the door, as the resplendent three hundred swept in, was a man, naked to the waist, barefoot, wearing a turban and sultan's-slave pants. His was the only skin of color in the whole crowd, and it was glossy with sweat. His massive arms were folded over his glistening chest.

"Aren't you—?" I began to inquire.

He smiled, relieved that someone actually had spoken to him.

"Yes." He was the former Dallas Cowboys football star Duane Thomas.

"What are you doing here, dressed like that?"

"I've been asking myself the same thing." He laughed ruefully.

I looked once more at his Oriental slave costume. "What are you supposed to be?"

"Not addressing the economic problems of the underdogs, I can tell you that."

Flash forward two years and two months to November 1986. When the Iran-contra scandal first broke, the president relied on the coping strategies that had worked for him in the past. First, the salesman's speech. Always before when his deep voice quivered with emotion and he talked of his "visions" and the "miracle" that is America, it was as though some divine afflatus had descended upon him to point the way for all of us—that was the Reagan magic.

Then, suddenly, his dream-spinning unraveled before our very eyes. During the first press conference he'd held in four months, he tried using the old Reagan charm on the media. His performance startled the nation. He was poorly informed, uncertain, and couldn't get through four points without forgetting the last:

"The causes that I outlined here in my opening statement, first of all, to try and establish a relationship with a country that is of great strategic importance to peace and, uh, everything else in the Middle East, at the same time also, to [pause], strike a blow against terrorism, and uh, to get our hostages back, as we did, and uh to, this, this particular thing was we felt necessary in order to make the contacts that we made . . . and there was a fourth item also as I pointed out."

Toward the end, he even appeared to some as if he were about to cry. To others, it looked as if the curtain had been drawn and, as Tom Shales wrote, we'd all glimpsed the Wizard of Oz before he turned and shuffled away, so as not to be exposed as a kindly old fraud.

The actor-president who had perfected the part we all so desperately wanted to believe was real—a bullet-proof, media-proof, crisis-proof leader, prerecorded for the history books as "the most popular American president in fifty years"—was cut down virtually overnight to the size of a normal politician.

How did we get from there to here?

Even those who have worked most closely with him, or covered him as correspondents, say, "Ronald Reagan is still very much a puzzle to me." His chronicler for seventeen years, Hugh Sidey, wrote breathlessly at the end of 1987, ". . . after seven years of unrelenting and often brutal analysis, few if any experts know exactly the qualities that sustain and propel this man on a journey that has taken him happily through three-fourths of a century." Sidey suggests those qualities may be destined to be known only to God and Nancy.

At the risk of seeming impertinent in trying to join such august company, I still find it compelling to attempt to piece together the puzzle:

How does Reagan's mind work? Does it ever change? Is he truly unaware of the facts or willfully ignorant? Does he still believe in his policies after everyone else tells him they've failed? How can he be known for both his "geniality" and his "detachment"? How is one to explain the contradiction between the "passivity" that allows him to be so easily manipulated and the "stubbornness" that fires his hard-line veto strategy to the point where he dares Congress, Clint Eastwood style, to "make my day"? And why, in the face of so many blunders and such a monumental insensitivity to the sufferings of the homeless, minorities, AIDS victims, and the millions plagued by drug abuse and related violence, why do so many Americans still believe Ronald Reagan is a nice man? His is a character study that challenges us all. Who *was* he?

Only now, as insiders leave and begin talking, are some of the myths that insulated Ronald Reagan ready to be stripped away. Several of his closest advisers, who were in day-to-day contact with the president, have shared their observations with me, while asking there be no attribution. Their insights, together with those in the most probing books written about his early childhood, political biographies, Lou Cannon's Boswellian columns and two books, and Reagan's own autobiography, make it possible to suggest some connections that might explain both the formidable strengths and the almost pathetic failings of the great pretender.

EIGHT

Ronald Reagan: Who *Was* That Masked Man?

"As a kid I lived in a world of pretend," Reagan has admitted.

He could conjure up a tiny fragile world from a collection of butterflies and bird's eggs discovered in an attic, or create a tropical forest by staring into the globes of glass over flowers. Fantastic griffins could be made to fly out of lumped horsehair furniture and wars fought on the wall with the shadows of lead soldiers. For a boy born shy and scrawny, but with a vivid imagination to keep him company, he learned the habit of solitary play early. A loner, they called him. A dreamer. Caught up in fantasies of a life as a trapper along the Rock River, or lighting out for the West to be a cowboy . . .

Reality was grimly different. Dixon, Illinois, was an isolated backwater village that might have been a hundred leagues under the sea, so culturally distant was it from Chicago. The Reagans moved frequently, but of necessity, not for upward mobility. Because of Jack Reagan's drinking, they were forced to move from the flat over a bakery with no toilet facilities where Ronald was born. Tampico, Chicago, Galesburg, Monmouth, try Tampico again, on to Dixon—the Reagans were always the new folks and were never long enough in one neighborhood to form friendships.

"Dutch," as Ronald was called, shifted to different schools every year between the ages of six and ten. His father, a footloose orphan, had quit school in sixth grade. Not much store was

257

set by academic achievements in the Reagan household. A natural tumbleweed, a joker, Jack Reagan talked himself into sales jobs by stretching the truth. Whatever money he brought in by whatever job he could temporarily hold was siphoned off by his Saturday-night drinking bouts. Nelle Reagan took in roomers and sewing to pay the rent. Still, the family could afford meat only on Sundays, and then it was liver the butcher would have otherwise kept aside as pet food or discarded.

The world was a blur to young Reagan. "Stop that blinking, boy," he'd be scolded at school. Dutch couldn't read the blackboard, even from a front seat, but he was good at bluffing his lessons. It never occurred to him to complain about the faint and fuzzy outlines of what he saw. In his mind, as he described it in his autobiography, *Where's the Rest of Me?*, "the whole world was made up of colored blobs. . . . I was sure it appeared the same way to everyone else."

His parents didn't notice the problem, either. His older brother, Neil, has said Ronnie had "a photographic mind," which helped him manage his schoolwork: He could rattle off dates in second grade the way he would do later with statistics as a politician. Content with taking in only the superficial content of the material world, never one to be curious, Dutch went along spinning out his daydreams.

"But by the time I was [eight or nine] I felt self-conscious about it," wrote Reagan. "People made fun of me . . . 'What are you doing, kid? Talking to yourself? Enough people make enough cracks like that, and a sensitive boy . . . begins to feel a little silly . . . So from then on he doesn't pretend openly . . . That was the way it was with me anyway."

Pretending, then, became a secret habit, but it also became, more and more, an essential escape. For soon the most sinister aspect of Reagan's childhood could no longer be ignored.

By 1921 Reagan's father had his own shoestore. Playing fast and loose with facts, he passed himself off as a "practipedist," a highfalutin title for a man with no credentials other than a correspondence-course degree and an X-ray machine in his shoestore. One winter day, at the age of eleven, Dutch came home from school to the nightmare every child of an alcoholic dreads: His father, flat on his back on the front porch, sodden with snow, arms flopped out, the sour smell of the speakeasy belching out of his mouth between snores.

"He was drunk, dead to the world," Reagan has written. "I wanted to . . . pretend he wasn't there. . . . I don't know at what age I knew what the occasional absences or the loud voices in the night meant, but up till now my mother or my brother handled the situation and I was a child in bed with the privilege of pretending sleep. . . ."

The boy managed to drag the deadweight of his drunken father into the house and upstairs to bed. Thereafter, the men who drank hard with Jack Reagan saw the boy come to the aid of his father when he was barely able to stand on his feet or out cold. Throughout adolescence, Ronnie did not mention his parent's behavior. And in public he always showed respect and affection for his father.

Saturday was the cruelest night of the week. Nelle Reagan, a devout member of the Disciples of Christ Church, would pray for deliverance from the rascality of Jack Reagan. "She was on her knees several times a day," Ronald Reagan would recall years later. "And she just refused to give up, no matter how dark things looked." But she could never drive away the demon, and always she forgave her husband. She sought escape from these realities in the more fervent embrace of her revivalist religion, proselytizing around the county. And in the same year as his initiation into the full degradation of having an alcoholic father, her Ronnie, at the unusually young age of eleven, was baptized by total immersion.

But something very different was apparently going on inside the boy. With a shy, introverted temperament and a cautious, constricted nature that sought out set roles rather than enjoying spontaneous and risky behavior, Ronnie not surprisingly shrank from his father's hard-drinking, rough-joke, saloon society. Anne Edwards, in her careful biography *Early Reagan,* writes that "Dutch developed two worlds—public and private—and was acutely alert to the dangers of Jack's benders so that when they came he could cope with them, a feat that took a tremendous amount of self-control . . . Nelle worried about Dutch's . . . ability to block out such things as Jack's binges."

It wasn't until Reagan was thirteen that he borrowed his

mother's glasses and, for the first time in his life, felt the full jolt of reality. He was woefully nearsighted. Although he reports that "the miracle of seeing was beyond believing," he soon became self-conscious about his immense, horn-rimmed eyeglasses. Vanity won out over curiosity. The glasses were worn only in private. And the boy slipped back into his fuzzy, fantasy-supporting private world at every opportunity.

Neither one of his parents ever had physical contact with their sons, unless it was Jack in a rage administering a beating to Ronnie or his brother, Neil, while Nelle cried and pleaded for him to have mercy. So Reagan developed his own habit to deny the darkest aspect of his childhood—the hard-drinking father who shamed him. If his father used alcohol to escape reality, and his mother used religious devotion, Ronald Reagan found his escape in daydreams.

Since early childhood, then, Reagan has been denying harsh realities and concocting his own, more pleasant alternatives. A born dreamer, whose active imagination was encouraged by the handicap of extreme nearsightedness, he saw a world of "colored blobs" where the line between fantasy and reality was *naturally* blurred. Even primal figures, like his father, were only present in that world when they were very close, but if the boy stepped away, his father would become fuzzy and—what relief!—he could make him disappear.

He gravitated toward his mother's world, and there he was able to build on his gift for creating fiction by becoming a performer. Herself a frustrated actress, Nelle Reagan scraped up the money to give her favorite son elocution lessons. The boy eagerly seized on the opportunity to improve his make-believe self-presentation. He acted out roles created for him by his mother in church skits. "Nelle's obsessiveness demanded a continuous performance by him in public—" writes Edwards. It was a much better stage for Dutch than the athletic field, for instance.

It wasn't much good making the Dixon varsity-football squad, when they kept him warming the bench for two years straight. Neighbor Ed O'Malley has said, "He always wanted to carry the ball," and "would go charging ahead." But without his glasses, Dutch Reagan was as helpless as Harpo Marx against older boys waiting to trip him up and send him flying. He was far more successful being gracious to adults and shouldering some responsibilities in his mother's church activities. The Dramatic Club adviser at North Dixon High School once said that Ronnie "fit into almost any kind of role you put him into." Even then, with his reddish-brown hair Brylcreemed into a perfect pompadour, Ronald Reagan impressed people with his speaking ability.

At sixteen, his legs having grown long and exceptionally strong, swimming was a physical arena in which Dutch could rightly show off. He went to work as a lifeguard at Lowell Park. Twelve hours a day with no books, no stimulating conversation, might well have been a crashing bore to a more curious or intellectual boy. But Reagan had his daydreams, and nothing disturbed them in that chair so high above the crowd, the guard stand he saw as being "like a stage. Everyone had to look at me." Of those six summers throughout high school and college, he points out as his crowning achievement, "my beloved lifeguarding."

He fished seventy-seven souls out of the Rock River. There is some suggestion, however, that he overacted the role of guardian of those who dared to take risks. Many of his rescues were of grown men, toward whose undisciplined behavior in eating and drinking before swimming Ronnie displayed the censorious attitude he dared not show toward his father. Many bawled him out, as Garry Wills documented in *Reagan's America: Innocents at Home.* Only one person—a blind man—ever thanked Dutch for saving his life. But the park's owners and the local paper praised him repeatedly for his record.

From then on, as he entered the radio business, then Hollywood, then TV, his gift for pretense was rewarded again and again. He earned his reputation in radio during the Depression by concocting whole ball games from scraps of paper that came off a telegraph relay while he sat in a studio three hundred miles away. His most famous radio story underscores his gift for fabulation. When the wire went dead in the middle of a pitch, Reagan held his audience in the thrall of make-believe, inventing so many foul balls he lost count. Dutch Reagan was saluted in the midwestern press more than once for his unfailing ability to pretend. It was clear that acting would be the ideal profession for him. Actors are in the business of borrowing personalities, which they change like costumes from a stage wardrobe. Although in real life he had no true friends, in Hollywood Reagan was successfully type-cast in the role of "best friend." He made fifty-one movies during the heyday of the big studios. And years later, in his political incarnation Governor Reagan was praised by the California press for refusing to acknowledge the unpleasant or admit mistakes.

It became axiomatic that "he just puts the negative behind him and goes on."

Reagan's idyllic first marriage, too, existed only in his mind. As he got out of the Army Air Corps, where he'd spent World War II making films in Culver City, adjacent to Los Angeles, he cast himself as the tired soldier heading home on a troop ship. "All I wanted to do," he wrote later, "was to rest up awhile, make love to my wife and come up refreshed to do a better job in an ideal world." Jane Wyman, a talented and serious actress, gave him a daughter, Maureen Elizabeth. She also threw herself into the tragic parts that would eventually lead to an Academy Award. When her sadness couldn't be buoyed by Reagan's unfailing sunniness, he told her, "We'll lead an ideal life if you'll just avoid doing one thing: Don't think." As Ronnie described the story of their wedded bliss, through Warner Brothers press agents: The Reagans of Hollywood "show signs of becoming one of the important first families of the film colony, a new dynasty."

Jane Wyman told a painfully contradictory story when she filed for divorce. She had found her husband a bore, obsessed with politics and union activities. "Finally, there was nothing between us," she testified. Lou Cannon reported in *Ronnie and Jesse* (about Reagan and California boss Jesse Unruh) that Reagan confessed to friends at the time that he was "shattered."

One night, at a small dinner party during his last term as president, Reagan began to talk about the worst year in his life—1949. In debt, without friends, no longer able to get acting jobs, desolate about the breakup of what he had believed was a successful marriage—the last straw was a dumb accident in a park baseball game. Another actor happened to throw the bat at Reagan's leg and shattered the bone in something like fifteen places. Reagan spent months in a full leg cast.

These grim setbacks all hit him at an age that is particularly vulnerable—thirty-eight—when one is approaching midlife and naturally fearful of peering into what is anticipated as the void. For an actor, the terror is not just existential, it is real. The parts for romantic leads dry up. Reagan wasn't even getting second-lead offers anymore. And even second leads did not get invited to Hollywood parties. Reagan had failed to make the transition to a peacetime actor.

And so—he spun out his tale of woe to the dinner guests—he took a boat to England that winter on the promise of a film role. He found himself in a country that was digging out of a world war, a country that in its desolation, in its bone-chilling climate, in its shortage of every kind of nourishment, and seemingly hopeless prospects for gainful employment, perfectly expressed his own predicament. Jobless, wifeless, friendless, and cold, the role he played in *The Hasty Heart* was a romanticized version of his real-life situation: He was an American soldier recovering in a Burmese hospital.

Enter Nancy Davis. After Reagan arrived back in the U.S., she engineered a meeting with him, the man on the top of her list of eligible Hollywood bachelors. Reagan would later rhapsodize about her effect on him: "How do you describe coming into a warm room from out of the cold?" Having had mediocre success in her own movie career, Nancy focused all her efforts on protecting, guiding, and advancing her interests through her new husband.

Reagan was an active Democrat at the time of his marriage in 1952. Nancy was apolitical. The crucial turning point in Reagan's political evolution was prompted by a personal experience: his struggle against confiscatory taxes. He and his bride lived in a heavily mortgaged new home in Pacific Palisades. Deeply in debt, but no longer under contract, he had to take any part that came along.

Reagan's fortunes changed dramatically while he was president of the Screen Actors Guild, where he used his position more effectively than he had as an actor to build a nice nest egg. Between 1952 and 1954, he performed a huge favor for M.C.A. (Music Corporation of America), his talent agency. Television was becoming the new cash cow of the entertainment business, and M.C.A. wanted to beat the major studios by producing its own TV shows, drawing upon its own stable of actors. It was long-standing S.A.G. policy to prohibit its actors from signing with agents who were also producers, which would mean turning over control of their contract negotiations to the very people handing out the jobs. In 1952, with the stroke of a pen, Ronald Reagan changed all that by signing a confidential blanket waiver for M.C.A. It allowed one, and only one, agency to produce TV shows.

Two years later, M.C.A.'s vice-president suddenly rescued Ronald Reagan's career with the offer of a million-dollar contract to host *General Electric Theater.* He went from a has-been movie actor, able to get only third-rate parts and deeply in debt, to a TV star who lived in a G.E. dream house overlooking the Pacific. In that same year, 1954, while Ron and Nancy Reagan still served on the S.A.G. board, the ban on agents producing for TV came up for extension. Reagan arranged a private session in which the M.C.A. waiver was extended. M.C.A.'s founder, the grandly ambitious Jules Stein, his monopoly now guaranteed, was able to build his fiefdom into the first and largest of Hollywood's superagencies. It became nicknamed "The Octopus." Stein did not forget the favor.

Taxes remained very high after the war; actors might pay 70 to 90 percent of their annual income, and Reagan was fit to be tied about it. Having never been rich before, he wasn't prepared for the pinch of a steeply graduated income tax at a time when income averaging wasn't allowed.

He went to Washington to testify against the discrimination imposed by the tax structure on creative people who have a short earning span. The fear of becoming financially dependent had permanently engraved itself on his mind, and made him loathe taxes. Going back to the doctrines of the Disciples of Christ Church that celebrated individual initiative, and the Horatio Alger stories he had devoured, he only needed someone with more political sophistication to provide him with a policy framework for his personal fears. Loyal Davis, Nancy's hard-line conservative stepfather, offered it. He presented Ronald Reagan with a "vision" of America that served the purpose of making him feel safe in a hostile world and of cementing his fantasies into a reality-tight construction: the conservative ideology.

As Reagan traveled around the G.E. circuit from plant to plant, making speeches in the conservative mid-fifties, his audiences responded fervently whenever he denounced government. This further solidified his feeling that big government is bad and all those who fall back on government assistance are welfare cheats. Nearing the end of the decade, Reagan was told by G.E. he was more in demand as a public speaker than anyone in the country except President Eisenhower. Although Reagan admittedly still didn't have a political philosophy, per se, he did now have a political prop for his fictions.

In 1962 Reagan told his agents he was thinking of entering politics and needed financial security. Stein went to Twentieth Century-Fox and engineered a fantastically profitable sale of Reagan's ranch, originally purchased at $293 an acre, for the inflated price of $8,000 an acre. When he was called before a grand jury to testify on why M.C.A. had been granted a monopoly, Reagan tried out two stratagems that would thereafter serve him well. He denied it, and retreated into forgetfulness.

The $2 million Reagan pocketed from the ranch sale, in effect, bought him his own stage on which to perform. He became, increasingly, a political gadfly. Reagan had first discovered his gift for political oratory by making a speech, as a mere freshman at Eureka College, that brought down the college's president. Public service had never entered even his wildest dreams; he loved the entertainment world. But deciding he had been "blessed" as an audience-pleaser (as he elaborated on his story in 1984), "I thought it was only right that I should use that in behalf of causes that I believe in."

Those causes became contained in "The Speech," as Reagan himself originally dubbed it. As a G.E. salesman and conservative rabble-rouser, Reagan delivered essentially the same speech he'd showcased around the Hollywood circuit under the label of "liberal." The content showed no fundamental growth or alteration over the twenty years between 1944 and 1964, according to Lou Cannon, who monitored it closely. The essential parts were a salute to economic individualism, tax reform, democratic ideals, and a crusty anticommunism. It was as dependable as a model airplane kit. No matter how many times The Speech was taken apart, it always came out the same way. Only the label and the audiences changed.

Switching parties was just another surface rearrangement. As a Democrat, Reagan voted for Eisenhower, worked hard for Nixon, and didn't formally change his registration to Republican until 1962. By that time, The Speech had become so blatantly political it drove *G.E. Theater,* and Reagan, off the air.

Reagan was always remarkably facile in being able to rewrite his own story in his head. By 1965, needing to reconstruct the reality he had lived to ready it for public consumption, he chose the genre of Mark Twain. His autobiography, *Where's the Rest of Me?,* reflects an idyllic Huck Finn-Tom Sawyer boyhood. He cast himself in the part of the loner Huck, who is always fishing for catfish, lying on the riverbank, and keeping one eye out for "Pap." *"But I reckon I got to light out for the Territory ahead of the rest, because Aunt Sally she's going to adopt me and sivilize me and I can't stand it. I been there before."*

Garry Wills's insights in *Reagan's America: Innocents at Home* challenged Reagan's rewrite of a classic American work of fiction. In reality, in Mark Twain's world Dutch Reagan would have been the *villain:* the model boy.

Young Ronnie's invention of a fantasy world to block out what really hurt him was a healthy way of adapting—for a child. But the grown-up Reagan's facility for self-delusion gave him an easy out when times of crisis were signaling the necessity for change. The work of development in adulthood, after all, requires letting go of some of the immature techniques that worked before, giving up some magic, some cherished illusions of safety, to allow for growth. Instead, entering mid-life, Reagan found in politics a secure construct for his fears. And from then on, he had a grand stage on which to perform his fictions.

The beauty of it is that Reagan's fictions are sentimentally idealized versions of American values—in many cases, the opposite of what he really lived:

He champions family stability. He came from utter instability. He talks as though, in the world he came from, the father was the unquestioned breadwinner; thus no need for equal rights, day care, or a woman's right to choose. In Reagan's rosy past, everybody knew everybody and when someone's barn burned down, the whole town pulled together to rebuild it; that fantasy was expressed in his volunteerism message. In fact, the father in his house was unreliable, the family knew nobody very well, and Jack Reagan and Ron's brother, Neil, were both out of work until Roosevelt became president and they were given jobs distributing federal relief to the community.

Indeed, it was the world of organized public welfare that kept his family from ruin and allowed him to finish college—exactly the kind of government bureaucracy he has been railing against throughout his political career.

"There are no second acts in American life," declared F. Scott Fitzgerald during his own midlife depression. Ronald Reagan has proved a stunning exception. At the age of fifty-three, he made a speech on national television celebrating the hopeless candidacy of Barry Goldwater. In a mere thirty minutes on that October day of 1964, using the medium of the times, the man formerly self-described as "a near-hopeless hemophiliac liberal" who bled for every cause transformed himself from a junked, middle-aged movie actor into the most vibrant up-and-coming superstar in the nation's conservative political firmament. Washington columnist David Broder pronounced Ronald Reagan's performance "the most successful political debut since William Jennings Bryan" more than sixty years before. By now, Reagan had the stratagems he needed to maintain and communicate his fictions.

He did not initiate the idea of running for political office. Shortly after Goldwater's resounding defeat in '64, a clutch of southern California millionaires brought together by Holmes Tuttle, a Ford dealer from whom Reagan had once bought a car, decided they might be able to use the actor to showcase their brand of politics. Reagan had been out there in the wilderness of southern California conservatism for years, enunciating the very democratic verities that the changes of the sixties threatened to sweep away. The millionaires would look him over as their man to run for governor in 1966. Tuttle brought in a prestigious firm of political managers, Spencer-Roberts, to assess how easily Reagan could be manipulated. When they okayed him, a two-man team of behavioral psychologists was brought in to "fit the personality of an unusual candidate to the demands of the political system."

The psychologists were shocked. What they found on visiting Reagan at home was a man who knew zero about California—and "I mean zero," Dr. Stanley Plog told Cannon. Drastic measures were in order. The psychologists insisted that three days be carved out of Reagan's campaign schedule so they could work on "the whole concept of the man." Holed up in a beach cottage in Malibu, the mental rearrangers went to work cutting and pasting Reagan's rambling generalizations into simple answers, arranged around eight different themes. Then they wrote out five-by-eight cards for him, and snapped them into eight looseleaf binders. Although Reagan kept pretty much to the same sentiments, stemming from his personal experience, before and after the psychologists got hold of him, the Basic Script now had been set into an indelible mold that would last well into his presidency.

Reagan himself found a made-to-order issue in the "Berkeley situation," in which he reduced the vanguard of the free-speech and antiwar movements to campus "sex-and-dope orgies." Through the marvel of television, his fervent John Wayne presence came into the living rooms of scared middle- and working-class parents and reassured them that fundamental American values would stand fast against so-called social change and rebellion.

Californians swept him into office by a landslide.

In those first few months of governing, Ronald Reagan was an eager listener and learner, not the least abashed by his ignorance of state affairs. Nor was he troubled by the fact that only one out of four of his small circle of advisers had had any experience in government. "We were novice amateurs," admitted Lyn Nofziger, the wisecracking correspondent who signed on with Reagan and who, after leaving the White House in 1982, was convicted of breaking conflict-of-interest laws. The gover-

nor's staff presented him with one-page "mini-memos." Reagan
chose from the alternatives with dispatch. Or, to put it another
way, he was an easy sell.

Although a well-known fact in the state capitol, it came as a
total surprise to the new governor that the state was up to its ears
in debt. The man who had begun his election campaign railing
against the unfair tax burden was faced with the necessity of
adding to that burden almost from the moment he took office.

On spending, too, he did a 180-degree turnaround. After
endlessly repeating his diatribe from The Speech against government spending, he had insisted in his inaugural address:
"The truth is, there are simple answers—there just are not easy
ones." The simple answer he'd proposed was to match spending
to income. The actual outcome was the first $5 billion budget
in the state's history.

He hid behind statistics. He hid from the most helpless
victims of his program cuts, such as mental patients. And he
carried it all off as if he saw no contradiction whatsoever. He got
home most every night by six, either took a dip in his pool or
showered, changed into pajamas, and unconcernedly spent
evenings with his wife watching *Bonanza* or *Mission: Impossible,*
and looking over correspondence or memos.

He continued to believe his own fiction—that he was executing his tough "squeeze, cut, and trim" policy—even as he was
mounting the largest tax increase in California's history. "Incor-
rigible optimism," some called it. Others remarked on Reagan's
"incredible ability to rationalize." He glided on, escaping accountability for errors and reverses that would have been fatal
mudslides for lesser politicians.

But almost unavoidably in public life, some dark scandal
will be uncovered that cannot be swept away or shrouded in
illusion. For Governor Reagan, it was a sex scandal.

His name was being touted as a top G.O.P. presidential
prospect when one night eleven poker-faced staffers knocked on
the door of Reagan's hotel suite in San Diego to break some bad
news. Silently, they handed him a report. Governor Reagan read
that a number of homosexuals were working in the top echelons
of his administration.

"My God." Reagan's face blanched. "Has government failed?"

He went into a state of shock that paralyzed his government for the next four months. He couldn't bring himself to disclose the truth. And when a story leaked by Nofziger finally surfaced in the press, Reagan lied with royal indignation— "I refuse to participate in trying to destroy human beings with no factual evidence"—apparently taking the high road in order to hold to the fiction that the situation simply didn't exist.

But here he was using a stratagem considerably more extreme than a gentle retreat into fantasy.

We are all familiar with the defense mechanism of denial. When one is first confronted with a shocking loss or crisis, the unconscious mind may generate a temporary "I don't believe it, this can't be happening" response until the ego is ready to deal with the new reality. This response is normal and temporary, and we all have it from time to time. But denial of unpleasant realities became Reagan's characteristic problem-solving style.

Denial, of course, is a primary symptom of alcoholism. Children of alcoholics tend to take on the same symptom to avoid spilling the family's darkest secret. The child of an alcoholic commonly spends years telling teachers, friends, employers that everything at home is "fine." The painful truth is that at home there is a parent out of control, who can turn into a drunk driver or a child-beater, or go off on a toot and disgrace the whole family. The distortions produced by using such defense mechanisms become part of a person's view of the world. Truths too uncomfortable to admit are unconsciously altered or postponed, and the altered truth then becomes *subjectively* true.

"The Scandal both hurt Reagan and revealed him as a man," wrote Lou Cannon. "He withdrew from administrative detail at the very time he seemed most ready to take real command . . . the Reagan administration never recovered its exciting, if novice, charisma of those first few months . . ."

Cannon, who wrote those words in 1967, might have reprinted them without change twenty years later, during the Iran-contra scandal. Again, Reagan would be paralyzed for four months. Again, he withdrew from administering just when the need was most crucial for him to take charge, and went from dissembling to dithering to silence.

Ronald Reagan drifted into presidential politics with all the incognizant charm of Chauncey Gardiner, the famous television-tutored *naïf* on whom others could project their pet philosophies, and who was adopted as a running mate by the president in the Peter Sellers movie *Being There.* The nation's most influential editorial writers didn't take Reagan much more seriously. As late as March 5 in the election year of 1980, Meg Greenfield wrote him off in *The Washington Post:* "Most of the journalists I know and much of the Eastern world I live in find Reagan's candidacy preposterous." In the so-called runaway election, Reagan got less than 51 percent of the vote. It was nothing like the "mandate" proclaimed by his party and much of the media.

The scene on the morning of his first inauguration is destined to become a classic. Michael Deaver describes it in his book *Behind the Scenes.* An old California retainer, Deaver turned up at Blair House shortly before nine A.M. to help the Reagans prepare for the big day. He asked Nancy where the governor was.

"I guess he's still in bed."

Deaver was incredulous. Still in bed at nine o'clock, on the morning he was to be sworn in as president of the United States?

He found Reagan under a heap of blankets in a pitch-dark bedroom. The dialogue has a decidedly *Being There* air of unreality.

"Governor?"

"Yeah?"

"It's nine o'clock."

"Yeah?"

"Well, you're going to be inaugurated in two hours."

"Does that mean I have to get up?"

History didn't so much catch up with Reagan as turn back to him, which is common during major crises of cultural confidence. As Reagan took office, political scientist James David Barber predicted his character type would be "passive-positive" with a "tendency to drift . . . the danger is confusion, delay and then impulsiveness." But the hype of his popularity was main-

271

tained with such intensity by the public-relations team who came into office with him that Ronald Reagan rode through his first legislative season like a hero on a white charger. The press was never able to lay a glove on him. He sold the so-called Reagan Revolution without the outcry over cuts in social programs that many expected.

The shock troops who came to power with him, charged by their own irrational conceptions of the world, were intent upon setting the United States on an entirely new course. His kitchen cabinet of self-made California businessmen set up a command post in the Old Executive Office Building. Ron could dress up as Captain Marvel while they pulled the strings. Détente was out. Arms were in, regardless of quality or cost. Human rights were swept off the agenda. "Authoritarian governments" were all the rage. Congress resisted this simpleminded formulation of the world, and the public fretted over the possibility that President Reagan would mount some foolish military adventure.

But always he kept the people entertained, using radio to deliver weekly homilies in a manner he'd picked up from the master, F.D.R., and mounting his sermons about fighting communism on the medium he had long since conquered as a G.E. made-for-TV salesman. Frequent photo opportunities kept the razzle-dazzle going and distracted attention from the massive structural changes the Reagan administration was beginning to introduce to the economic system, the social contract, and the courts.

Indeed, as president, Reagan continued to act like a candidate. Still running, instead of governing.

Candidates, even more than presidents, are engaged in "impression management," as Dean Keith Simonton calls it in *Why Presidents Succeed.* And however much people may pay lip service to the ideal of the philosopher king, with his high intelligence, sophistication, and intellectual curiosity, in practice the American masses prefer middlebrow candidates with an anti-intellectual "common touch."

But once the candidate becomes the president, a different standard of mental abilities needs to come into play. A 1981 study of ten presidents by Philip Tetlock traced how well and how quickly they shifted from the simplicity of campaign rhetoric to the complexity of their postelection statements. The shift was found to take place very quickly, if it happened at all. "Within the first month the complexity level was attained that would be sustained in the next couple of years."

What Reagan's new team began to notice in the first month was his laid-back, drifting inattentiveness. Lee Atwater, then a lean and hungry operative working for the president's political advisory team, could hardly contain his glee. After two weeks in the White House, he went to his boss, Lyn Nofziger:

"This place is a fuckin' candy store. Just waiting to be stolen," meaning, no one was minding the store on political strategy and they could do anything they wished in Reagan's name.

Another member of the White House team soon recognized that Reagan saw only what was right in front of him. He dealt with that and nothing more. "Long-range planning in the Reagan White House was lunch."

Michael Deaver, long one of Nancy Reagan's closest friends, knew Ronald Reagan to be a man of simple beliefs and with a striking lack of intellectual curiosity or depth. Those new to the president's team, however, had to find out the hard way.

Among the true believers, Richard Darman stuck out like a sore thumb. A former member of Elliot Richardson's team at the Justice Department who resigned over Nixon's "Saturday night massacre" during Watergate, Darman had been thoroughly schooled in the northeast-corridor view of Ronald Reagan: This guy is a caricature bureaucrat and a lazy ideologue; he reads his cards, period.

Ronald Reagan had used three-by-five cards as far back as his General Electric days. The only thing that had changed over the years was the size of the cards. As he got older and his eyesight even poorer, he switched to four by six, then to five by eight. He used to write them out by himself. Throughout his 1966 campaign for governor, the cards worked as the firing mechanism for several minutes of oratory, or a one-liner, and they took advantage of his "photographic mind." Since then, they have been passed on and worked over by one set of political handlers after another. His staff members found that Reagan, as one of them describes it, was "totally unashamed to pull out the three-by-five cards we'd prepared for him, and read from them even at a meeting with *us.*"

Darman took encouragement from watching the new president work on his speeches himself. A very astute pencil editor, Reagan edited every speech he gave, quickly and well. Reagan was also extremely orderly in his work habits (vestiges of his mother, Nelle). His desk was clean every night, and each and every item in his briefcase would be in exactly the same place when he returned the next day. Darman found him to be very much a creature of organized work habits; in fact, he was easily rattled if others deviated in the order of the day.

One matter on which he was always alert, even vigilant, was keeping track of his contact lenses. This was important since the extremely nearsighted president was hypersensitive about being seen in glasses. In the office he always wore reading glasses, although he never allowed himself to be photographed with them on. In public he wore one contact lens to read the speech or TelePrompTer, and relied on the other eye to see the world. Imagine the world through Reagan's eyes, then: It is a strangely dreamlike distortion of some sharp images—the lines of his script—and beyond them a faint and fuzzy infinity.

The experts who were called in to suggest programs to the new president, just like the earlier advisers to the new governor, found he was a quick sell. The key was to lock into one of his fantasies. In fact, they scarcely got the chance to do any explaining at all.

The blueprint for the Reagan Revolution was David Stockman's hastily prepared, thirty-five-page, hard-sell job résumé, prepared under the tutelage of Jack Kemp. Reagan bought it on the basis of one anecdote that connected with his past. He never asked about the figures. And in forty days the whole concept of "Reaganomics" was born.

Most sweeping policy changes are nurtured and debated over years. Not in the White House of dreamer Reagan. Transforming the rough computations of a few ideologues into a tempest of change that would send waves around the world, to the end of the decade if not the century, Reagan stood like Prospero the magician on his beautiful little island—aloof from it all—and remade America's economic world in forty days.

Stockman wasn't sure whether to laugh or cry. In the few informal sessions he attended with the president-elect, it appeared as if Edwin Meese were the acting president. The chief simply listened, nodded, smiled, asked no questions, issued no orders. He seemed so "serene and passive." Stockman, of course, was all fired up to mount a bloody, head-chopping assault on the whole American welfare state to pay for a massive tax cut. Reagan, he found, grasped only half the equation—the happy ending.

Stockman was back in the Oval Office six months later. The blow-dried revolutionary had gone back to his hand calculator and discovered overnight that there was no $60 billion surplus at the end of the supply-side rainbow. Instead, there would have to be $100 billion in spending *cuts* every year just to balance the budget.

He tried to uncouple the engine of his ideas from Ronald Reagan's fantasies before they had a head-on collision with reality. No luck. They had become fused. It would be twenty-four months before the illusion was shattered and Reagan's vulnerability to any "preposterous, wantonly reckless notion" that supported his fantasies was first exposed.

Reagan's most cherished daydream—an across-the-board tax cut—took effect on September 30, 1981. During the first week in November, the president met with his economic-policy team every day. By now they had compiled for him all the facts and he heard all the arguments against Stockman's original formulation.

Their consensus forecast showed the tax cut would mean that over the next five years the deficit would mount up to more than $700 billion. That came close to the entire national debt it had taken America two hundred years to accumulate. "It just took your breath away," writes Stockman. "No government official had ever seen such a thing."

Reagan remained serene. He did not see the numbers. He only heard those words that echoed his well-meaning fiction.

Stockman was one of the first to realize Ronald Reagan was not only fiscally incompetent, he didn't seem to care. Meese stayed away from economic policy. James Baker concentrated on politics. Deaver was busy social climbing with Nancy and her friends the Alfred Bloomingdales. It was Richard Darman, the most patient of the bunch, who took the trouble to try to understand how the president's mind worked.

Darman was confounded: Why couldn't the boss take in new information? He watched Reagan's eyes when he was given a briefing book. When the president looked at a sheet of paper, his eyes scanned the whole page, rather than focusing on it line by line, as people do who are reading. He seemed to be taking a snapshot of the page.

It must be true, as his brother had said—Reagan had a "photographic mind." It had allowed him to glide through a course like high-school civics, never cracking a book yet able to pass. But as that mental reflex naturally declined with age, Reagan had no other habits of study to compensate.

One common definition of intelligence is the ability to keep two opposing ideas in mind at the same time and still think. Reagan could not integrate opposing ideas on his own. Somebody else had to do it for him, and condense the result. The full realization of how Reagan's mind worked hit Darman like a ton of bricks. The president could not take in two new ideas at the same time unless they were on one page.

Even then, the most alarming predictions and inspired graphic tricks could not guarantee that Ronald Reagan would be able to look reality in the face. He would accept a *Reader's Digest* bromide from a sycophantic adviser every time.

"You might as well know it," Darman told the agitated Stockman, as reported in the latter's *The Triumph of Politics*. "When you sit there going over the deficit projections, the man's eyes glaze over. He tunes out completely because he doesn't fully appreciate that the pony is already built into the numbers."

The reference was to Reagan's favorite story. We all have an anecdote or two we tell about ourselves, quite repetitively, long after the story has worn out its dramatic value; the reason the joke or tale persists is that it captures an essential part of our personal myth. The longest-running story in Reagan's repertoire concerns two boys who each get a Christmas present. One boy is a pessimist, the other an optimist. The pessimist gets a roomful of toys. He is miserable, certain there is some catch involved. The optimist gets a roomful of horse manure. But he's thrilled. With all that manure, he's sure there must be a pony in there somewhere! According to Reagan's fantasy-fused-into-ideology, the coming economic recovery would drastically shrink the deficit numbers by 1987 or '88. And the president could not think in terms of more than one year at a time.

So President Reagan's economic advisers did what the smart men around Reagan had always learned to do. They inched the process along, encouraging the president's self-delusions to the contrary, and then tricked him into doing what they wanted. It wasn't really a tax increase, it was a "management adjustment." *"Hold on, less make up the deffisit . . ."* It's a scene right out of Reagan's own favorite Huckleberry Finn script, where two clever men trick the children of a dead man out of part of their inheritance. Darman, along with Baker, helped guide the tax increases of 1981 and '82, the Social Security compromise of 1983 and the tax-code overhaul in 1986, before Darman left an administration reduced to almost total disarray.

I tested out my denial thesis on one of President Reagan's closest advisers, a man who saw him almost every day for six years. He said, "Yes, he uses denial all the time. Normally, there's a grain of truth in what he's doing to support his denial. That's the reason he's normally very comfortable with his fictional constructs. They're teleological—they serve a higher good, certainly in his mind, and frequently in fact."

Those aspects of life that do not fit Reagan's optimistic fantasies are either not perceived, or when perceived, denied. He is able to put across his daydreams for a very simple reason. As an adviser who has been close to him for many years sums it up:

"Once Reagan creates a fiction, it's real for him."

Ronald Reagan *knows* what he wants the world to look like—like his daydreams. And once those key daydreams are fused into ideology, they are impervious to challenge or the introduction of new information. It is with chilling awe we should regard the result: that such genuine, heartfelt belief projects an image of leadership.

Reagan's performance was sharpest when the Baker-Deaver-Darman group was writing his script (it would weaken in the second term when Donald Regan "let Reagan be Reagan," and still more when the nondirective Howard Baker replaced Regan as White House chief of staff). But no matter how many gaffes or slips or blatant misstatements the media might point out, Reagan brushed them off like an actor who'd blown a line, and hurried on to get through the scene.

"Tell me what you want me to *say*," he'd tell his staff. *Direct me.* Most politicians are doers, and much better as officeholders than as candidates. Reagan was the opposite, happiest when performing as a perpetual candidate.

Edward Rollins, his top political adviser, accompanied the president on a triumphal drive through downtown Manhattan after an award ceremony at the precinct used for the old *Kojak* TV series. A million people or more thronged the streets, straining for a glimpse of that magnetic smile. To Rollins, all this adulation was a tremendous thrill. But to Ronald Reagan, he noticed, it seemed commonplace. It made Rollins realize that "here was a guy, over seventy, who'd been a celebrity all of his life, from his days as a lifeguard to radio to the movies. It's the most natural thing in the world to him to have crowd approval." It was comforting to the adviser, who had seen Richard Nixon's pathological insecurity up close. This Reagan, Rollins told others, is a very secure man, and that's what we need in a president. He wasn't going to use the Oval Office to fulfill his own ego needs.

But it soon became a running joke around the White House that if any one of the political operatives had a chance to be alone with the president, the others would pounce on him when he came out and ask, in mock breathlessness, not "Which policy did you talk about?" but "Which movie plot did he tell you?" Reagan had no interest in talking about politics, none. "I could sit with Richard Nixon and chew over every precinct chairman in the country," a member of the political staff recalled. "Reagan wouldn't even know what a precinct chairman was. But he could tell you every storyline in every old movie that was made."

"Never forget, they're both actors," Lyn Nofziger once reminded his colleagues about Ron and Nancy. "And they'll always put the performance on." After watching Reagan, another adviser's scattered observations ripened into an insight: "He's not sitting there day after day making the tough decisions. He is acting, he's basically *playing* president."

A year before Reagan would stand for reelection, the United States was bogged down in Lebanon, with our marines in jeopardy, and the Democrats warning every day of some dire result. Reagan needed a show of military might to personify his own strength as a world leader. When the president of a small Caribbean island friendly to Cuba was suddenly assassinated, throwing the political situation into chaos, the stage was set for a blockbuster. Reagan hit upon the plot—crush a Communist threat in his own backyard! Invade Grenada!

"Myopic," ironically, is the characterization of the misadventure given by our then ambassador to the Organization of Eastern Caribbean States, Sally Shelton Colby. When Ronald Reagan went before the American people to warn in the gravest tones, "The United States national security is at stake in Grenada," Ambassador Colby was shaken, having seen no evidence of the huge military buildup he was claiming. The president showed aerial photographs of a 10,000-foot runway in progress, warning it was obviously for military purposes. Colby later told *Frontline* she had the impression that "the president was almost *wanting* to see these installations in Grenada, as opposed to actually seeing them or having evidence they were there."

"Wishful thinking," it was dubbed by former Ambassador to Costa Rica Francis McNeil. Hastily dispatched to Grenada as the president's special envoy to assess the need for invasion, McNeil says today candidly, "We pretty much lived by our own rhetoric rather than seeking the reality of the situation on the island. It was kind of 'I'll huff and I'll puff and I'll blow your Marxist house down.' "

Even as the president extolled the rescue-invasion on national TV as "a brilliant campaign," American medical students were being put in jeopardy by their own government. The 9,600 American servicemen committed to "Operation Urgent Fury" were provided with no intelligence whatsoever and issued tourist maps upon landing. Many of the students were still awaiting rescue four days after the American invasion, *Frontline* reported. Although they'd been under the guns of Cuban and Grenadian forces all that time, not one was harmed or taken hostage. But nineteen American military men were killed and eighty-five seriously wounded. As the crowd chanted his name at the 1984 convention, Reagan would play General Patton: "One year ago we liberated six hundred Americans from Communist thugs."

That fall Reagan was reelected, in part, on the wave of popularity he gained from showing "America is back." The Grenada invasion had served his fantasies as well as his political purposes. Which were, as ever, short-term.

Reagan's perspective on the "big picture" was rather like his eyesight. One incident crystallized it for Edward Rollins in late 1983:

Reagan had spent a rough day in Chicago, wrestling with the ego of Mayor Jane Byrne. On the last leg of the trip back to Washington, Ed Rollins sat directly opposite the president as his helicopter stirred the air over the South Lawn. Reagan looked up and sighed. On the bulkhead was a little picture of his California ranch.

"Oh, God, I wish I was going there instead of back here," he said.

"Mr. President, history will be kind," soothed Rollins. "It will all be worthwhile."

Reagan turned to Rollins, a deadly serious expression on his face. "Ed, I don't give a shit about history. I'll be dead, and they'll distort it anyway."

By 1984 a growing number of political analysts were on to the extraordinary disparity between Ronald Reagan's performed fictions and the facts. "Give Mr. Reagan a good script, a couple of invisible TV screens, and a half hour on prime time and he'll convince the people they have nothing to fear but the facts," wrote James Reston of *The New York Times* in January 1984. David Broder noted in *The Washington Post* a month later, "It is apparently President Reagan's belief that words can not only cloak reality but remake it." If his prestidigitations were purely calculated, meant to mislead the public, they might have been less ominous. But at least a dozen people in his inner circle now knew better: They knew the president lived in his own reality.

He was protected by at least seven myths. His success in

convincingly projecting those myths was phenomenal and, for many, is sustained to this day.

Leadership Myth: Ronald Reagan gave a theatrically convincing *performance* of leadership in his first term, and that swelled public confidence in him to a degree desperately needed.

But critics and even some friends had been saying behind his back for years that Reagan, being both uninformed and not particularly worried about being uninformed, was very much at the mercy of his aides. A leader needs the ability to spot what's missing when presented with presorted facts. This was never in the cards for an older president who liked living in a world of pretend and preferred leaving the details to a revolving cast of aides and advisers. One White House staffer says he came to understand that the president's natural passivity had been reinforced by his movie career: twenty years of taking direction.

Ed Rollins was struck by the president's quiescence when he managed Reagan's 1984 reelection campaign. The opponent, Walter Mondale, always wanted to pick the spots to stop, rewrite his commercials, change the script. Reagan's team found the president to be the exact opposite.

"Reagan never asked, 'Where are we going? Why are we doing this? Why am I saying this?' " says Rollins, the incredulity still fresh in his voice. "Never once did he ask a question. Nothing. Nothing." Nor did he call to thank anybody after winning the election.

"He's not an analytical man, not an inquisitive man," decided one member of his new team. "He's like a sponge. He can suck up and remember anything."

As Michael Deaver saw it, "Ronnie Reagan had sort of glided through life, and Nancy's role was to protect him." It was predictable that Nancy Reagan might assume as much, if not more, power than Rosalynn Carter, although unlike Mrs. Carter's loftier human-rights agenda, Mrs. Reagan's instincts were for public relations. It wasn't what the president did, but how it made him *look.* As Nancy Reagan has often said, "My instincts are for protecting the president." She never ran short of political parasites, like Deaver and Regan, bent on convincing her she couldn't protect the president without them.

So, the battle for real leadership all took place behind the scenes. And some of those who seized the most power were the weakest in mental balance. Deaver admits he was then imbibing half a bottle of scotch a day and having "terrific mood swings and bouts of depression." He told the president as much even before he left the White House in May 1985. National Security Adviser Robert McFarlane also had bouts of severe depression; indeed, he would later attempt suicide after his failure to cover up the Iran-contra affair. And C.I.A. Director William Casey was masterminding covert operations while suffering from a massive brain tumor. Casey told Bob Woodward that he continued to be struck by the overall passivity of the president—"passivity about his job and about his approach to life"—and he used that insight to run rings around Reagan.

It was, ironically, the alcoholic on the team, a most unlikely acting president, who managed to get Reagan to do something about the Israeli bombing of Lebanon in 1983. As Deaver recalls the scene in his book, he told the president: "You're the one person on the face of the earth right now who can stop it. All you have to do is tell [then Israeli Prime Minister Menachem] Begin you want it stopped." Reagan got Begin on the line and told him that he had to stop the bombing. Twenty minutes later, Begin called Reagan to report that he'd issued the orders for the bombing to cease. And then, as Deaver tells it, "Ronald Reagan looked up and said, seriously, 'I didn't know I had that kind of power.'"

It was little wonder that by the second term the coldly calculating John Poindexter would learn to play straight man for the president. Or that Oliver North, a younger, zanier version of Reagan's own Rambo fantasy, would become the president's stunt man.

In reality, Reagan has been one of the most passive and easily manipulated presidents of this century.

Amiability Myth: On the surface, yes, Reagan was always personable. His greatest gift is not verbal, it is the instinct for knowing how to make other people feel comfortable. Even in his last term, people who attended small private dinners with the Reagans couldn't get over how the Leader of the Free World would enter the room, smile, as if to say "Relax, guys," immediately and easily dispel any discomfort, and before they could even figure out how, erase any apparent distance between himself and his listeners. And they always became listeners, his audience.

Even with Secret Service men crawling around, and the inevitable doctor hovering nearby, Reagan could entertain the whole table for hours with his stories. He never talked about the substance of state business, unless someone pressed him on one of his pet peeves, like taxes. Then the appropriate speech would roll out like a continuous loop tape. But as soon as it was finished, the president would go back to what he has always done with the most gusto: telling Hollywood stories. Nancy, presumably bored by listening to the same tales for thirty years, would usually pick out one of her dinner partners and monopolize him with a one-on-one conversation.

Those who have worked for Reagan over the years nod, with knowingly half-closed eyes, on hearing such stories. "If you sat down with him for dinner, you would think, 'This guy is one of my dearest friends.' Then you may never see him or hear from him again."

Reagan has always had difficulty remembering people's names, including those of his staff people, as if they, too, are "one big blur." People close to the Reagans often remark on how Nancy "isolates" him. But a loner likes it that way; he needs only one person to depend upon, who will keep the rest of the world at bay.

Even Reagan's family affiliations have always been tenuous at best. He found the thirty-mile drive from West Hollywood to Malibu too long to bother visiting his young children, Maureen and Michael, after his first marriage broke up. And once Nancy entered his life, all their children—his, as well as theirs together—were kept at a distance. Michael Reagan, who was an all-state high-school quarterback, never once looked up in the bleachers and saw that he was important enough to his dad to bring him out. A man who dated Maureen thirty years ago remembers her as a pretty, tiny-waisted, blond adolescent "tied up in knots all the time about her relationship with her father." Maureen was not wanted at either parent's home on holidays. Her former beau remembers Maureen's pain one Christmas when she asked to go home to her mother, Jane Wyman. The actress sent her $500 to fly home to her father. Nancy Reagan, however, suggested she go somewhere else, perhaps take a nice vacation.

"The picture we see of the public Reagan is one of a warm family man, concerned about family values and the sanctity of the home," says Maureen's old friend. "The reality is just the contrary." That truth of thirty years ago has now been documented by dozens of articles and even books by Ronald Reagan's own children—a scathing *roman à clef* by Patti Davis, who hasn't visited her father for several years, and an autobiography by Michael Reagan, who writes that he was never able to tell his parents that he had been sexually molested as a child.

Reagan really never formed strong attachments to anyone except his mother, his first wife—who devastated him by saying she felt no connection with him and had to divorce him—and Nancy. In this regard, he is no different from his father, who was "able to escape from real life, and that generally included the lives and feelings of his family," as Anne Edwards has documented.

Friends—he has none. Not among the old California crowd. They attached themselves to Ronald Reagan for their own advancement. Not among the Zipkin-Bloomingdale-Sinatra pack. Those were Nancy's pals. People think Reagan has a close relationship with Edwin Meese. But Meese is not the kind of self-made millionaire the Reagans admire (though it's not because he hasn't tried), and insiders say there is no personal attachment there. People thought Reagan had a close relationship with Michael Deaver. Reagan was very angry when Deaver walked out of the White House, although the president did continue to consult with him by phone; but as for friendship, Deaver was Nancy's sidekick.

Those who deluded themselves into thinking that Reagan really depended upon them, or—folly of follies—that they were indispensable to him, were in for a rude awakening. Ed Rollins, who ran Ronald Reagan's winning 1984 campaign and was seen as one of his closest advisers, confessed a painful fact. "I've had two phone calls from Ronald Reagan in the course of five years."

Senator Paul Laxalt moved in Washington circles for the last seven years as the president's closest friend. One night, over a bottle of wine, a former Reagan aide asked him, "Laxalt, how often do *you* talk to him?"

"Once a month."

The aide observed that the way it sounded in the newspapers, Laxalt and the president were on the phone together every day. "Does he call you?" he persisted.

"Nope. I call him. He never calls me."

The only occasions when the president would pick up the phone to call Laxalt were when he wanted something, and then one of his aides would put a sheet of paper in front of him with the Nevada senator's name on it.

Michael Deaver was another person who believed his own self-promotion, that he was closest to the throne of the holiest of holies, and that without him the whole temple of pretend would collapse. "How the hell did the old man go on without Deaver?" one of the president's men asked Joe Holmes while the staff was kibitzing one day. Holmes was a movie press agent who had followed Reagan since the early Hollywood days.

"The old man could get along without anybody," avowed the movie man. "What you have to understand is, for twenty years Ronald Reagan made a movie every three or four months. That means every four months he had a brand-new director, brand-new script, brand-new lead to play 'best friend' for, brand-new love interest. Then they finished and went on to the next director, the next script."

The "old man" not only got along fine without Deaver, he jettisoned him emotionally and mentally. As Deaver tells it in *Behind the Scenes*, he and his wife were invited to the White House for a small dinner party, about eighteen months after he'd left the administration. Deaver carefully avoided mentioning the newly controversial Iran arms sales, but suggested to his former boss that instead of giving the *Voyager* crew the Citizenship Medal, he give them the Medal of Freedom.

"The president cocked his head and said, 'Mike, I've got competent people at the White House who make those decisions.' It seemed as if the twenty years I had worked for him had vanished in the blink of an eye."

He let his advisers come and go, literally interchangeably.

And as soon as they were out of sight, Reagan never attempted to make contact again. After James Baker moved out to become treasury secretary, the president did not initiate a call. When Richard Darman left after six years at his side, the president never got in touch with him.

Reagan doesn't get his affection, approval, or nurturance from real live individuals, according to others who have been up close. He gets it from audiences. The closest thing to a friend is "Barney," a former California state policeman who drove for him when Reagan was governor. When Reagan bought Rancho del Cielo, there was only a beat-up three-room ranch house on the property. He and Barney, whom he'd hired as caretaker, built the patio, cleared brush, posted fences. Aides say the president enjoys himself most when he's out at the ranch because he is most comfortable with that kind of simple, hands-on outdoor activity. Nancy hates it. "Barney is his only real relationship," says a staff member who traveled everywhere with the president. "It grows out of their working together manually."

One of Reagan's political operatives came to this conclusion after five years: There is *nobody* in the president's inner circle. "They're all just directors and press agents and stagehands. And he's the performer." When the operative finally saw the Reagan mystique in that context, he decided it didn't matter *who* was around the president.

"Ronald Reagan lives in a world without connections," says a former longtime, day-to-day adviser. "He has no real human attachments. People come and go almost as if they're cartoon characters you could erase."

It is now known that decades after their parents die, children of alcoholics do not find it easy to trust anyone and have difficulty forming intimate relationships. Above all, the child has to deny his or her own deepest feelings about the alcoholic parent.

In reality, Reagan has no human connections in any meaningful sense.

Loyalty Myth: Many ambitious people wanted to work for Reagan, claiming he inspired tremendous loyalty.

"He never reprimands," says William P. Clark, Reagan's former national security adviser. "If he had nailed the first guy down the path, and made an example out of him, then people would have thought a little bit," observes a former staff member. "But no one was ever cut loose. It was a White House without discipline." Those who got into trouble were not the experienced members of the government bureaucracy, who tend to outlast the peculiarities of mere presidents. The men and women who made up the sleaze parade of administration members forced to leave because of charges they had violated ethical if not criminal codes were the ones who came in with the Reagan Revolution. They brought the ethics and practices of the more permissive business world. And they operated at the pleasure of a president who saw nothing wrong with someone enriching himself while in office, or with rubbing shoulders with power and going back to the marketplace to peddle his contacts before they went stale.

One top law-enforcement official heard William French Smith, Reagan's first attorney general, telephone the president and mince no words in warning him that Ed Meese just wasn't up to the job. A longtime financial adviser to the Reagans and the president's own personal lawyer, Smith was much closer to Reagan than Meese ever became. From Meese's confirmation hearings, onward through a maze of ugly charges of financial improprieties and dereliction of duty during the "shredding party" period after the first Iran-contra revelations, and right up to the accusations about the Iraqi-pipeline scheme, Smith's warning was borne out. And Ronald Reagan has never uttered a word of surprise or criticism.

He continued to insist that he had "every confidence" in Meese's integrity (although some insiders see signs that the president is withdrawing from the controversy over his attorney general's activities), and hotly disputed the oft-cited statistic that more than one hundred of his officials have had to leave for ethical or criminal reasons. He is fond of pointing out that two indicted officials—Labor Secretary Ray Donovan and N.A.S.A. chief James Begg—were cleared by juries, ignoring the fact that six top members of his administrations have pleaded guilty or been convicted. Two of his closest former aides, Michael Deaver and Lyn Nofziger, both convicted of criminal charges after they left the White House, are defended to this day by the president as "the very soul of integrity."

The president has charged that criticism of his administration's ethical climate is creating a "kind of lynch mob atmosphere." In the end, he may even avoid the consequences of his tacit acquiescence in the actions of his officials. The administration has challenged the constitutionality of the special prosecutor law, and the case will go to the Supreme Court in early summer. If the appellate court's ruling that the law is unconstitutional is upheld, or the high court comes to a four–four tie (Justice Anthony Kennedy has disqualified himself from the case), the results could wipe out Deaver's conviction and cast doubt on Nofziger's conviction. Reagan himself was expected to pardon Poindexter and North after the fall election.

Again, a clue to Reagan's behavior can be found in studies of adult children of alcoholics. They often show extreme loyalty, but of a childish kind, sticking up for those who are undeserving of such loyalty.

As for the loyalty he ostensibly received from his staff, there is another way to view that, too.

One Friday afternoon well into the first term, a reporter was chatting with then White House Chief of Staff Jim Baker in his office. Selected senior White House correspondents were invited for regular private sessions by the totally imperturbable Texan with the cool monotone, who most of them believed was really running the United States. All at once, Baker looked up at the clock and turned white.

"Oh my God!" he gasped. "Reagan's leaving and I won't be there to say good-bye."

Something like a look of panic crossed his face, according to the stunned reporter, and Baker bolted from the room—running. He ran all the way to the president's helicopter, to stand there in a clump of people who waved, as they did every single Friday, and shouted, "Have a nice weekend, Mr. President!"

When Baker returned, the reporter asked, "Did you have something you had to tell the president?"

"No."

"You mean you ran just to say *good-bye*? When he's going to Camp David for two days?"

"Yes."

Perhaps that was how the otherwise passive Reagan "inspired" loyalty, the reporter mused, through fear. The aloofness, the chilling distance he maintained with the most powerful men around him, sent a subliminal signal that one day he could cut them loose and never look back.

Nancy Controls Him Myth: Nancy did indeed isolate her Ronnie, from the moment she married him, drawing her own formidably protective circle around him. As far back as his gubernatorial days, she was the dominating presence in his life. She told him even then when to turn off the TV and go to bed, when to put on his coat and rubbers, which newspapers not to read.

From her first days in the White House she started urging the president to get rid of the far-right-wingers, to ease up on the religious and social issues, and to set up a summit meeting. Having no luck with a direct approach, she connived with Mike Deaver. Among the victims of their backstage maneuvering, Deaver claimed, were Al Haig, Don Regan, National Security Advisers Richard Allen and William Clark, and Interior Secretary James Watt.

But, according to Lesley Stahl, CBS national affairs correspondent, "even Nancy, it appears, won't go head on with Reagan. She does a devious number . . . She would have these little dinner parties, people were invited specifically to tell him that he ought not to do the religious breakfasts, he ought to shut up about abortion, that he should just cool it on the social issues. She would tell them ahead of time that their function was to bring it up, and halfway through the meal she'd give them a hand signal—*now*—and they wouldn't want to do it. Reagan sort of sent off some body signals, *Don't do this to me.* But she would say, 'Joe is here to tell you, Joe was telling me something interesting on the phone the other day, Joe, tell him what you told me . . .' And then Reagan would cut the conversation off."

When Reagan dug in his heels, there was no moving him.

Nancy could not keep him from visiting the Nazi graves in Bitburg; by then his chief handler was Patrick J. Buchanan, whose rabidly reactionary views had ascended over those of the pragmatists who stage-managed Reagan's first term. She failed totally to dissuade her husband from his fantasy of "Star Wars." And she gradually despaired of restraining his support of a massive increase in defense spending long enough to divert more funds to social programs.

As easily as criticism rolls off Ronald Reagan's back, it sticks in the craw of his perpetual bride. And where he has no stomach for personal conflict, Nancy can get angry, in Chief of Staff Howard Baker's phrase, with a "dragon lady's" venom, and nurse a grudge interminably. A scapegoat must be found when Ronnie's world of pretend is punctured by unpleasant leaks. Nancy blamed Lyn Nofziger, whose slovenly grooming she'd always held against him, for Governor Reagan's loss of credibility during the homosexuality scandal. And despite the fact that Don Regan was a snappy dresser, a good talker, and appeared always to support the president rather than correct him—criteria that counted with Mrs. Reagan—she turned on the White House chief of staff when he began trying to upstage her Ron. He was her scapegoat for Ronnie's poor preparation at the Reykjavik summit. The battle over making Regan responsible for the Iran-contra scandal brought the Reagans head to head. The president publicly snapped at his wife, "Get off my damn back."

In fact, Nancy Reagan plays the role of the nagging mother, but usually only wins on small things. Some of those who are close to the couple see a connection between Reagan's wife and his mother—Nelle Reagan, too, was something of a nag. Ronnie often calls his wife "Mommy," and behaves toward Nancy like the model child who goes along with his mother on a lot of things, but on others flagrantly ignores her.

So Nancy, who has celebrated their long romance with full-court Hollywood press-agentry skill, may not be as influential as she would like us to think.

Compassion Myth: As one White House adviser explained it to me, when Reagan is faced with a real live human situation—provided the human dimension is evident—he is the world's softest touch. Lobbyists usually confront him with an abstraction, whereupon he relies on his ideology. "And his ideology is against the kind of intervention his humanity would be for." Another former member of the president's team says, "Reagan sees only the particular case. Bring him a child who needs a liver transplant, he'll pick up the phone and make it happen. But he can't extrapolate to groups." I asked if that was a deficit in intelligence, or simply indifference. "I don't think he's interested," said the aide. "It's only what's right in front of him that Reagan deals with."

Again and again, the scene was played out in the first-term White House, as mayors and governors and directors of social programs taking the brunt of budget cuts demanded to plead their case with the president. They would go in fuming mad. "We'll give him a piece of our mind," they would vow to White House reporters. "He's ruining the country, he just doesn't care." Coming out, they would have stars in their eyes. "He agreed with us! He saw the light. We are saved."

Later Larry Speakes would brief the press on the meetings. When correspondents played back the comments that had been made, the president's spokesman would reply, deadpan, "No, they didn't hear him correctly. We are sticking with cutting the program." What was going on? Did the president really not know what was being asked? Did he fake his lines just to get through the scene?

To some degree, this is the essence of political fraud. Most skillful politicians are artists at making people think they have been persuaded. But with Reagan it was more than politics, it was a puzzle with two different sets of pieces. One set was colored in soft pastels—Reagan as the "world's softest touch." The other set was colored black and white—the "stubborn" Reagan who could personify and dismiss the whole welfare problem with his anecdote about the "Chicago welfare queen."

Again, the blurred line between reality and fiction he engineered so as to be able to adapt to his boyhood can be seen as a key to the puzzle.

His message is always: *Do not derail me from my mission. My mission is to make things positive.* Thus, he can clap his hands and superimpose a vision of American civil rights over the

reality of apartheid: "The [South African] government has eliminated the segregation that we once had in our own country—the
type of thing where hotels and restaurants and places of entertainment and so forth were segregated—that has all been eliminated." The war on drugs, President Reagan proclaimed, "is an
untold American success story," and the use of illegal drugs, he
said, "has already gone out of style in the United States." He
cannot allow himself to *see* real people in the little heaps of scrap
humanity around the White House, so he makes them invisible
by describing ". . . the people who are sleeping on the grates,
the homeless who are homeless, you might say, by choice."

He cannot deal with them, or with suffering on a mass scale,
any more than he could face his father laid out dead drunk on
the front porch.

In reality, Reagan sees what he wants to see, and lets you
hear what you want to hear. It is up to his press secretary to
announce later that you misunderstood.

Most Popular President Myth: The media's frequent references to Reagan's "phenomenal popularity" and "personal
goodwill" surrounded his first term like a warm blanket.

But even during that charmed period when the legend of the
Great Communicator grew, Reagan's average approval rating
was significantly lower than that of his predecessors. After the
first two months in office, his rating of 60 percent was 15 points
lower than Carter's approval rating of 75, and did not rival
Kennedy's 73, Eisenhower's 67, or Nixon's 65, according to
figures reported by Thomas Ferguson and Joel Rogers in *The
Atlantic*. After the first year, he was down to a rating of 49
percent, also below the others at the same point in their presidencies (except for Nixon).

At the end of two years, Reagan's 37 percent job-approval
rating looked dismal next to Eisenhower's 72, Kennedy's 70,
Nixon's 56, and Jimmy Carter's 50. Some pundits took note of
the low poll ratings, but explained them away as if Reagan's
personal popularity had a life of its own. In fact, it is typical for
presidents to enjoy much greater *personal* popularity than support for their policies.

Why did the media take Reagan's unproven popularity for

granted? One theory is there existed an enormous subconscious desire in Washington for the president to succeed after a string of failed presidencies—a desire that Washington may have projected onto the American people. If so, it went a long way toward helping to establish the myth of Ronald Reagan's invincible popularity as the truth.

Ageless Myth: In the first of two television debates with Walter Mondale during the 1984 presidential campaign, Reagan appeared sluggish and somewhat befuddled. He had several serious "Where am I?" kinds of lapses. One lasted seven seconds. When the networks commented on candidate Reagan's mental fitness after that uncertain performance, they were swamped with irate calls. But the president's staff had felt the cold sweat of possibly swift defeat. They called in an emergency media consultant, Roger Ailes, a tough TV producer from New York.

Ailes listened to David Stockman rehearsing Reagan by clobbering him with facts. Reagan kept fumbling, his mock audience of aides correcting him again and again. Ailes took Deaver and Baker aside: "If you think he was bad in Kentucky," he said, "wait till he gets to Kansas City. It'll be a disaster if you keep this up."

Ailes knew the president hadn't been elected on facts. Indeed, facts were his nemesis. He'd been elected because he talked in broad emotional generalities, or "themes" as they'd been packaged, but, even more important, because he made voters *feel comfortable.* The main thing the American people wanted from the president, Ailes told the staff, was some reassurance that he wasn't too old for the job. Deaver warned him not to raise the age issue: "We don't want to introduce anything new." As Ailes recounts the scene in his book, *You Are the Message,* he plunged in anyway:

"Mr. President, what are you going to do when they say you're too old for the job?"

The president blinked, struck dumb. But after thinking a moment, he came up with an old line he'd used before.

"Fine," said Ailes. "Don't get drawn into the age question at all. Just say your line and stand there."

And so, in Kansas City, when the age question inevitably surfaced, Reagan turned to Mondale, and with fifty years of performance experience behind him, delivered his line with just the right timing and tonal blend of self-confidence and self-deprecation:

". . . and I want you to know that I will not make age an issue of this campaign. I am not going to exploit for political purposes my opponent's youth and inexperience."

Reagan's highly visible exhibitions of energy did the rest of the trick. Cameras never failed to record the incumbent president walking briskly across the South Lawn every Friday and bounding up the steps of his helicopter. Only in his second term did stiffness begin to set in and did he seem increasingly to be leaning on Nancy, so the cameras began to stop filming before he got to the steps. The deterioration in his hearing became noticeable very quickly after he turned seventy-three, with Nancy covering for him, as in her memorable prompt—"We're doing everything we can"—when the president hesitated over a reporter's question about arms control. He picked up the cue. Like the veteran performer he is, Reagan simply incorporated his handicap into the act. He *used* his hearing problem and the noisy helicopter as props, to avoid answering questions from newsmen who could only catch him as he came and went on weekends.

Lesley Stahl tells of going to the Oval Office with her husband, Aaron Latham, who writes movie scripts, to introduce her family at last to the man she had covered for six years. It was Christmas 1986. "Up close, the president looked like a cadaver. No light in his eyes, age spots everywhere, wattles of skin hanging from his slack jaw, you could practically see light through his skin." She thought, "This is shocking, really shocking!" His press secretary stepped forward and said, "Mr. President, Aaron's made a movie that you like very much, *Urban Cowboy.*"

"And instantly—not gradually—but like a pop-up figure in a children's book, the man's whole demeanor changed," describes Stahl. "The age spots faded, the eyes took on light, the wattles tightened up, and he engaged with my husband on the level of a mutual excitement over movies. Whatever it is about Reagan, it's not senility."

Just give him an audience and he'll lose twenty years, for the time being. The stories are many about how the president will hunch over to get out of his limousine, tired, slow-moving, an old man about to make what looks like his last speech. Then the band starts, he skips up onstage, and boom!—he's on. Reagan loves being the star of stars—the state dinners, the worldwide photo opportunities, the cameras.

Professor Dean Keith Simonton has found that the optimal age range for seizing the presidential nomination is between fifty-five and sixty, and the same range holds true for a wide assortment of postwar world leaders. Republican strategists were worried it would be an issue in the '84 reelection campaign, and they were right to be worried.

Few people knew that President Reagan's mother, who worked as a hospital volunteer in later life and was well liked, had developed Alzheimer's disease. From the age of seventy-seven until her death at eighty, she was severely impaired by it. Alzheimer's does carry a hereditary factor. Some medical experts told me the chances of inheriting the disease are as high as one in four.

In 1984 I had asked Dr. David Arenberg of the National Institute on Aging whether Reagan would be able to spot what's missing or see the opportunity for a possible breakthrough at a summit meeting. He replied, generalizing, that "the direction is clear: There's a decline. He's going to have more and more trouble." He added a qualifier: "There are, however, those rare individuals whose mental alertness and memory defy all the studies or norms over age seventy."

A group of gerontologists at U.C.L.A. had made it a practice to monitor Reagan's TV appearances weekly and discuss changes. Even from a distance, these experts were struck by how he had been slowing down. What appalled Marilyn Albert, associate professor of psychiatry and neurology at Massachusetts General and Harvard Medical School, and an expert on Alzheimer's, was not Reagan's zigzagging in his first debate, but "how scared he looked. Even when he was summing up at the end, with a speech he had prepared ahead of time."

Yet when the Republican convention anointed him in the summer of 1984, I couldn't get an article printed that even raised the issue of the possible effects of aging on our oldest president. Most news organizations wouldn't touch the subject with a ten-foot pole. Opinion research showed that Americans reacted very negatively to stories that made any connection between Reagan, age, and decline. Moreover, the redoubtable Nancy Reagan was quoted as being "goddamned angry" about the attention given to her husband's age.

What an admiring public did not stop to consider about Reagan's advanced age was the impact it could have on his ability to sort out problems. Deficits in mental functioning among people over seventy are most evident in problem-solving. In problem-solving studies at the National Institute of Aging, participants of that age group characteristically cannot remember all the information they are receiving. They appear to reach a saturation point, but feeling they have to make an inference, rush to do so before they have all the facts. As a result, the first inference is usually wrong, but the older person will often cling to it stubbornly.

Given the problem-solving style he had used all his life, the seventy-five-year-old president ran true to form, for example, at the Reykjavik summit. He couldn't remember all the cards that had been put into play. Some accounts suggest he leaped to the inference that this was the first time in history that a Soviet leader had mouthed the ideal of total disarmament. He confused ballistic with strategic missiles, and toyed with the abolition of all nuclear weapons without regard to the threat of Soviet superiority in conventional weapons. Confronted with contrary evidence on his return to Washington, the president clung stubbornly to his snap judgments.

People are quite consistent in using problem-solving strategies that have worked for them over the years. If an individual is accustomed to relying on experts or underlings for facts and analysis, rather than demanding of himself that he master complex issues, he will predictably depend more and more heavily on that strategy as he ages.

On February 6, 1988, Ronald Reagan turned seventy-seven. *Parade* magazine saluted it as a triumph: "No other president in U.S. history has attained that respected old age while still in office."

In actuality, Reagan's advanced age increasingly limited his alertness and capacity to solve problems. He did not turn out to be one of the rare ones.

Two elements were essential to support the magic of Ronald Reagan's great fictional constructs. They had to be closely tied to idealized American mythology; i.e., his strategic defense initiative (S.D.I.) was John Wayne, Flash Gordon, and Luke Skywalker, all starring in a spaghetti western set in outer space. Second, in any classical Reagan formulation, there was a happy ending. And Reagan would identify himself with it—at the last moment finding the pony in the pile of manure.

Both elements must have seemed guaranteed in Reagan's mind when he began negotiating with Teheran for the release of the hostages held in Lebanon. Presumably he was dreaming ahead to the day, preceding the crucial 1986 congressional midterm elections, when he could stand on the White House lawn and reenact one of his favorite roles, that of Commander Reagan welcoming home freed American hostages. It had worked to elect him the first time. Why not use the same script in time to save the Senate from "falling to the other side," as he called it? There were at least six, and possibly eight, meetings in the summer of 1985 at which Reagan was told about the proposed discussions with Iran, including the suggestion that eventually arms transfers would be involved. According to Bud McFarlane, then his national security adviser, the president was "excessively enthusiastic," and said words to the effect, "Gee, that sounds pretty good."

Throughout 1986 the president was briefed on the Iran initiative at almost daily meetings. But his questions were perfunctory, and he preferred doodling and telling anecdotes. When he did ask questions, they were confined to the hostages' well-being and the timing of their release. It was as if he were dreaming of a double feature: *Hostages Come Home* and *Contras Rid Marxist Threat in America's Backyard.*

Until that happy ending, the plan would be wrapped in secrecy and ensured against backfire by the policy of "plausible deniability."

Now added to the deficits of aging and the habit of denial

were the sudden depletions of political standing and physical health suffered by the president in the months before his greatest fiction was found out. His periodic bouts with colon cancer had begun in the summer of '85, when he underwent major abdominal surgery. New polyps were found and removed both in January and in June of 1986. A few months later came the first great political blow—losing the Senate to the Democrats—a stunning exhibition of his failure to transmit his personal popularity to his party. In six years as president he had raised over $800 million for his party, yet not a single Republican had been added to the numbers in the House or Senate. And then, to be caught swapping arms for hostages with the most hated enemy of America—his defenses were under maximum stress.

George Bush told *Time* magazine, "I know for a fact the President, in his own mind, does not see it that way." Even after the White House released written proof that Reagan knew arms for hostages was one of the initial goals of the directive he signed, the president kept up his incredible pretense. Nixon observed, "He's stubborn." That is more than stubbornness. That is denial.

To learn that half the country believed him to be lying, to be caught in a quagmire over the very dilemma that had pulled down his predecessor, to be hounded week after week by leaders of his own party to wake up and face reality, to undergo surgery again only to come back to the White House in January and be confronted with unpleasant facts about what the government did under his stewardship—all this may have strained Reagan's mental defenses to a dangerous degree. For denial is a slow poison.

What happens when a lifelong denier comes up against a problem the world simply won't allow him to deny? He does all the odd, disconcerting things that people who watched Reagan over the first four months after the Iran-contra scandal broke reported as "monumental indifference," "stubbornness," "sloth," "shuffling," "drifting into oft-repeated anecdotes," and refusing in every way to come to grips with reality. Eleven of his answers at the first press conference on the Iran-contra affair began with the word "no." He refused to apologize for what was euphemistically called his "management style." He was adamant with advisers about saying he would not change. Everybody in the world—his own party leaders, Nancy, even Margaret Thatcher—tried to get him to face the situation and fire Oliver North and John Poindexter, as well as Don Regan. So close was he to being stripped of his ultimate defense mechanism, he even swore at his wife.

Reagan had always relied on two ways of coping with unpleasant reality. He'd deny it, and if denial didn't work, he would rewrite the script. But here was a script, try as he might, that confounded his every effort. He really did convince himself it wasn't arms for hostages, according to an insider who was accustomed to Reagan's gift for self-delusion. The reason he did poorly, publicly, was twofold:

Ordinarily, his fantasy world, his vision, whatever he was fighting for, could be defended as holding out for America's most cherished ideals. In Iran-contra, he found the thing he had to defend was trading weapons with the leader of a terrorist nation, the Ayatollah, who had burned this nation's flag. In Ronald Reagan's fantasy world, this is the character he should have been smashing. But in the real world, he was doing business with him. Rather than a celebration, this was a desecration of traditional American values. The president, adamantly refusing to listen to the protests of his Cabinet officers, had dispatched two marines (Bud McFarlane and Oliver North) to pay off the government that bankrolled the Beirut barracks bombing in which 241 of their fellow marines were killed.

Second, there was no way to find a happy ending in this case. He didn't get the hostages out.

"I've never seen him so depressed," recalls a White House staffer who stuck it out with the president. "The only thing he would hang on to—and it was pathetic—was the fiction that it wasn't arms for hostages. For a while, he could convince himself. But this time there was no grain of truth to support this denial."

During the course of the long, inconclusive Iran-contra hearings, disillusionment seeped through the electorate. It was almost like waking up to find one is living over a toxic-waste dump. The president in whom so many had believed so fervently, the well-meaning outsider who championed eternal verities and would never lie to the people, turned out to be just another slow contagion. America's long-term economic health and international position of respect had been weakened in critical ways under his leadership, and many Americans felt doubly betrayed.

In the autumn of 1987, after the October 19 stock market crash left almost everyone else shell-shocked, Ronald Reagan was still sleepily reciting his view of America's economic future from five-by-eight cards. His denial system was functioning even more blatantly by now. After three days of silence, the president announced, "This is purely a stock market thing."

The world's financial markets clamored for his political leadership. Reagan dithered. A prominent European ambassador said on October 28, "We are seeing definitive proof that the United States and the rest of us cannot get along without a functioning government in Washington." Other world leaders implored him to give some sign he would try to deal with the U.S. deficit. No response.

In late October, Treasury Secretary Jim Baker assembled a group of business leaders to figure out how to staunch the bleeding. Baker asked Peter Peterson, former secretary of commerce under Richard Nixon, chairman of Lehman Brothers until 1984, and now chairman of another New York investment bank, what impact he thought the crash would have on the deficit. Peterson minced no words. This was a very interest-sensitive market, he said, "and if you guys don't pass this lousy package you have on the table [the budget compromise] it will be a signal to foreign investors that you can't do anything. The dollar will sink even lower, and when interest rates go up the market will freak out again."

Baker said, "You've got to tell the president." He said he would forewarn Reagan, but that sometimes the president forgets, so Peterson should be certain to bring it up.

The president came in and sat down, took his cards out of his pocket, and propped them in front of him. There was no discussion. For fifty-five minutes of the hourlong meeting, Reagan read from his cards, still spouting the same ideas he had brought with him into the office seven years earlier, with no indication he had integrated any conflicting evidence.

Ronald Reagan's presidency went wrong because he came into office quite unable to change. The American people caught on that his story was imaginary. They discovered what Ronald Reagan had tried to hide as a kid—that he lived in a world of pretend. He didn't have a strong second act. And finally he couldn't find a happy ending. Not to Iran-contra. Not to the doctrine of Reaganomics. Not to the war in Nicaragua.

The only happy ending was, ironically, to change the oldest plot line of all those in his head—to rewrite the Soviet Union's role as an Evil Empire that could never be trusted, and remake it into a partner in seeking peace. This did mark genuine progress in his thinking. Close observers say that only personal experience changes Reagan's mind. And the experience of meeting Gorbachev face to face, three times, made a profound impression. Before the summit meeting of December 1987, Reagan told a group of TV reporters that Gorbachev is the first Soviet leader who has not said his goal is world communism. After that meeting with the Soviet chief, Reagan called Gorbachev "a different kind of leader" and compared him favorably with Lenin. While the rest of the president's set speech still contains lines he used thirty years ago, the automatic anti-Communist diatribes have all but disappeared.

Reagan is unfairly accused of a last-minute flip-flop on arms control or of caving in to Nancy (who *does* give a damn about how history treats her husband). At least since 1982, Reagan had been telling those around him that he wanted to be the president who reversed the arms race and began reductions. He had read an article by Senator Daniel Patrick Moynihan convincingly articulating his own belief that arms-control agreements accomplished the very opposite of what most people thought they did: They *accelerated* the arms race. They all leveled *up*, and so created a new asymmetry between the two sides that ensured an even higher level of arms production. What Reagan kept talking about was an arms-*reduction* agreement. The zero-zero option was proposed by Reagan in 1981, but no one took him seriously at the time. He did finally engineer, with Gorbachev, the first verifiable arms-reduction treaty—and that is brand-new in the nuclear age.

By February 1988, Reagan wanted to go to the people once more on national television to rail over the threat of Nicaragua and the necessity to aid the contras. The networks refused him. It was by now an old movie, and everybody had seen it. The medium dominated for seven years by the Great Communicator simply turned off the president of the United States, and then the trashing began.

On the domestic front, the reality behind the fiction was equally stark. Following the same script he had used as governor, Reagan came into the presidency billing himself as a tough fiscal conservative and ran up the biggest debt in the history of the nation. With a straight face, he submitted a $1.1 trillion budget to the Congress in January 1988, about 16 percent higher in constant 1982 dollars than Carter's last budget.

The only way the United States can pay its way in the world now is by sucking in even larger sums of foreign capital. This dependency has already transformed the world's largest creditor into the world's largest debtor nation—all in the space of a few years. And this debtor nation now has a $10- to $15-billion-a-*month* habit. It has all happened so fast, Reaganomics might be renamed "crack economics." Yet, even as the Reagan administration pumped up the bubble of illusion year after year, voters surveyed door-to-door back in the summer of 1987 knew it would burst. The only question was how soon. And a *New York Times* poll taken in early 1988 found that for the first time since Reagan had taken office, Americans did not believe the country's future would be brighter than its past or present. The poll conveyed a national sense of uneasiness unmatched since the darkest moments of Carter's presidency.

If Ronald Reagan came to assume he was above reality, it was in large measure because we the electorate coddled him into believing it. For leaders are surely projections of the fondest fantasies of the led. Ronald Reagan's fictions coincided with the new narrative America wanted to hear. Following John Kennedy's death, the country had started floundering, and for the succeeding two decades we experienced an identity crisis. Reagan was able to restore our confidence in traditional American values and the position that America had held in the history of human development as a "shining city on the hill."

In relief, Congress and the media and large portions of the public all lowered their standards to accommodate this hypnotically happy president. He didn't have to work a full week or keep notes or referee policy disputes among his advisers. No amount of press reports of his misstatements of fact seemed to register. On the contrary, they became part of Reagan lore. It was his stock-in-trade to "forget" facts that interfered with his perception of himself as pure in motive and true to his word. He had entered the Oval Office sleepy; now he was preparing to leave it indifferent to history. All that the nation had to look forward to from its premier performer in his last act were the reruns. By the end of his presidency, Reagan was reading even the simplest and most natural "ad-libs"—"Thank you all for coming here today" or "God bless you"—from prepared scripts.

And so, to all the other questions about America's search for leadership, we must add this crucial one. Are the American people ready yet to hear the bad news along with the good intentions? To take the bitter medicine along with the bromides? To get on with the reconstruction of a productive, competitive country that can hold its position in the world? Or, hoping to put off paying the piper as long as possible, will we prefer to elect another president who hides the truth but tells us what we want to hear?

After eight years under Reagan, many Americans, too, have developed the habit of denial. The sobering possibility is that, content to partake of the president's self-indulgence as our own, we will simply roll over and beg to finish the dream.

It is our choice.

Or perhaps, building on the resurgence of national pride that is Reagan's strongest legacy, we will recapture the spirit to look to the future and risk bold experiments, a spirit that has made this country unique, and envied the world over, since its original declaration of independence.